IN
HER
TIME

IN
HER
TIME

Iris Sangiuliano, Ph. D.

WILLIAM MORROW AND COMPANY, INC.

NEW YORK   1978

Library of Congress Cataloging in Publication Data

Sangiuliano, Iris.
    In her time.

    Includes bibliographical references and index.
    1. Women—Psychology. 2. Identity (Psychology)
3. Married women—United States—Case studies.
I. Title.
HQ1206.S25   155.6'33   78-9662
ISBN 0-688-03377-6

BOOK DESIGN   CARL WEISS

Printed in the United States of America.

First Edition

1 2 3 4 5 6 7 8 9 10

FOR

LEO AND LUCIAN

AND OLGA

PREFACE

ABOUT THE WOMEN, THE METHOD, AND ME . . .

FOR THREE MONTHS I WAS ON MY BACK RECOVERING, OR TRY-ing to, from two ruptured spinal discs. I was vulnerable, incapacitated, and in pain. Not only was it a shock to my self-image, but it also jolted my perception of the world. Frozen in time, I'd watch the passing clouds by the hour, or I'd take a sudden interest in the slope of the slate-gray roof of the Gothic church visible from my window. I didn't know it then, but I was faced with one of those jolts about how our lives *should* be that gives us the breathing space for reflection and change. I'd always been a doer and, most of the time, I'd been busy doing my thing, which was the practice of psychotherapy.

It also happened to be that notable Watergate summer of '74 when we, as a country, were shocked into sober ques-tioning and change. Being, perhaps, unduly sensitive to the arbitrary fates of nations and people, I felt personally identi-fied with the unfolding national drama. The chiseled images of the political wives, appendages to the men in power, will-ing victims most likely, ignited my curiosity.

I began thinking about women and their lives. I wondered how such women maintain a separate identity and any measure of autonomy if, indeed, they do. What had been a familiar circumstance for me as a psychotherapist—troubled women—now took on new dimensions. Before long my curi-osity spread beyond the Watergate wives. I wondered how *any* woman, centered in marriage and family, evolves her own definition—relinquishing, as she often does, her name, her work, sometimes even her friends and community—when she chooses the intimacy of union. Specifically, I became intrigued with the pattern of women's adult development.

Trussed and corseted, I was determined to find out. I spread the word among friends, some in the public eye, some colleagues, and some in education, that I was interested in interviewing women. Did anyone know women, married to successful men, who'd be willing to talk in depth about themselves and their lives? I wanted to speak with women like the political wife, the corporate wife, and so on—homemakers who might easily live in the shadows.

Since my interest at first had been aroused by women married to public figures, I started my interviews with that kind of woman. But this was clearly only a beginning. Soon I became concerned with contrasts. I was made aware, for example, of the different periods in the life cycle at which I'd met some of the women. Like a tumbleweed, I gathered my variants as I went along. In age, the youngest women were in their twenties, most were in their thirties, forties and fifties, and one, the blithest spirit, had just turned seventy.

Each woman was deliberately selected because she represented some variable. One woman had been married as long as forty years; another was a newlywed. One woman had divorced and remarried; one had divorced and was living alone; another had been widowed and had remarried. Still others were about to have their first child, or were in a quandary whether or not to do so; others had launched, or were about to launch, their last child into the world. Some had large families; others had none. Although the majority had college degrees and a few held advanced degrees, some had been college dropouts, one didn't go beyond high school, and another had finished only tenth grade.

My source of supply gathered momentum. It was usual for

a woman after days of "talking" to suggest: "I think I know a woman you'd really be interested in." The women themselves frequently suggested many of the variables. In all I collected two dozen interviews that stretched for the most part to several sessions over a period of days and in some instances over the almost four-year span of study. In addition to those women, of course, were countless others who came tumbling out of my current practice of psychotherapy, enriching the depth and dimension of all the interviews.

A word about numbers. It has been my firm belief, supported by common research practice, that we can learn more by the careful scrutiny of a few individuals in great depth than by glancing at a great number of people in survey in the hope of gathering trends. My intent has been neither a definitive study of women—a swollen ambition, at best—nor a survey. My motives for looking at the adult woman over her life span, rather, arose from my observations in treating women and men, as well as from research evidence, pointing to a need for different theories of growth and development for women and for men.

I'm acutely aware that my sample consists of women who at some time in their lives have been married. That's because an overwhelming majority of women are, or have been. Even in the seventies women report marriage as the preferred state. The married woman still centers her identity in her marriage; the single woman still centers in the fact that she's *not* married.

Throughout these pages I shall often refer to "women" or "the women." By that I mean those women whose lives I've brought under scrutiny—middle-class white women, who are or have been married to middle-class white men. My observations, obviously, concern American middle-class women during this time in history. Each event or period of their life that we'll explore, moreover, as we trace their personal and sexual unfolding could be a book unto itself. True to my intent, however, my thrust has been developmental, that is, the changing patterns of woman's identity and autonomy over her life course.

My interviewing method was that of a biographer with a trained ear and diagnostic tools at her disposal. The interviews were also a study in contrasts. I wanted to maximize fully the potential of each encounter, influencing the women as little as possible with theoretical preconceptions, allowing them the freedom of their own reflections and interpretations. A humorous incident occurred when I asked one woman, who flailed her hands this way and that, every gesture coated with refinement, what was more important to her: Building a nest, or "making it." "Making out, without a doubt," she replied. "Being popular was really important to me." In subsequent interviews, I've asked, of course, "What is most important to you: Building a nest, making it, or making out."

I also wanted the opportunity to pursue my hunches. I set about sifting through the facts and fictions of their lives, probing not only their conscious realities, but also their dreams and daydreams—past, present, and of the future. That took a special kind of listening.

Too often we may say what we *think* is socially acceptable within a certain context, but our deeper feelings are at odds with what we profess. One woman, for example, said that if she could she'd choose a very different life-style: She'd prefer living with a man and having children without the shackles of marriage. Sinking my stockinged feet into her wall-to-wall beige carpeting, I pursued the subject: "What life-style would you want for your daughter?" Without pausing for breath, she answered: "Oh, marriage. I want my daughter to marry someone who will take care of her."

Our relationships are determined by more than the rational, thinking part of ourselves. I listened hard to each woman, mostly with my third ear. I listened for her image of herself, how she thought she was supposed to be, and how she had come to that image. I listened to her expectations—

what she'd imagined marriage would be like—and to the disillusionment of those expectations. I listened not only to what was being said, but also to what remained unsaid.

I was listening for something special—something that would identify each woman. I was listening for her single voice. Although the woman may have been J. J. Bowen's wife, or Sandy's mother, or the daughter of Mr. So-and-So, that's not what made her special. That's what defined her roles and status. I was listening, instead, for those central critical events in her life—the disruptions that jolted her from what she'd expected—and how she'd met those jolts. That's what made her special. That's what shaped her personal identity.

In most instances, at least one session took place in the woman's home; I wanted to sample her life-style as well. Prizing the privacy of each person, I've altered identifying details. Where two women experienced similar life-dilemmas, composite word-portraits were constructed to preserve anonymity. Anonymous, the women were more self-revealing and less self-protective. The dialogue, however, is verbatim, and the tone of each journey is true to life.

I've told something about the women, but since I'm their filter, I should tell something about myself. When one writes a book about women, one of the first questions asked is: "Are you a feminist? Are you pro or con?" Although I've lived my life as what is presently termed a feminist, I felt the label narrowed me in my approach to different kinds of women. I wanted to be with each woman with what the French novelist Robbe-Grillet describes as an "innocent eye," devoid of any urgency to prove anything. I wanted no sexual politics to blur my vision. I came to each person with an open attitude and more than a dollop of curiosity about the inner and outer reality of the particular woman —and myself—as a woman.

Along the way I chose to become a psychotherapist, marry, and have a family. Each aspect of my life fed the other and I've been enriched. I was fortunate, too, that by temperament I was a rebel of sorts and fought swallowing the social ideal of womanhood as exclusively wife and mother. I grew up at a time when the prevalent truism was, "If you get a doctorate, you'll never get a doctor." Like most choices between a this and a that, it was a false dilemma. I chose both.

I am fortunate also in having been born a woman. Had my fate been otherwise, being an "achiever," I might have been entrapped in the male clichés. As it is, I am free to have feelings and intuitions, and free to play my hunches. I am free to be nonrational, and to abide by my dreams.

At first flush, the *raison d'être* for this book was to explore the female experience of adult development. Still, the years I'd spent in the practice of psychotherapy precluded my being a pure theoretician. The unmined potential of a number of women, or at best the late blossoming of personal interests, brought out a bit of the reformer in me. So, as the book unfolded, I became aware of still another purpose for my writing. Through listening to other voices, I hoped to offer women an opportunity to broaden their knowledge of each other, and of their own growth process, supporting their quest for a separate self and a singular voice. That, I trust, would be the case whether they are single, married, mothers to a new generation of daughters, or whether they're daughters, looking at the track ahead.

While I'm proffering all my hopes, I should mention not the least of them. It would be gratifying if our male counterparts—husbands, lovers, sons, potential mates to our daughters, colleagues, and particularly men in the health disciplines—medical and psychological—would care enough to listen to what makes *us* grow.

ACKNOWLEDGMENTS

My thanks to:

Leo Chalfen for listening, disagreeing and agreeing, lending invaluable assistance in hammering out my thoughts. And for suggesting the title.

Lucian Chalfen for opening many worlds to me that otherwise would have remained unknown.

Olga Sangiuliano Menaker who has been since my birth the staunchest believer. It was said of us as children: The little one dreams and the other swears by it.

Mildred Newman for catching my enthusiasm about a book devoted to women and setting the wheels in motion. Betty Anne Clarke, my literary agent, for her comments and for her constancy in nurturing the manuscript from a study of women to the seeds of a book. My editor at Morrow, Pat Golbitz, for her skillful and enthusiastic assistance in completing the process of producing a full-fledged book. And Hillel Black for his interest.

Colleagues and friends, who must remain unnamed, for assisting in my search for the women—and the women, for allowing me to enter their lives. One woman, who sent me a Peanuts card, best expresses my feelings. On the cover Charlie Brown says: "Thanks from the bottom of my socks." Inside, he explains: "Somehow thanks from the bottom of my heart didn't seem deep enough!"

And, by no means least, S.C.S.

CONTENTS

LIST OF FIGURES

I

BEGINNINGS

Give birth to me, sisters, in struggle we transform
ourselves, but how often, how often
we need help to cut loose, to cry out, to breathe!

—MARGE PIERCY,
The Magician

1

ABOUT ADULTHOOD,
FEMININE IDENTITY,
AND SELF-DEFINITION

"Whatever happened to Edith?" one of the women asked.
"What do you mean?" I inquired.
"Well, she used to be so . . ."
"Invisible?"
"That's it! She used to be Bill's wife."

A separate identity is just a flip of the coin, the other side
of invisibility. But it isn't a mere flip. It requires moments
when we are coerced into taking a new look at relationships
that have become invisible simply because they're there. It
requires a new way of experiencing ourselves as daughters,
wives, mothers, and as women and persons in the wide, wide
world.

Nothing is as devastating as invisibility, even though it is
reputedly safe. How often have you heard, "Aren't you Bill's
wife?" or "Johnnie's mother " or "The daughter of So-and-
So?" Our life course has been narrowed by our gender
identification as women. We have been defined as daughters
by our parents; as wives by our spouses; and as mothers by
our offspring. And for many of us that has meant that we're
forever and only daughters, wives, and mothers. We are
identified by what we've been—little girls, and what we will
be—wives and mothers. It was the French existentialist Si-
mone de Beauvoir who said, "Female destiny is foreordained
and repetitive."

But that's only one part of a larger landscape. The late

poet Anne Sexton reminds us that "women are born twice." And indeed, some of us are. Anne Sexton never attended college. She was the "little wife" who'd lived a doll's-house existence. Her second birth took place the day she happened to hear some poetry and thought, I think I can do that! and did.

That yearning for a singular voice—a personal identity—exists in us all. Some of us are only too aware of its absence. Others drown ourselves in daily routines. More and more women, however, are discovering with regret that their lives cannot be reduced to making this or that choice unto perpetuity. The choice we make in our twenties to marry and have children cannot be the lifetime choice of our thirties, forties, fifties, and sixties. Relationships change as we change. Marriages can and do dissolve through divorce, death, shattered illusions, and emotional distances. Children grow and leave us, as they should.

Divorced at the age of forty-five, her daughter away at college, one woman explained that ever since childhood her dream had been to be a wife and the *best* mother ever, unlike *her* mother. She'd even limited her family to one child so that she could give her daughter everything. Wistfully, she continued, "Now I wish I'd latched my dreams elsewhere, to something that has a bit more mileage."

And more mileage is precisely the concern of this book. Throughout these pages, we will follow the path that women have taken toward a second birth—journeys strewn with their share of by-ways and dead ends—and we'll explore what's given some of us the impetus to move from that sheltered *we* to seek the *I* within the *we*.

Since our concern is with mileage, or technically, with life-span development, let's turn for a moment to some of the theories about how adults develop. Once all but ignored, adult development in recent years has been smothered with attention.

About Adult Development: Stage Theories. The theory

of adulthood as a series of developmental tasks, or crises, that the adult must resolve at various stages of his life underlies the notable works of Erik Erikson, Robert Havighurst, Lawrence Kohlberg, Daniel Levinson, and Freud. That view, although a popular one, is one among many theories proffered by a broad spectrum of social and behavioral scientists. Like most theoretical constructs, it has its shortcomings. One of them is in the area of predictability.

Predictability has always been the hornet's nest of social scientists, and well it should be. Has anyone known a woman's life that was predictable? There are a myriad of influences that shape a life: the social climate and expectations; the personal psychological response to those expectations—which makes every woman unique; and the values and meanings, at first borrowed, later personally derived.

Paradoxically, however, not only do the stage theories fall short on the issue of predictability, but they also fall short on the flip side—that question of *unpredictability*. The view of adulthood as a series of orderly, predictable, linear progressions—steps that are age-specific—makes little room for the impact of those "unexpected" critical events that have changed the focus and direction of women's lives. Those are the kinds of events, in one woman's words, that turned her life around and planted her in another direction.

It was just that kind of "unexpected" off-time event that caught my attention as I began exploring the lives of women. Using both biographical data and my own observations of women in psychotherapy over a number of years, I was struck by the fact that women's lives unfold, not in a rigid, predictable progression of conflicts, identity, mastery, and autonomy, but rather in great surges of billowing change. Interestingly, one distinguished researcher, Harvard's George Goethals, has suggested that the more appropriate metaphor for adult development is a sine curve and not a straight line.[1] For those of us who've forgotten our high school trigonometry, a sine curve looks like this:

The stage theories, nevertheless, have an appeal. Most recently, for example, adult life has been characterized by two authors, Gail Sheehy [2] and Roger Gould,[3] as a sequence of predictable crises or changes that are age-related and follow a predictable pattern. For women that is an incomplete concept since it leaves little room for the unpredictable, which, paradoxically, we'll discover, is the seminal female ingredient of change. If an event is predictable, it's unlikely to be experienced as a crisis, and if it isn't experienced as a crisis, it's unlikely to "shock" women into growing.

By the unpredictable I mean the unique and personal response to those central common events in a woman's life such as leaving home, getting married, taking a job, as well as the unique response to those "unexpected" but also critical events which disrupt her innocence and shake her dependency. Those are the events that women have indicated as markers in their lives.

For example, she expects a perpetual honeymoon, and abruptly her lover or husband begins working far into the night, and she's on her own again. Or, she is expecting a baby, and her husband expects her to go scuba diving. Or, the baby arrives—that bundle of joy—and she's so depressed she can't get out of bed!

Those are just a few moments of truth that have "shocked" women into reassessing past, familiar meanings. Those are the events that contradict what we've been led to expect. They are the events that isolate and separate the "I" within the "We" and the "All of Us." And, for many women, they're the conflicts and contradictions that have moved them to change.

Change is a reality whether we seek it or not, welcome it or not. Women, paradoxically, are groomed to be docile and dependent, and in a sudden moment are confronted with the realization that they're required to be resolute and independent. How we face those contradictions will determine if and how we'll earn that second birth. When we learn to *meet* those contradictions not only as losses, but also as potential gains, not just as obstacles, but as challenges, we grow and stretch our skins.

Adult life also has been described as normal and as predictable as the infant's sitting up, then crawling, and finally walking. Somehow, child development, which leans heavily on physical maturation, has been equated with adult development—an unfolding with its own, quite different complexities. Neither Spock nor Gesell provides sufficient analogues of the adult's journey.

To begin, fundamental psychological change in the adult is not directly a function of age. It is, as we'll see, closely related to pivotal events that trigger us to take another look at ourselves and our relationships. It wasn't being thirty that "threw" one woman, but the fact that at thirty she felt the pressure of time. Her childbearing years were crowding in on her; conflicted, she was pressed to look at her life and make a choice. Similarly, it wasn't turning forty that "jolted" another woman, but rather the fact that her husband had become dissatisfied with his life and had joined a "back to the earth" movement, sold their home, and retired to a farm —and she was expected to rejoice and follow. She was "jolted" into questioning those familiar *meanings*, who she *should* be—a good wife and helpmate—and who she'd just discovered she was—a person in her own right with her own interests and leanings.

Women grow by leaps and bounds. In the chapters that follow, we'll consider those jolts that have been the fertile soil for reassessing our past as we revisit old assumptions and attitudes that we've held sacrosanct. For the adult, obviously, the issue is no longer one of increments of age or of physical prowess—although some of us persist in seeing our lives that way—but of *meanings* that grow and change as we do. Unhappily, we haven't been prepared for that—perhaps because the area of personal meanings is not so easily codified. I'm grateful, therefore, for the work of Nancy Datan, a developmental psychologist, who observes: "While the self and its solitude are major themes in existential psychology, the developmental model of the transition to young adulthood has focused on the fit between self and society. . . . The problem of youth in developmental theory is often conceived in sociological terms; and it would be unkind but not at all untrue to say that a brief overview of Erikson's (1963) description of the core problem of ego development, identity vs. role confusion, might lead the reader to conclude that the problem of ego identity can be resolved by competent high school career counseling." [4]

About Feminine Identity. Why does it seem so much more arduous for women to come into their own than for men? "It is a difficult point to admit," essayist and novelist Joan Didion writes. "We are brought up in the ethic that others, any others, all others, are by definition more interesting than ourselves; taught to be diffident, just this side of self-effacing. ('You're the least important person in the room and don't forget it,' Jessica Mitford's governess would hiss in her ear on the advent of any social occasion. . . .)" [5]

At long last, social scientists, predominantly women social scientists, have made considerable inroads into the misty matter of feminine identity. [6, 7, 8] We learn that men, in the very process of identifying themselves as masculine, are groomed to *do*; women are taught to *be*. That makes sense. By the nature of things, mother is the primary source of identification for both male and female infants. However, in order for the boy to identify himself as masculine, he is required to labor early to separate himself from his primary source of nurturance and security. Lest he become a "sissy," he must be supported and encouraged to venture from the apron strings. Thus, it has been pointed out, a masculine identity must be achieved.[6]

And girls, how are they made? Until adolescence, feminine identity is a *given* attribute. We needn't labor for its acquisition; feminine identity is said to be "ascribed." Girls are expected—indeed, taught—to imitate mother. Psychologists Bardwick and Douvan explain: "When boys are pressured to give up their childish ways it is because those behaviors are perceived as feminine by parents. Boys have to earn their masculinity early. Until puberty, femininity is a verbal label, a given attribute—something that does not have to be earned. *This results in a significant delay in the girl's search for identity, development of autonomy, and development of internal criteria for self-esteem.* Because they continue to depend on others for self-definition and affirmation and are adept at anticipating other people's demands, girls are conformists." [7] (Italics mine.)

Conforming for the girl, until puberty, includes high grades at school. She's rewarded for "good" behavior and learning such skills as spelling, reading, grammar, and so on —tasks that require little independent thinking. "With the onset of the physical changes of puberty," Bardwick and Douvan continue, "definitions of normalcy and femininity change and come precipitately closer to the stereotype. Now behaviors and qualities that were rewarding, especially successful competing, may be perceived negatively." There grow the early sprouts of our ambivalence, in which we come to fear both success and failure. We become boxed in by limiting images of femininity.

During adolescence, girls are bombarded by several coalescing events that create feelings of helplessness. Adolescence is the time when *she* must begin to labor to earn her feminine identity. It is the time when she begins to separate from mother, a task for which she's ill-prepared, rarely having had to exercise those muscles of autonomy. Separating—being different, or "better than" mother—she feels, will threaten an already ambivalent relationship. It is the time, as well, when her sexuality is beginning to burgeon, and being "better than" can threaten not only her relationship to mother—the original competitor—but also her relationship to boys. Rather than meet those paradoxes of separating, of loosening those original ties, and achieving a personal identity, conflicted, too many women choose to remain little girls

Although the boy's task may seem more arduous at first, in the long run he has been better prepared to meet the alternating life currents. I'm particularly struck by one concept in those formulations, that of laboring. It was Louise Nevelson, a sculptor of international repute, who at the age of seventy-seven observed: "I don't say life was easy. For forty years, I wanted to jump out windows. But I did feel I had the strength and creative ability. There was never any doubt about that. No one could move me till I got what I wanted— on my terms, on earth. And I do. And it did take, maybe not the greatest mind, but it did take courage. And it did take despair. *And the hardship gave me total freedom.*" [9] (Italics mine.)

About the Process of Self-definition. Laboring, separating, and birthing is the process in achieving a personal identity. Separation is the moment of birth; labor, its means.

It is crystal clear that in our laboring, women and men are coming from a different place. Those very actions in women that trigger and separate the I—so deeply rooted in the We of mother, father, mentor, lover, spouse, children—are considered unfeminine. Angry, aggressive, assertive, doing, laboring, and venturing are not the social images of how a woman should be.

Laboring conjures images of a kind of physicality that women simply are not supposed to possess. In the psychotherapeutic treatment of men I've been especially impressed, as a woman, with the centrality of the physical for the boy. Women have no such measures as confronting the bully and winning, or the team spirit—being fiercely competitive and still functioning within the We.

In a compelling autobiography, *Not So Wild A Dream*, Eric Sevareid reflects on his boyhood. "By competitive sports (vastly overdone) a boy may acquire the invaluable easy confidence with his fellows which can last him the rest of his life, which is the basic touchstone among young men all over the world, for the relationship of most men during at least one half their lives has a physical basis."

Those reflections are particularly impressive from a man who is a noted journalist and an intellectual. He goes on to describe a harrowing summer and fall when he was seventeen, paddling twenty-two hundred miles! Having survived and returned home, he observed: "A boy does not grow up so imperceptibly that there are not sudden moments when he is acutely conscious of change within him. I walked carrying my pack and paddle, toward my father's house, past the castellated red-brick high school, scattering the drifts of dry autumn leaves with my broken boots. The boys and girls on the sidewalk seemed unprecedentedly young. . . . My chief return on this investment, outside of a fleeting local notoriety which got me a job on a newspaper—as office boy—was that for several months thereafter, until sedentary habits softened my flesh, my older brother could not lick me."

Men's bodies are the inner source of their pride and pleasure. It's not only acceptable for them to venture and compete, it's necessary. Such are the rewards that are independent of anyone's approval—rewards that are central to the core spirit of the self-esteem and self-image of masculinity.

Women's attitude toward their bodies is strikingly different, coated as it is with ambivalence. Pubertal girls are both proud and embarrassed by their burgeoning breasts, proud and sometimes ashamed of the monthly flow of blood. "I've got the curse," we whisper in school corridors, with pride and pain—aware in the back of our mind of the pleasure and pain that our sexuality holds for us, of those images of a sagging body in pregnancy and the pain of childbirth. Unlike that of our male counterparts, our bodily pleasure seems always tinged with the shadow of pain.

As we grow older, the single consistent relationship we seem to have to our bodies is in their malfunction. Physicians' coffers, I suspect, are filled by women, and it can't just be that we have more parts that can go wrong!

So what stories do *we* have to tell?

One woman, twenty-eight years of age and expecting her first baby, confided: "I'm scared. I don't want to have a marriage like my mother's and I don't want to be a mother like my mother. I'll never forget those family dinners. My father, my sister, and I monopolized the table. We always had a story to tell. My mother never had a story to tell; she was out of it. And baby or not, *I always want to have my story to tell.*"

In the chapters that follow we will lay bare and buttress that urge in every woman to have her story to tell—a story quite as compelling as her husband's deal with AT&T, or her children's adventures at the skating rink.

It's been said that everyone has at least one story in *him.* Indeed, so do women! Have you ever tried plotting *your* life? Think back. Consider *your* experiences growing up female. What were those events that propelled you from then to now?

At one point I began asking women whose lives we're about to explore to trace their life course—quite literally with pencil and paper.

The results invariably jolted them.

The idea itself is not new, but its application is. Originally the Life Line—a line representing one's life over the span of years—was devised for a Life Planning Workshop intended to involve the participants, usually college students, in "the process of influencing their own futures." [10]

Try drawing your life course—before we look at what shape other women's lives have taken. The results may surprise you as well.

Draw a line representing your life. It can take any form or

direction. Place an X where you are now. With small circles
indicate the important events in your life and label them.
Put down the approximate ages at which they occurred. With
a plus or minus, indicate whether you considered the event
as a positive or a negative experience.

Now sit back and take a hard look. Where does that X fall?
Where are you between "time-since-birth" and "time-left-to-
live"? Have you given yourself a future? A life beyond wnere
you've been?

Let's begin our journey with some of the stories, graphically plotted, that women have had to tell. As you'll see, what
is striking, despite the variety in size and shape, is the path
they trace—hardly a straight-line progression. There are periods of stability, instability, transition, and synthesis. Women
have indicated certain markers, crucial events that they've
experienced as significant in directing the course of their
lives and, in many instances, the changes that took place.

Consider Ellen, who is twenty-eight, married six years, and
expecting her first baby.

From a low point of childhood and adolescence, Ellen's
life course is generally on the ascendancy—with disruptions
of even greater depth now, however. Currently, thick in the
unsettling period of deciding to have a baby, she'd neglected
to give herself a future. I pressed for one. Her projection of
the future—based on her experience of the past—is noteworthy. In her early thirties, she explained, after the disruption of having a baby and the first few years of caring for it,
she will be on a high with a successful career. But that too
will bring another time of unsettlement—in terms of a possible breakdown in her marital relationship and also with
herself. In her mid-thirties, after all that success, she wonders, what will she do for an encore? A prophetic question.
Following that disruption, she foresees another period of
stability in her forties.

Standing away from her drawing, she laughed. "My life

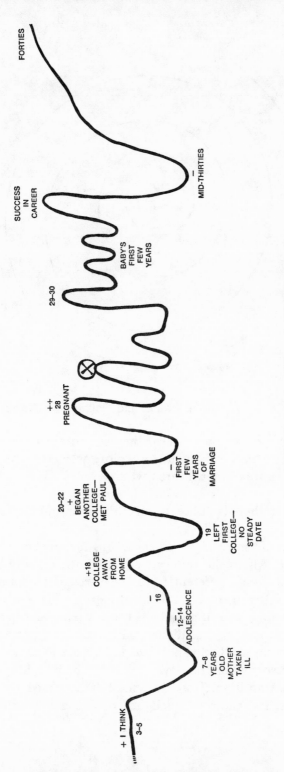

FIGURE 1 / Ellen: A "Cardiogram"

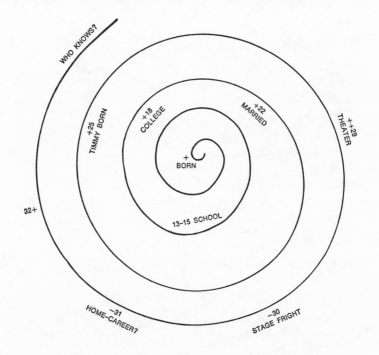

FIGURE 2 / Millie: Round and Round She Grows

looks like a cardiogram!" she observed—an apt description. What better way, I thought, to explore women's lives than by the measure of their heart rhythms?

And then there is Millie, who is thirty-two and the mother of a seven-year-old girl.

Millie's life space began to expand as she left home to go to college, where she came in contact with other ways of being and doing, different from the parental admonitions. She married with the traditional images of what a wife and mother should be. But as she was thrown more and more on her own resources, she discovered an old interest in the theater. In the conflicting pull between what a mother should be—a homebody—and her love of theater, she hit a low point, a time of transition. Unsettled, she felt disrupted until, at thirty-one, she chose to quell her doubts and pursue her interest.

* * *

Evelyn had just turned forty. At the age of eighteen, she had married a young man whom her parents had selected for her. She had one daughter, divorced three years later, remarried, and after eleven years divorced again. Shortly after, she began living with Sam.

From what we already know about the facts of Evelyn's life, it is apparent that she has obliterated the disruptions and the hurts, indicating only what for her have been the positive events. She neglects to note, for example, her first marriage, a time of considerable upheaval; her childhood, which was a particularly painful one; and her current love affair, about which she is ambivalent. What she fails to take into account, however, is that, except for those disruptions, she would not have reached the point which she has at forty.

As Evelyn was tracing her life course, she recalled a recent dream that had been particularly distressing. In the dream, she was driving a car when suddenly a wind came up of such velocity that she couldn't make any headway, and she got stuck trying to cross a bridge with the motor revving. She observed: "It was just as if I were kicking up sand."

Experiencing herself in transit, Evelyn struggles to bridge the familiar assumptions about her life in order to reach fresh meanings. As she studied her life course, she pointed to the Now on her journey, explaining: "I was in my twenties when I was divorced and left with Nancy to raise. I landed this terrific job, with all kinds of opportunities for promotion, and from nine to five, there was nothing in my head but getting home to Nancy, and figuring out how I could get David, who eventually became my husband, to marry me. And tucked away was another me—the me I've just met, a me that never got aired. Only after I married David and things began going downhill did I begin to percolate. At forty, I feel more like a twenty-year-old boy with a dream than a·forty-year-old woman. I've gone from acne to my change in one leap."

In transition, she projects a turning point, as we can see,

in the not-too-distant future, returning to the quest the boy-child launches at eighteen or so.

At age fifty there is Kate, who has been married for twenty-seven years. She has graphically depicted her life, with its high points, low points, and turning points.

To begin, the high points in Kate's life had been associated with pleasing others—that was the way she made herself known, and the way she gained a feeling of personal worth. She married, and shortly after the birth of her firstborn her life literally went downhill. At age thirty-eight, she was faced with a serious illness, a totally "unexpected" event that turned her life in another direction. (Who of us expects to be faced with dying in our thirties?) At forty-four, she faced another turning point when she discovered her husband's love affair.

"As I reached forty," Kate explained, "well, until that time I'd kept myself hidden in the shadow of my husband. Slowly, I began establishing my own roots. And those roots began to nourish me." Kate had faced dying and she'd faced the death of a relationship that had been the center of her identity.

And then there was Betty, in her late forties, a historian, married and childless, whose life course traces sharp contrasts —peaks followed by chasms.

Historian that she is, Betty "talked" her Life Line, mechanically drawing peaks and valleys. I've included her life course because it vividly illuminates the generational gap in women—a matter not of qualitative, but of quantitative difference. The woman who is middle-aged placed a greater stress on being "popular." (Note Figures 3, 4, and 5.) However, that element was certainly not absent from, say, Ellen's Life Line (Figure 1) where her decision to leave the first college she attended was based pretty much on the fact that she had no "permanent" boyfriend. And she is a woman of the sixties.

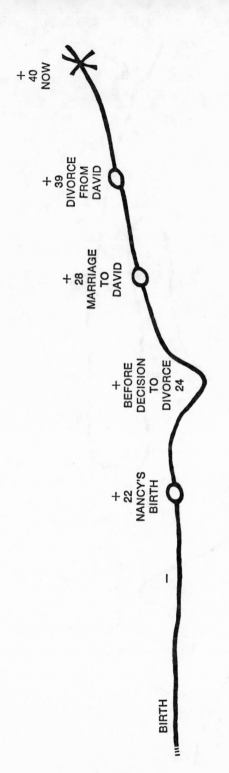

FIGURE 3 / Evelyn: "The Only *Important* Events Are Positive"

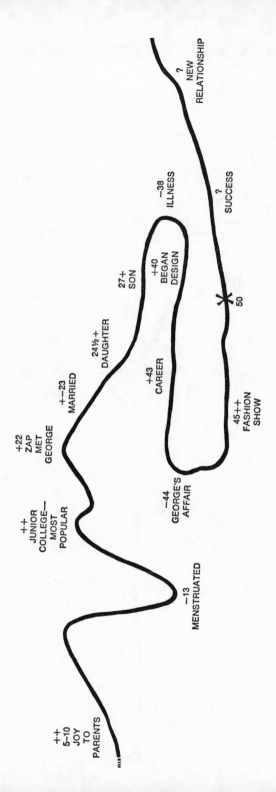

FIGURE 4 / Kate: High Points, Low Points, Turning Points

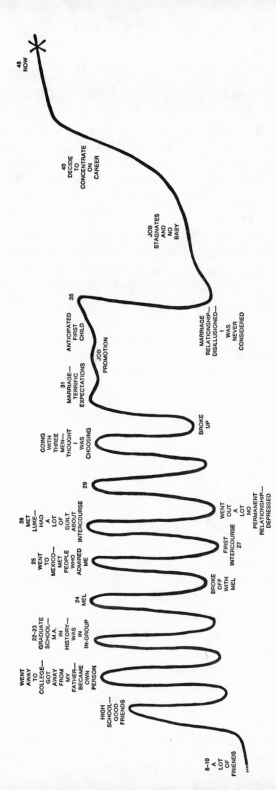

FIGURE 5 / Betty: Life Through the Eyes of Men

One could say that Betty's life traces the pulse of her popularity at first with little girl friends, later in heterosexual relationships. Thus, her life begins in early adolescence, a time when she started making friends, obliterating the earlier pangs of growing up. A high point and certainly a transition in many women's lives is going away to college, which Betty notes also as "getting away from my father," and "becoming my own person." Working toward her Master's degree is also a high point, thickly colored, however, by the fact that she was part of the in-group. From that period, every event is shaped by the nature of her relationship with men—either their absence, or their uncertain presence. Only as she reaches fifty is there a glimmer of a *me*.

What are those events you've considered important enough to note? What are those that you've anticipated? And those you've omitted or even completely obliterated?

Some women indicated:

> Their birth
> Graduations
> The onset of menstruation
> The cessation of menstruation
> Their first sexual intercourse
> Their first job
> The decision about a career
> A promotion
> Love affairs
> Marriage and the emergence of a We
> The birth of a first child
> The departure of a last child
> The discovery of their husband's love affair
> Divorce
> Death: Parents, Spouse, Mentors
> A life-threatening illness
> A critical choice; a time of freedom
> The birth of a dream

A career change
Their second birth; the emergence of an I

How have you looked upon those events? As losses or gains? As obstacles or challenges? Were they anticipated or unexpected? Those are some of the noteworthy circumstances in the women's life course. Some are bridges, others mark turning points—moments of critical choice and upheaval, periods of impending fundamental change.

Perhaps some events have been omitted because you wish they'd never occurred. Some may have been omitted because they'd been anticipated, like menopause or a child leaving home, and so were discounted. Still others, such as the birth of a dream, or the emergence of an "I," may not have been indicated because they have yet to happen.

From time to time as we move through other women's lives, turn back to your own Life Line and look to see how you can add to your future.

Chapter 1. / About Adulthood, Feminine Identity, and Self-definition

1. Albin, R. "The Long View: Looking at the Life-Span." *American Psychological Association Monitor*, July, 1977.
2. Sheehy, G. *Passages: Predictable Crises of Adult Life.* New York: E. P. Dutton, 1976.
3. Gould, R. *Transformations: Our Adult Dilemma of Choice, Safety and Self.* New York: Simon & Schuster, 1978.
4. Datan, N. "Forbidden Fruits and Sorrow: Aspects of Adult Development Dynamics." Paper presented at

American Psychological Association, Chicago, 1975.

5. Didion, J. *Slouching Towards Bethlehem.* New York, Farrar, Straus & Giroux, 1961.

6. Chodorow, N. "Being and Doing: A Cross-cultural Examination of the Socialization of Males and Females." In *Women in Sexist Society.* Edited by V. Gornick and B. Moran. New York: New American Library, 1971.

7. Bardwick, J. and E. Douvan. "Ambivalence: The Socialization of Women." In *Women in Sexist Society.* Edited by V. Gornick and B. Moran. New York: New American Library, 1971.

8. Bardwick, J. *Psychology of Women: A Study of Bio-cultural Conflicts.* New York: Harper & Row, 1971.

9. MacKowan, D. *Dusks and Dawns:* Taped conversations with Louise Nevelson. New York: Charles Scribner's, 1976.

10. Johnson, R. "Life Planning and Life-Planning Workshops." *The Personnel and Guidance Journal,* 1977, *55*, 546–549.

2

UNION AND IDENTITY

"What do women want?" Freud was reputed to have asked. Most women will tell you that they want to be loved, they want security, and they want to be provided for; at the same time, they want to be independent, adventurous, audible, and visible.

Marriage? Marriage, it seems, is meant to be the answer to every contradictory need expressed in every maiden's prayers. Almost every girl's dream is to get married and finally be her own freewheeling self, with no more being told: What do you mean, you're thinking of quitting school? Or, who's that fellow you're dating? His eyes are shifty. Or, when are you ever going to settle down and get some sense into your head?

But what's a freewheeling self? Where does the self end and the other begin? What are the sharp limits of me? Can a woman enter a permanent union and not betray herself? And just how does one come by a self? Perhaps there are only single women on that journey. Certainly those surveys of professional women who are either avoiding or dissolving their marriages or their careers cause us to wonder.[1]

Or, is it the other way around? Is it only in establishing and maintaining our separateness that a genuine intimacy, appreciation, and love can flourish?

Those are the timeworn questions preoccupying women, and never more so than today. In Gail Godwin's elegant novel, *The Odd Woman*—odd referring to the odd number one, juxtaposed with the even number of coupling—the author sensitively probes the mind of her unmarried protagonist. In an assignation with her married lover, Jane queries obliquely:

" 'Can two selves have a permanent relationship?' she had to ask. . . . 'Can two selves, do you think, after they have cleaned themselves up, got their *egos* in hand, can they have a permanent love relationship, say, a kind of love that—that exists in a permanent, eternal way?'

" 'No,' he said, simply and matter-of-factly, as though he had long ago thought out this question and come to terms with it.

" 'Oh,' said Jane crestfallen."

Ten Years from Now? "What would you most like to be doing ten years from now?" researchers asked a group of teachers. The unmarried woman wanted most to be married; the married woman wanted most to have a home and be a housewife.[2] That study was undertaken in 1952, and according to the Virginia Slims ads, we've come a long way, baby.

Maybe. According to a 1974 Roper women's opinion poll —sponsored by Virginia Slims!—marriage, with traditional or shared roles, is still the preferred way of life for more than ninety percent of the women surveyed.[3]

We can safely state that, although women in the seventies are exercising greater choice in marrying than women in the fifties, their expectations have not changed. Changes in the concept of marriage are yet to be reflected in women's concerns.

It is still fact—according to the U.S. Bureau of Census— that in 1974, 95 percent of all women thirty-five and older had been married at least once, and all but 10 percent of those women had had at least one child.[1] It is also fact that 80 percent married with religious ceremonies.[4] It is another fact that, even as late as 1974, the American woman married at the median age of 21.1—barely out of school and into the working world. That, by the way, is considered an improvement in the changing status of women, who, according to the census figures of 1950, married at the median age of 20.3.[1]

If we add still another statistic, the fact that people are living longer, we come to the striking figure that the life expectancy of a marriage can stretch over a fifty-year period! In terms of a life-span perspective, it is indeed the case that woman's self-esteem, identity, and social roles are centered in her marriage. As a consequence, we have developed an elaborate mythology, as psychologists Roxanna Van Dusen and Eleanor Sheldon point out, of "well-defined notions of what activities and roles are appropriate for women of different ages." [1]

NOAH'S ARK: COUPLING

Identity? Intimacy? There's little doubt that autonomy, identity, and intimacy are the complex female strands that need unraveling if we're to understand the woman's journey toward that separate self.

The recent attention given to appropriate developmental activities for particular ages undoubtedly is a reflection of the collective state of our psyches—enough of a mirroring to even have insinuated itself on prime-time television in a "Mickey Mouse" version of Erik Erikson's eight stages of man! [5]

The work of Erik Erikson has been pivotal in drawing attention to the fact that adults, as well as children, go through major transitions. He postulated eight stages of development, from infancy to late adulthood, emphasizing the kinds of mastery that are appropriate to each stage. Each stage focussed on a turning point in the life course. It was important to his theory that each turning point was critical for a particular age period, and that resolution of one phase was requisite to growth in the next. In short, the process of adult development was seen as a series of critical steps at critical ages.

His theory of the developmental sequence of adulthood is worthy of study in some detail in view of what we're about to observe in women. Let's start with adolescence, the launching pad of adulthood. According to Erikson, adolescence is a time for resolving those Who Am I? confusions, and shaping one's identity or self-system (Identity vs. Role Confusion). Once that is on its way, man is ready to take on the phases of adult development.

The next phase is of particular interest. This stage, which Erikson identified as Intimacy vs. Isolation, is a time when the young adult (early twenties) "emerging from the search for and insistence on identity, is eager and willing to fuse his identity with that of others. He is ready for intimacy, that is, the capacity to commit himself to concrete affiliations and partnerships. . . . Body and ego must now be masters of the organ modes of the nuclear conflicts, in order to be able to face the fear of ego loss in situations which call for self-abandon; in the solidarity of close affiliations, in orgasms and sexual unions, in close friendships. . . ." Commitment without the threat of betraying the self becomes possible, then, when the man feels he has a handle on who *he* is.

Following his achievement of a self-system and union with another, man moves to his next developmental task: becoming productive/creative, caring and parenting in his work and his family (Generativity vs. Stagnation). And lastly, at age sixty or so, he is required to come to grips with perhaps the most awesome reality of them all: the acceptance of this as his one and only life. At this time he must achieve an ego integrity—a creative summing up—lest he fall into the despair —of "what might have been" (Ego Integrity vs. Despair).

I've used the term man deliberately. Erikson (and most of those who've followed him) based his observations essentially on men. For men, success in establishing a self-system not only *precedes* but also buttresses success in establishing a union with the opposite sex—not the other way around.

The work of Yale psychologist Daniel Levinson, until recently exclusively with men, also supports an underlying order in the life course of the adult male. He, too, emphasized developmental tasks that must be mastered before men can move successfully to the next stage of growth. Interestingly, he identifies the period between sixteen and twenty-two as the search for autonomy—"Pulling Up Roots." The time between twenty-two and twenty-nine he describes as the time to shape a vision of oneself in the world—"The Dream Emerges"—which later can be converted into a career goal. It is the time to find a mentor, and the time to form the capacity for intimacy *without betraying the self*.[6] (Italics mine.)

So much for man's timetable.

But are we always to be squeezed under the umbrella of man? Or dragged in as an afterthought? Even those studies describing couples seem to fall into the same trap as they report essentially on the man's life course and then on how woman does or does not accommodate to his developmental rhythms.

The emerging self—shaping one's identity as a separate person—is not the same process for women as it is for men, as we'll learn. Neither the sequence nor specific events nor age can be used as a gauge for woman's development. Women, we'll discover, are late bloomers, by and large. In the woman's life journey, the striving for union precedes and postpones the labors of a personal identity, and sometimes sends it underground.

Whether we label that launching period as the time for developing autonomy (Levinson) or the time for developing identity (Erikson), the fact remains that men can commit themselves to marriage without seriously threatening the self, simply by the ordering of their priorities.

Having observed such a sequence of development in the adolescent girl, some researchers have suggested that the developmental stages from identity to intimacy in males may well proceed in the opposite order for females.[7] Still another researcher, trying to make order from seemingly discrepant data, theorizes: "While marriage is an important milestone for a man, it is typically merged with an enduring vocational commitment and is an additional manifestation, but not a definition, of his masculinity. For women, marriage may mark the resolution of her identity crises (perhaps symbolized by her change of name)." [8]

Significantly, the developmental ordering of a woman's life is a misty area still. Mostly, we persist in seeing her in the reflected light of men. Indeed, it has been the case that girls are overinvested in interpersonal relationships. Popularity is their yardstick for self-esteem. And marriage, to be sure, does serve women, as a vocational commitment serves men. Where men have used career goals to crystallize and enhance their definition, women have used marriage to affirm their identity as female, feminine, and worthy. For women, "we" carries more clout than "I." However, for most women, marriage has not been a resolution of an identity crisis, rather it's been a postponement and a submergence of those developmental tasks that Erikson describes as leading to a self-system. Not until women have committed themselves to coupling—or failed in that striving—does the quest for a single, solitary self emerge. And changing her name, seen in that context, is not the symbol of resolution, but rather the symbol of an identity that is in flux. When we stop to think of it, a man knows his name from the crib to the grave; a woman waits for hers.

Customs rooted in symbols, however, die hard, since the symbols carry the images of our time. Adopting the husband's surname is a custom meant to symbolize the unity of the couple—a unity, unhappily, that pockets the identity of the woman. As a matter of fact, legally, the name change is required only in Alabama, Indiana, and Hawaii.

It wasn't nit-picking, I realized, when a woman chose to retain her own surname. It was rather a subtle communication of the individuality within that union. That is especially the case where both partners are professionals. Still, how many professional women do you know who all-too-happily drop their own name and adopt their husbands'? And how many boys do you know who are Juniors or Seconds, and how many women?

It was Elaine Cole who first brought my attention to the painful price of merging. Forty-one years of age, Elaine had been divorced and remarried. Currently struggling with an emerging, gnawing sense of self, she explained: "I feel more important as a couple. After I divorced, alone, I felt like a pariah. There is a certain solidness in being a couple. For instance, when Matt and I would go to the annual Yale reunion I'd always introduce myself with: 'I'm Matt Cole's wife.' Last year, a friend overheard me and she said, 'No, you're not. You're *Elaine* Cole.' That landed on me like a thunderbolt!

"But as I think about it, that's not unusual. When I was divorced for several years, even though I'd been miserable in my first marriage, my only goal was to remarry. I didn't feature myself alone. And friend after friend, I've noticed, even if they're successful, have professions, are beautiful, married before, or what have you, they all seem to have one obsession in common—to fall in love, and have a permanent relationship with somebody. We can't seem to settle into ourselves, to discover who we are, unless it's in relationship to someone else. It's that Noah's Ark, two by two thing. Is that it?"

That, and women's priorities.

Somebody Loves Me! Those feelings. Ecstasy. My Aunt Dee would brush her shimmering auburn hair, and with each deft stroke she would softly sing that old Gershwin lyric: "Somebody Loves Me. I Wonder Who? I Wonder Who It Can Be? Somebody Loves Me. It Worries Me. . . ." Absorbing my aunt's words as by osmosis, I swallowed up the wonders of being loved! I've often thought about my aunt and her life, but not until last night, reading Marge Piercy's collection *To Be of Use,* did it all fit together like the pieces of a giant anagram. I read:

That willingness to hang on a meathook and call it love,
That need for loving like a screaming hollow in the soul.

Speaking from a less poetic viewpoint, Newman and Newman state: "In the traditional sex-role conceptualization, women in society acquire their adult social standing from

their husbands' occupation. (Brown, 1965) Where this condition holds, there is no way for the late adolescent woman
to engage in serious deliberations concerning her occupational choice which would, in turn, facilitate the development of personal identity. In fact, women in this situation
spend more time thinking about the characteristics and re-
quirements of their future husband's occupation than they
do about their own." [7]

Now we can understand why the brightest college girl,
siphoning her energies into the task of achieving a permanent and intimate relationship, is hard put to compete in the
outside world—except for a man.

Mr. Right. Not just *any* man, of course. The *right* man.
Setting aside *why* we marry, consider *who* we marry. Matt,
David, Brian, by any other name, is Mr. Right! Like a Greek
chorus, the women's voices came spilling out. "It was that
romantic thing. *Zap.* I dated a lot and suddenly I met *the
right person* and all I could see were those great big blue
eyes, so tender and melting," one woman said. "My father
had eyes like that."

And then another voice: "I married David to continue my
life story. His inaccessibility attracted me. He was hidden,
and like my father, his life was not dominated by a need to
be with women." Each in her own way pointed to what was
familiar about the stranger they'd embraced. "Without my
father's brutality," still another woman explained, "my husband treated me like my father did. When we were dating,
he thought I was the prettiest, sexiest, most interesting
woman he'd ever met."

Is marriage a visitation of our past? A revisiting of those
haunted Oedipal grounds? Most of us do marry the person
we marry to continue our life story. And the problem with
that is that woman's life story doesn't go very far in fostering
the requisite strivings for autonomy that lead to a separate
identity.

Paradoxically, what connects and enchants us has the seeds

of its own disenchantment. "I'll please him. I'll get him to be interested in me," we tell ourselves. "I'll soothe and heal; I'll give my man what mother wasn't able to give hers." Replaying dead dreams and dead rhetorics, we find it impossible to encounter our own significance.

Late Bloomers: The Sleeping Beauty Syndrome. For many women, marriage is a tangle of rescue fantasies. The prevalence of this state of affairs causes us to pause and wonder: Just what is it that we want rescuing from? Like so many Sleeping Beauties, we await the awakening.

Sleeping Beauty has become one of those archetypal dreams, marking the "ideal" pattern of coupling, victimizing not only women but also men. P. I. Travers in *About the Sleeping Beauty* suggests that Briar Rose, the British original of our Sleeping Beauty, has long been the dream of every man, and the hope of every woman. (An interesting aside. In the earlier versions, the prince does not awaken the girl with a gentle kiss, but rapes and impregnates her.)

No matter. If the dream of every man is to rescue and awaken the dormant beauty, then the hope of every woman is to be rescued and awakened. Obviously, the myth is a *folie à deux.* So let's not neglect the significance of the man's dream. After all, it is he who seeks out the dormant beauty, the damsel in distress—that certain helplessness that affirms his potency. The couple, however, do not live happily ever after. The myth comes at too high a price for both.

What is noteworthy in this ancient tale is the symbolic process of woman's dormant condition and subsequent awakening. What are the aspects that lie dormant? In real life women have used their couplings to defer their personal development. The self is what lies dormant. The woman's awakening comes slowly as she discovers that what she has been identified with are her social roles—daughter, wife, and mother—and not with the whole of who she is.

Roles are not definitions—although they have been used that way. Role functions are performed through patterned tasks and duties. They are the palpable witness of aspects of our femaleness, *not* the total mark of who we are. I'm reminded of Roger Gould's trenchant observation that a role can lead to "two opposite results in the change process. A role can be an opportunity to come to a more comprehensive understanding of oneself in action or a role can become a simplified definition of the self that does not do justice to the whole complex human being." [9] Thus, being a wife and mother can be "vitalizing" at one stage, and "justifying" at another.[10]

From widely different sources, again and again, we are told of women's hibernation. A study at Columbia University suggests that "Women perceive themselves and their ideal woman with equal components of activity and passivity. They perceive man's ideal woman, however, as significantly more passive and subordinate in both personal development and place in the family structure." [11] In short, Sleeping Beauties. Therefore, to sustain a woman-man relationship, they tuck themselves away.

Certainly, marriage does offer some rescue; it structures our time. It tells us what to do with our day. And what we do with our day identifies us—for a while. But how can marriage not be disenchanting? It not only has to fulfill our need for intimacy, but also to shape our identity, self-esteem, and self-image, determining who we are and who we will become.

THESIS AND ANTITHESIS

What is it like, this process of self-generating one's own meanings, of not leeching off parents, spouse, or offspring?

The common denominator in the woman's life course has been the paradox of coupling. Every significant merger carries the seeds of its own dissolution. If anything can be said to characterize woman's quest for a singular voice, it is those conflicts and contradictions of merging and distancing in endless repetition.

With those "givens" of feminine identity, we may well wonder how we overcome. Still, many of us have. Endings, you'll discover, bear the seeds of new beginnings. Gathering the women around us, let's explore the process of changing as it occurs in the reality of everyday living. Let's listen to how some "ordinary" women, like you and me, found their lives full of some "shocking" events—and how they unpredictably met the unexpected.

Chapter 2. / Union and Identity

1. Van Dusen, R. and E. Sheldon. "The Changing Status of American Women: A Life-cycle Perspective." *American Psychologist,* 1976, *31,* 106–116.
2. Kuhlen, R. and G. Johnson. "Changes in Goals with Adult Increasing Age." *Journal of Consulting Psychology,* 1952, *16,* 1–4.
3. Roper Poll: *The Virginia Slims American Women's Opinion Poll.* Vol. III. A survey of the attitudes of women on marriage, divorce, the family, and America's changing sexual morality. Spring, 1974.
4. Lopata, H. *Occupation: Housewife.* New York: Oxford University Press, 1971.
5. Erikson, E. H. *Childhood and Society.* New York: Norton, 1950.
6. Levinson, D., C. Darrow, and E. Klein, M. Levinson, and B. McKee. "The Psychosocial Development of Men in Early Adulthood and the Mid-life Transition." *Life History Research in Psychopathology,* *3,* University of Minnesota Press, 1974.
7. Douvan, E. and J. Adelson. *The Adolescent Experience.* New York: John Wiley & Sons, 1966.

8. Kimmel, D. *Adulthood and Aging: An Interdisciplinary Developmental View*. New York: John Wiley & Sons, 1974.

9. Gould, R. "The Phases of Adult Life: A Study in Developmental Psychology." *American Journal of Psychiatry*, 1972, *129*, 33–43.

10. Gould, R. "Growth Toward Self-tolerance." *Psychology Today*, February, 1975.

11. Steinman, A. "Studies in Male-Female Sex-Role Identification." *Psychotherapy: Theory, Research & Practice*, 1975, *12*, 412–417.

II

JOURNEYS

However certain our expectation
The moment foreseen may be unexpected
When it arrives.

—T. S. ELIOT,
Murder in the Cathedral

3

TWO BY TWO:
THE COUPLE IDENTITY

IN THE EARLY SIXTIES A GROUP OF YOUNG WOMEN FROM A prestigious women's college were asked to write essays on the way they expected to be living in ten years. "From the fifty women studied, 46 to 48 projected the following picture:" [1]

1. Marriage to a successful professional man or junior executive.
2. Three or more children.
3. A home in the suburbs.
4. Daily activities that included: chauffeuring, shopping, and food preparation.
5. Family income of $20,000 or more.
6. A station wagon.

And so on. The picture requires no elaboration, I think. Those were middle- or upper-middle-class women who purportedly had all the options. Like most women, however, the trajectory of their future was mouseholed in the prescriptive images of marriage, motherhood, and homemaking—right down to the station wagon.

Coupling: Wed and Unwed. "After graduation, we were all many times each other's bridesmaids. The marriages were in Maryland, Boston, New Hampshire, California, Georgia, Maine," the narrator of Renata Adler's *Speedboat* writes. We women married in the glow of romantic attraction, or in the social pressure that two is better than one. And we built our nest among the sturdy oaks of suburbia.

This is the way that's done. By waiting. We marry and

wait for our life to begin. We tell ourselves, I'll marry and my life will be in order. As a girl, we'd waited to be found. Then we'd met. We waited for his phone call. We waited for his letter. We waited for his valentine. We waited for him to put it in so many words. "Let's get married," we said finally. "Let's not wait." It's our last semester in college and out there is the "real" world. He'd be leaving soon (for the Air Force; the Navy; Europe; a fellowship; graduate school; a job—any one will do). He really didn't want to *marry*; he wanted to wait. "Finish your degree," he'd said. "Or, let me finish my (med school; law school; graduate studies; residency; training . . .)." We talk him into it. We marry sooner than he'd planned. But it would have been her, he tells himself reassuringly.

Waiting is the dead space, the empty in-between.

Unwed. We live together, because two is still less lonely than one. Living together, we tell ourselves, is the best preparation for a permanent relationship—like a practice run. So we turn up our noses at the sturdy oaks of suburbia and build our nest with tarpaulin, canvas, and plastic. We're only camping, we tell ourselves.

This is the way that's done. "Freed," we rent our own pad, or share it with a roommate—who spends all *her* evenings at her lover's place. Being alone is tantamount to being lonely, and it's lonely without a roommate, so our lover sleeps over three or four times a week. "Let's live together," we finally say. "Let's live together and split expenses." He's living in the apartment half the time anyway. Cloaked in practicality, we talk him into it. "Why pay two rents? Two phone bills? Two electric and gas bills? Two grocery bills?" If we share, maybe we'll be able to afford a nicer apartment or a larger TV set. We don't have to get married . . . not now, anyway.

How we've changed! Now we're totally prepared—or at least we know what to expect. Or do we? Unwed coupling has been common enough this past decade to shed considerable light on the woman's process of coupling, unwed and

wed. Still, I hadn't expected the sources of my enlightenment
to be marriage counselors or family service associations.
There is an anomaly in the fact that one tenth of the family-
service case load consists of unwed couples, most of them in
their twenties and early thirties. The phenomenon, and indeed, it is a phenomenon, is sufficiently widespread to war-
rant coverage in an article for *The New York Times Magazine*.[2] The ultimate in "liberation" has found its paradox:
Marriage counseling for unwed couples!

To be sure, the prescriptive images have changed. Living
together and *not* getting married is now the thing to do.
The rhetoric and strategies also have changed, but apparently
the webs and nets of bonding remain unchanged. The changing patterns of coupling are not reflected in the changing
patterns of women's *expectations*. Women still fall back on
establishing a couple identity through which, we tell ourselves, we'll come into our own. "Together, we'll conquer
the world," one woman said. After that marriage dissolved,
years later, she said of her lover, "He'll build me a stone
and concrete house on a hill with trees and a brook. He will
do for me what I can't."

The seventies axiom—that if we know what to expect,
we'll be prepared and different—implies that we have only
to practice and we change. The rise, however, in uncoupling
and recoupling—in search of what?—tells us something else.
While divorce rates increase, so do the number of remar-
riages.

What can we learn about the female journey of union
and identity—the process of coupling—from the so-called
singlehood of the seventies—from the coupling, uncoupling,
and recoupling? Has living together truly "liberated" our
relationships, buttressed our intimacy, diminished our disillusionments, reshaped our expectations, shaped our identity, strengthened our autonomy? Is living together truly the
marker of shedding the last vestiges of our female past, of
our changing?

No longer locked into the traditional styles, women are

inclined to make of the nontraditional patterns still another imperative and another cage. Women, especially, are uneasy with difference. We function more comfortably when we bond, affiliate, and merge. I'm reminded of an observation by literary critic Anatole Broyard, who nails down his thoughts as sharply as a lapidarian pins his fluttering Monarchs. Although it was written in another context, the comment is apt. He wrote: "I hate to see any differences disappear, in fiction or in fact. We are diminished enough as it is." [3]

Let's explore the process of coupling, unwed and wed, as we listen to Erica Childs. Let's listen, in particular, for that expectation of rescue, followed by the emerging couple identity and its crisis, leading to the emergence of a personal identity—the common elements in the woman's journey of self-definition through coupling.

WE BUILD OUR NESTS

From Tarpaulin and Canvas . . . When we met, Erica was twenty-eight, an active feminist, and married for the past two years to Harold Shaw. She and Harold had lived together for two and a half years before getting married—and before that she'd had a tumultuous affair with Sandor. She hadn't always been a feminist. Not until the late sixties, she tells us, did she come to a point of "heightened consciousness" when suddenly she could look back on her life and understand for the first time those growing-up miseries.

We begin our odyssey with Erica because hers is a story of a metamorphosis in coupling and in selfhood that starts with a first love affair, and every woman's dream of rescue and fulfillment, and unfolds with a marriage to another man, and another vision of herself. As she traces the byways of her changing, she brings her journey into sharp relief with all its longings, expectations, contradictions, and "shocks."

"Take the first right on Simmons Square, go south three

blocks, and take an immediate left. If you get lost, phone me. It's a perfectly safe neighborhood." Erica sounded brisk and efficient.

I left my hotel forty-five minutes ahead of schedule, to finally pull up before a concrete and brick building on the fringe of the "arty" part of Boston. I waited before a heavy door until a lean, attenuated man unbolted the latch and led me silently up one flight of stairs. Later, I learned that was Erica's husband.

We went up another short flight, and I burst on a profusion of sun and warmth and foliage—a veritable greenhouse. Erica and Harold were reconverting a commercial loft into their own nesting ground, housing their separate careers and their home. Erica is an independent TV producer with several documentaries to her credit; Harold is an architect. Their living quarters seemed a complete reflection of their life.

She was on the phone when she looked up and motioned me ahead. She had small, delicate hands and was fine boned. The fact that she wore no makeup heightened the luminosity of her skin. She continued her conversation. My eyes bounced from the proliferating ferns and palms to the comfortable-looking leather couch, to an old-fashioned rocking chair, to a portable Singer sewing machine, to the brick wall of whisks, ladles, spoons, and carving knives glinting in the sun. Nearby the refrigerator stood as an unobtrusive presence—nontraditional, I thought, but organic, much like the encounter that was to follow.

If you were to ask Erica, "Who are you?" she'd answer quick as a finger snap, "What do you mean? I'm a producer!" Her manner can seem querulous even when we're in perfect agreement, but then she'd fought and labored from an early age.

As a girl, Erica was subjected to a number of contradictory messages—in psychological terms, double binds. Those are situations where the child is caught in a network of "can't win" communications with verbal injunctions to Do, while

other verbal and nonverbal messages imply Don't! To begin
with, she was named Erica because her parents couldn't agree
on a name, and compromised by giving her the same name
as her mother. Her parents, she explained, had assumed that
there'd be no reason for a mix-up since, being a girl, she'd
marry and her husband's name would then identify and
distinguish her from her mother. As an infant, however, to
avoid confusion, she was nicknamed Eric, and it stuck.

Moreover, her mother, an accomplished photographer and
college instructor with occasional gallery exhibits, was her
"best friend" and "role model," who made it clear that her
daughter was to excel. But *not* while she bore the identical
name as her mother, Erica Childs.

Erica's interests were supported by her mother, she was
taken seriously, and it was always assumed that she'd be a
professional, like her mother—until the actual day arrived.
"You see, I've got the kind of public attention because of
producing that my mother always wanted," she explained
matter-of-factly. "With one side of her mouth, I was told,
You should excel and go beyond your parents. With the
other side, I'm told, Don't you dare! It's weird. She even
wanted me to change my name when I first started becoming
known."

Like a good many contradictions, however, it was an opportunity for growth. It was the first step in separating—in
sifting herself out—and in seeing the world through her own
eyes. "It made me realize something," Erica continued. "In
spite of all her accomplishments, my mother was desperately
insecure all her life. My grandmother was a handsome
woman, and my mother felt like the ugly duckling. Those
feelings of inferiority actually prevented her from getting
the kind of recognition she wanted. She always held back.
That's where I decided to be different from her."

That, too, housed its own conflict. Erica was different,
and differences are difficult to support when we yearn so
for approval. Temperamentally, she was an assertive, questioning child—attributes, per se, that foreshadowed her ca-

reer, and may well have salvaged her life. But they were also qualities that aren't readily accepted in a girl. So she plummeted into still another bind. Although she was reared to excel, she also was made to feel that her assertiveness was "wrong" and that some day it would "destroy" her.

"I was blamed for being persistent and aggressive," Erica explained, playing with the massive sculptured ring adorning her middle finger. "In school, because I was a girl, I wasn't being taken seriously. I didn't understand that then. Then, I thought it was because there was something wrong with *me*. At home, I was told that I was too aggressive. My family image was: 'Well, that's Eric, she's always the first one through the revolving door.' I was made to feel that was wrong. Really it was a means of my surviving—of making sure I got what I wanted, because nobody else was going to get it for me, but me. But I hated myself for that. I hated those traits in me. If I could have done something to change the way I was, I would have. I was miserable. I realize it now, that had I been a boy, I would have developed a confidence in myself that I didn't have. No one imagined that some day I might be in business for myself and would need those qualities. I was told: 'You'll never be able to work for anyone. You'll never hold a job!' "

Erica was also different from her peers in interests. Although uncertain of her direction, she was strongly drawn to the theater. Raised in a university town in Connecticut, she had the opportunity of seeing many plays, and while still in high school she spent all her free time doing just that. But the intensity and the nature of her interests also served to separate her from her schoolmates. Once again she was the alien one. She didn't fit. She wasn't popular.

She reflected, flatly: "I was a wallflower. The boys that were interested in me, I wasn't interested in. Besides, I didn't like me, so how could I like anybody who did. Anybody who was stupid enough to like me, I thought, had to be worse off than me. And if that wasn't bad enough, I was the tallest girl in class, although I'm only five eight now. And I was flat-chested, a source of great anguish, because I was always poked fun at. This preoccupation with conventional beauty is so destructive to women. It's a long, painful process before you come to realize that it's what's inside that counts."

Paradoxically, what caused Erica to have a "miserable" adolescence also caused her to confront her own identity earlier than most. Burrowing herself in the theater, she may, in part, have been escaping the painful reality of being "different," but she also was thrown into cultivating those differences. Moreover, the fact that she wasn't popular, or "pretty" in the conventional sense, caused her to turn inward, nurturing other aspects of herself—a common enough experience among women achievers.

"All the women I'm close to today," she continued, "women who've made something of themselves, all of us were miserable as children. But out of that suffering came a drive—whatever it takes to make you determined to amount to something. The sense to prove you're worthy."

For most women, however, self-worth is measured in terms of our worth in the eyes of men. And Erica was a female, after all. She'd been reared to believe that when she'd marry, she'd find her own identity and her own name. Like most women, she had to lose her way in order to find *her* way. She wanted very much to belong, to feel loved, and to feel worthy. Like most women, she sought to find herself through coupling.

The Watershed Years: Separating. In college Erica continued to feel an outsider and continued, as well, her intense interest in the theater, particularly in producing. But at the time, she had no inkling that she wouldn't be a photographer like her mother.

She also had no inkling of the direction her life would take. "My ideal," she admits, "what I was searching for, wasn't exactly *my* future. I had the image of someday meeting the perfect genius of a man, and through him I'd find myself. Someone with whom I'd work, who'd be my partner in every sense, and through him I'd achieve what I wanted. It would be *the two of us*. And would you believe it, I met him! It's such a melodramatic story that if I'd ever produce such a play, they'd say it was rotten even for melodrama."

In her senior year in college, she won an Honors Program abroad and went to Milan for a year of study. That year proved the final break with home and with mother. "I was twenty-one. I left for Italy. I let my hair grow. I changed my name; I wasn't Eric anymore. I insisted on being called Erica. And I also lost my virginity. That was the watershed."

It also was the watershed in directing the course of her future work. It was there that she met a friend with a similar interest in the theater. Walking home one night, after a particularly moving performance at La Scala, her friend casually observed: "You know, some day you're going to be a famous producer." Erica recalls that until that moment, it had never consciously entered her head. It was as if her friend had identified a hidden part of her, and planted a seed. What happened after that is melodrama.

"My junior year in college I fell madly in love with a professor," Erica began. "We dated. When I went to Milan he decided to visit me during spring vacation, since he wanted to visit his family in Paris. I wanted to sleep with him; I would have if he'd initiated it, but he didn't. He asked that I meet him in Paris. I agreed. As it happened when the owner of the *pensione* where I lived learned that I was going to Paris, she asked me to deliver some things to her nephew, who happened to live there and who also was a political refugee. I became the courier."

Coupling: The Couple Identity. Erica arrived in Paris a few days ahead of schedule, knowing not a word of French. An outsider once more. "I looked up this guy my landlady asked me to, since I was carrying this bag of stuff. Well, he turned out as if I'd invented him. He not only was a gorgeous man, but also in his own country he'd been a noted producer. I was twenty-one, a virgin, and here was this intense, romantic man, my first trip to Paris. Well, I never located the professor from school—we got our signals mixed and he went to Milan while I was in Paris. Sandor didn't believe there was a professor. I slept with Sandor the first night, and spent this strange week in his apartment. I bled all over the place. You could have wrung out the sheets."

Erica got up to make some coffee; she walked with quick, decisive steps, never once interrupting her narrative. At the end of the week, she recalled, she had to return to her studies, but she kept up an unflagging correspondence until once more she could rejoin him in Paris for the summer. By the time she left for home and her graduate studies, they were "engaged" and making plans for his eventual transfer to the States. Until then, he was to write and set a date for another visit during winter vacation. All told, they'd lived together only a handful of weeks.

Typically, Erica pushed toward merging; Sandor toward distance and ultimately a final separation. Having found her ideal image, Erica planned her future around him. In fact, she felt he was her future.

"My whole identity had been wrapped in this man," she said. "He was a brilliant genius I'd found, and he was going to marry me, and I was going to work with him. That's how I started graduate school, and majored in production—even though I'd decided that before I'd met him. I suddenly had a new confidence and a new identity. Or so I thought. That was all pre- my enlightenment. He was the bedrock of my identity. I was engaged to be married, and my life would be within that marriage. The last letter I received from him was in October, setting a date to meet in Paris for the holidays. I didn't hear from him again, ever."

Uncoupling: The Couple "Identity" Crisis. She wanted to shrink into herself, become the size of a tear. She was anguished, wrenched from a dream and an identity. She wrote. She phoned. She cabled. She was unable to reach him. It grew closer to the time she was to leave, but she feared going without word. Her world, Erica tells us, collapsed. "All my dreams about the future were shattered—who I was, what I'd be doing in my work, everything I'd been doing in school, for which I received a lot of recognition, was tied up with my belief in myself as Sandor's wife! It doesn't make sense. I was still the one doing it, but I'd given *him* the power. My confidence in school fell apart."

As an afterthought, she added: "I was very lucky really. Once I came out on the other side of hell, I understood that." Indeed, if not lucky, she was fortunate. The image she had of herself as a woman—not coupling but uncoupling, not merging but distancing—"prepared" her for living her own life. Living together, per se, would not have been a preparation for their future together, nor would it have been a preparation for her future as her own person.

She'd hurt as if stung by a swarm of killer bees. I asked about how she began to change. Flooded by a downpour of memories, Erica traced her personal epiphany. "I had to hit bottom before I could come up again. I felt so wretched that anything would have been better than where I was! So I was willing to do whatever I had to, to change and grow. That was the beginning. But it wasn't anything specific that I *did*. It was how I *felt*—feeling so shredded and so desperate. I'd always been so controlled before. Well, I cracked and lost control and that opened me up to see. I consider it a rebirth. I date *my* life as beginning from that point. It was the point at which *I became the person I wanted to be*. I began to know myself, and my own vision of me. Before that I'd felt as if I had a black pit inside me. A void. Things happened to me, I went through a lot of experiences, but nothing ever connected. I didn't learn anything from my experiences.

"One night I wrote Sandor to say that if I didn't get an answer to that letter, I'd assume that it was the end. At the time I didn't know . . . well, I was miserable so I threw a big party at school, and I got stoned! I'd smoked pot before, but I was so shut off that nothing ever happened. Suddenly, I was different; I had opened up and I felt like a light went on.

A flash of illumination. It was as if suddenly everything I'd been through came together. I connected. I saw how really badly Sandor had treated me all along. I also saw that my friends liked me for me. I saw . . .

"A few days later I found out that he'd died in a car crash. A suicide. But he had stopped writing long before his death and I'd come through the relationship and already faced the end of it." Erica learned that something had to die to make room for something to be born—another truism. The death of the dream of a life lived through him gave birth to the vision of *herself* in the world. His silence, even before his actual death, threw her back on her own resources. That black pit—that empty space—wasn't really empty. If we take a hard look, we may discover all those experiences we've had, but haven't connected with. To deny them may keep us from feeling the hurts, but it also keeps us unidentifiable and undefined.

Think about that.

Erica's childhood prepared her for her next leap of growth. She'd always been a fighter and a survivor. To her good fortune, she learned of Sandor's actual death *after* she'd gone through her own small death and rebirth—enabling her to relinquish the last dregs of an idealized image. It would have been so easy to hold on to him as a tragic hero.

"Of course, news of his death threw me back on all sorts of guilt trips," she said. "But I realized that I couldn't live someone else's life for him. Here was this great man, and he was crippled in a number of ways. And like so many women, I thought, I was going to heal and soothe and devote my life to *his* wholeness! I realized then that I had a right to my own life."

Recoupling. I felt as if I'd been through a bad melodrama with its countless gratuitous connections—a chance meeting in Paris, a tragic antihero, a reunion, a crack-up, and a suicide. "And Harold?" I managed. Erica responded, "When Harold and I started going out together it was different. I was twenty-

four and professionally established. The me he first knew was
the professional me. We lived together almost two and a half
years before we married. But getting married didn't mean a
thing. It was hocus-pocus for five minutes before a judge. It
didn't change our perceptions of each other, or our *expectations*."

If Erica had been subjected to double binds as a child, as
a woman she created her full share of her own double messages. And she was the first to admit that what she thought
didn't always coincide with what she did or felt. "Why did
I get married then?" She repeated my question, turning over
her thoughts. "Because there are still a lot of socially controlled reflexes in me that wanted that final step in our commitment. And it made my parents happy. Also we intend to
have children. Of all the feminist battles I've fought, that's
not one I intend to waste my energies over."

I thought this was an appropriate juncture to ask what she
thought about couples living together. A woman of strong
and definite opinions, she replied quickly: "I think anyone
who gets married without having lived with the person is
crazy. You can't know whether you're capable of living with
another person, whether you mesh, unless you have."

I suppose. But I continued to wonder. Isn't it the contradictions and incongruities of coupling that jolt us into a new
way of seeing our relationships, and ourselves in those relationships? Wasn't it really the fact of Erica's *being together
with* Sandor, and *then distancing*, that began the process
of sifting herself out? And also that permitted her to re-
couple with an awareness of her expectations? Don't we need
both sides of that dialectical coinage?

Erica answered my unspoken questions. "Although living
together doesn't necessarily mean you've worked through a
relationship. I know a lot of couples that, once they married,
the expectations have changed and they've had problems.
One couple I know has been living together seven years, and
they're better off not marrying.

"I firmly believe that you have to be capable of being alone and to have worked out your own point of view as a separate person, which I never could have done if I'd lived with Sandor, before you're capable of really having a relationship with someone else. What I imagined marriage would be like—the values and the fantasies—I played out with Sandor. After I broke through those, I changed. Yet I brought a lot of those feelings and expectations into my relationship with Harold. But in living with him, I became more secure. I found out I could be the first one through the revolving door and still be loved. I grew and changed. Not that we don't have our problems. I'm very greedy."

Paradoxes. Paradoxes. However much Erica espoused the freedom and the value of living together, once again some part of her also was impatient for bonding and cementing the union. Within the first six months of living with Harold, she became pregnant, not once but twice. In the shadowy corridors of her psyche, she began to build and even people her nest. On some level, she also needed a final proof of her womanliness. She observed: "Not consciously, but in some ways, I wanted a baby. The first time I was relieved to find that I could get pregnant. The second time it was awful. I was ten weeks pregnant and the whole experience of an abortion was upsetting."

And yet, however much some part wanted to cement her union with Harold, another part still was cautious. So they drew up an elaborate prenuptial marriage contract, separating them financially and also spelling out their shared obligations. "We don't have any joint bank accounts, for example," Erica explained. "I support myself and he supports himself and we share joint expenses, like rent, food, and so on. Since we both free-lance, neither is liable for the other. But it operates on other levels too. There are clauses related to child care. When we have children, the duties are to be shared equally. We talked and worked out all those things ahead of time."

I asked Erica, since they'd lived together and there'd been an open communication between them, why the necessity of a *written* contract?

"Why not?" she shot back. "If you trust each other, why not have it written down?"

"If you *trust* each other . . ." I persisted.

"That's not true," Erica explained. "By the time a relationship has degenerated to the point of divorce, people aren't rational anymore, and their best instincts and their feelings that come out of loving and trusting someone are eroded, and we wanted to straighten out and clarify and deal with and codify all those things out of our *best* feelings for each other, which then may be binding if it got to some point later when that wasn't operating anymore, and we wouldn't be in control. It's in terms of a rational dealing with possibilities. Most women don't ever confront those things; they assume everything's all right and later find out it's not."

Of course. Still, can change actually be predicted, codified, and executed? Wasn't this another attempt to control and bring stability into what is ultimately a changing relationship? Certainly, financial agreements can be codified—but can emotional ones? To buffer against more hurt, wasn't Erica attempting to control and cement her relationship?

Verbal and written agreements aren't new in the course of coupling, but their stipulations and the kinds of persons utilizing them are. In the past, prenuptial agreements were drawn up by the very wealthy to protect rights of descent and inheritance. Currently, there seem to be two categories of contracts—those drawn up by the young couple before marrying to insure an egalitarian partnership; and those drawn up in the middle years when the partners are attempting to negotiate compromises in their marital conflicts. Currently, in addition to financial arrangements, they also include stipulations concerning child care and household labor. Some also stipulate place of residence, decisions about careers, and extramarital relationships. A small number of those agreements, such as economic arrangements, may be legally binding; others are not likely to be.

An important note. For Erica, her marriage to Harold meant a sharing of responsibilities—financial, household, childrearing, and also personal development. Marriage, for too many women, comes to mean an abnegation of responsibility and a total merging of interests and activities.

Before we parted, Erica took me on a tour of their home. She was a proud guide. She showed me the work areas, where they worked separately but "contiguously," so that if she felt like a hug in the middle of the afternoon, she could run over. "It's the way we planned our living space," she explained as we squeezed past sacks of plaster, wooden beams, and cinder blocks. "We eat together twice a day. I make dinner because I enjoy it. And we see each other every night, but we don't spend a lot of time doing things together. In fact, we do very few social things together. I'm active in my professional life and with organizations. Most parties I go alone because he's not a big social person. Most people don't even know I'm married, and even those who do don't relate to us as a *couple*. We're two separate people."

Stepping over a thick cable, I couldn't resist one last question: "Extramarital affairs? I'd be furious. But I know he wouldn't." It was the first time Erica had laughed. "I'm not concerned with other men either. It's not a big belief in fidelity. It's just that for me sex is meaningless if it's not connected to the expression of the way I feel about somebody. That's probably part of my female sex scripting."

Off the main living area, we entered a small red-brick room. "That's designed for a baby's room," she volunteered. Grounded in their concrete and mortar, they'd made room for their next project!

As I left, my eye caught sight of two bronze plaques over the doorbell. Harold Shaw, Inc., one read. And next to that, splitting the rays of the sun: Erica Childs.

THE COUPLE IDENTITY

Erica has described, at a dizzying pace, the female process of coupling in which critical fantasies are played out—fantasies that are lamentably reductive to the woman's image and sense of autonomy and personal definition. Wed or unwed, swaddled in romantic illusions, the woman couples and suffers a common journey.

Coupling and Identity. We live together or marry and fully expect to share an identity. We do things Together—Together we'll conquer the world. That's the fabric of our first interactions and conflicts! The woman's identity is dependent on being two. She thinks in terms of a couple and with a typical incongruity, as she gains a new esteem in her own and society's eyes, she also loses a personal sense of self. Women in the early phase of coupling—identified, traditionally, as the newlywed—understandably are greedy and easily threatened. They're greedy for the reassurance of possession and threatened by any difference. Dependency and rancor seem to go together with romantic love and coupling.

Again and again in my treatment of couples, I've been struck by the tenacity of that couple identity—for the woman. In therapy session after session, the woman devotes her time and energies to discussing her husband or lover and her hurts, trying hard to fathom who and what *he* is, and how *he* can and "should" change. Occasionally, she'll even bring in a dream. His. In the reverse situation it is rare, indeed, for her counterpart to mention her, and if he does, it is because he is especially annoyed by something she'd done, but certainly *not* in order to plumb her psyche—even though they'd both purportedly entered psychotherapy because of a troubled relationship!

From that couple identity grow several contradictory yet consistent correlates.

Jealousy. To see our worth only through *his* eyes can't do much for our own sense of security. It's been reported that if the newlywed differs in any way from her elder sisters, it is with regard to two attributes: She shows both greater jealousy and greater warmth.[4]

Those seemingly contradictory emotions make sense when we note the initial expectation: "We were going to be all wrapped up in each other forever and ever." For the woman, coupling becomes a complete merger, in which the sense of a personal self is blurred over. So, logically enough, anything that threatens that merger will give rise to fits of jealousy, acute hurts, and the slamming of doors. The greater warmth and closeness, paradoxically, leads to more friction, more emotionality, and more *talk*. Compared to older couples, the new couples not only talk more, they also talk more *personally* about their hurts and expectations.

The early years of coupling, generally, are a time of—if not better—more sex, more demonstrativeness and more companionship. The couple has "fun" together;[5] they ski, play tennis, share a summer cottage with friends. They begin to unravel the cord that binds them as sons and daughters, and they even learn to "rap" against their parents. United they stand. The wife turns to her spouse for approval, concern, sympathy, and support. She looks to him for parenting. He becomes the source of her security and meanings. It follows that when those expectations aren't met, he also becomes the source of her jealousy, anger, feelings of betrayal, and sometimes even rage.

When we speak of the parenting she's lacked, I don't mean traumatic childhood experiences that are replayed in neurotic or psychotic marital interactions. Rather, I refer to the more frequent and usual lacks we suffer simply in the process of growing up female—the way that women go about assuming a feminine identity. What for the woman is Togetherness, for the man, having labored to *separate* and *achieve* his masculine identity, is s-mothering!

Twisting themselves to conform to an Us, women flatten out. I'm reminded of a study begun at Michigan State Uni-

versity with women freshmen. When those women, all in
the top 1 percent of their class, were followed up after
graduation, those who'd married tended to have lost their
independence and drive, appearing more compliant and con-
servative.[6] We tunnel our vision and tame our drive; some
women have suggested that they've tamed their sexual drive
as well.

Possessiveness and Commitment. Most women marrying
in the forties, fifties, and even mid-sixties have not had the
sexual freedom that their younger counterparts have experienced. It has been common for the woman of the past generation to have had her first and only sexual education at the
hands of her husband, at least until she reaches middle age.
By and large, extramarital affairs have been uncommon for
women in the early years of marriage. The younger woman,
in contrast, has been quicker not only in entering premarital
sexual relationships but also extramarital relationships—and
at an earlier point in the marriage.

Now out into the world and exposed to the same garden
variety of sexual attractions as their spouses, a good many
women encounter the same pulls, and the same opportunity
to explore facets of themselves that otherwise might have
gone unnoticed and unknown. For most women of the
younger generation, it is no more than that. Their encounters
are neither prolonged, nor do they seem to be particularly
disrupting to the coupling. That is, if she is the one to have
an affair. Although the younger woman feels she has more
sexual options, and doesn't feel bound by any great ideas
about fidelity, as Erica frankly admits, the possibility of *his*
having an affair is another matter. Rationally or not, that is
construed as a betrayal and an abandonment. Sexuality for
the woman, Erica points out, is connected not as much with
a physical imperative, as it is with a romantic illusion. (More
on the woman's sexual development later.)

"Shocks" of Coupling. As the merger of coupling draws
tighter, our male counterparts—reared to labor for separate-

ness—subtly inch their way toward the open space. To be sure, we're coming from a different sense of space. For the woman, the first jolt is experienced as a couple "identity" crisis. It is a time when those first cracks in "being all wrapped up in each other" suddenly become visible. Cushioned in the image of Sandor's future wife, Erica was shattered by his silence. Her experience was one of total abandonment.

For most of us, however, those first marks of fissuring are far less dramatic. They may be in as innocent a form as his desire to take up the guitar, play tennis with his buddy, hike with the Sierra Club, or work overtime, scaling the heights of his ambition. It matters little. All that matters is that both time and emotional investment are leaking away from Us.

Unsettled, women try harder. At first she falls in with his step. She accommodates, or tries to. "Those early years were painful," Roberta reflected. "I dropped out of college, married David, and went to Rome, where he had a glamorous job waiting for him. I'd expected adoration and David turned out tame in every way. In and out of bed. He worked into the night, bent on fulfilling *his* future. I had no outlet for my feelings. I could have taken some courses but there was nothing that interested me. I learned the language and worked in a secretarial pool at the U.S. Embassy. He was in international banking even then, and I thought, that way we'd be together. But he left me out; he shared very little with me. My options were limited. So what was the next thing to do? Babies. I was bottled up, angry and resentful, and he was totally involved with his career."

Nested in a traditional marriage, Roberta filled the void with more and more babies. We fill the growing space *between*. She reconciled herself to being, like her mother, a *"hausfrau."*

That was the fifties. What of the seventies? At the age of twenty-eight, married six years, Ellen is an involved working woman. She'd been through the rebellions of the sixties, had a brief affair with a "revolutionary," and then married Paul, who has a passion for scuba diving. She confides that although many of her expectations are different from her mother's, many are still the same.

"I was the one who talked Paul into marrying," she said. "He wanted to wait until he was out of school. He always says he got married a year or two earlier than he would have liked, but it would have been me. We share a lot and we've been good friends. We share in all the household routines, like the laundry, cooking, and cleaning. And I even took up scuba diving. Not to mention jogging.

"But he isn't quick to initiate certain things. Like I talked him into marrying. I've talked him into other things too. I fill in the space too quickly. Why? I wonder. I guess it's out of fear. I can't seem to stand a space. My girl friends are that way too. I pounce. I can't give myself time for something to develop. Maybe I can't face that we're different. It upsets me when I'm not connecting."

The One-Source-of-Supply Syndrome. Despite all the couple's talk, each is hard put to understand the other—be it in the traditional role-differentiated marriage, in which the husband is the breadwinner and the wife is the home-maker, or in the post-sixties shared-role union in which both share in the household routines.

For the woman, her husband is her most important activity. Particularly during the first years, if it is a choice between taking that training program or staying home with him, she is more likely to choose staying home. No matter how involved she may be with outside interests, the woman makes being sensitive to his feelings her primary career. So, she reasons, why shouldn't he feel the same way? That, after all, is part and parcel of the couple identity. We're a perfect match! Or, we should be.

The attitude toward work, for example, which Roberta identified as her first jolt, points up a striking difference between the sexes. Where men look upon work as a crystallization of their definition, enhancing their masculine identity, women view work in a rather more romantic and more practical light. One out of ten young women, it is said, hopes that her future husband's work won't be too demanding, so that they'll be able to spend more time together. For a woman, work doesn't define her husband; rather, the demands of his family's needs define his work![1]

From the young husband's viewpoint, he seems to feel that he has been pressed into curtailing his freedom sooner than he would have liked. And small wonder. Traditionally, although the man makes the final decision about when they'll marry, it is the woman who "talks him into it." Women, it's been pointed out, have a shorter range of marriageability and a longer span of life,[5] which contributes to the asynchrony in needs and pressures.

An early coupling, however, seems to be a disservice to both partners. Clearly it muffles the woman's development. I should be precise about the "it." It's not coupling or marriage, per se, that aborts her growth, but those corrosive attitudes and expectations: waiting for her future to begin; waiting to be fulfilled; waiting to be completed *through* another.

Perhaps the most corrosive illusion that we labor under is the expectation that the other will meet all our needs. In real life, couples are more likely to reinforce certain aspects of each other's person, while discouraging or ignoring others. How else could it be? It isn't the reality that's at fault but the fantasy—the illusion that one person can give us everything. This is something I've often referred to as our One-Source-of-Supply Syndrome. The reverberations of that attitude trigger the first disenchantments, but not until the middle years—if we continue to wait—do we feel its full impact.

Making the Connections. There is a strong need in us to belong and to connect. But too many women dissipate too much of their energies making those connections with others —husband, lover, children—before they've connected with themselves.

How the couple deals with the first shocks of distancing—those fissures in their togetherness—foreshadows the nature of their relationship and their interaction for the next several years. The traditional attempt at resolution is to fill the space *between*, not within. In a marriage of the transitional sixties, Millie straddles the old and the new, offering a glimpse of how she managed to bridge the two. Although she started out in marriage with the usual images of Togetherness, she also faced the gnawing emptiness.

"I'm not as dependent as I thought I'd be," she explained. When we met she'd been married ten years. "It wasn't my *image* of what marriage would be, but as it turned out, I'm not as much an extension of him as I thought I would be. You see, we married in '65 and in many ways marriage was still pretty much like in the fifties. We hadn't even slept together before we married. When we married I thought we'd be completely wrapped up in each other. I'd had this image of the ideal wife who would always be there for her man. And then a combination of things happened. Don became very involved in his work and started to travel a lot. And I was alone a lot. I was thrown on my own suddenly. I was really thrown. So I started looking around for something to do and I rediscovered my interest in drama.

"I discovered I couldn't depend on him for *everything*. Since he wasn't around as much as the first year, I had to find my own outlet. It would have been unfair to him to have me just waiting at the door with bated breath. So many women I know can't function if their husbands aren't around. I didn't want to be like that. So I told myself, Okay, you're not going to be around so much; you've gotten more independent. So now I'll find something to do too. Something that's all *my* own.

"I'm kind of embarrassed to admit it, but in college I didn't have a specific interest in mind because I knew I was going to get married. I liked children and I wanted to have a family. That was the ideal image.

"But when Don got more and more into his work, the

image didn't work. When the baby came I had all my time swallowed up with her. So between his being away so much and the diapering, laundry, and ironing, there wasn't much left for me. It became hard for me to see how my life could be fulfilled only through him, through his work. He's a financial investment broker, and that's very technical. His work is so different from anything I've done or been interested in. He's scientifically oriented and I'm interested in theater arts. I said to myself, How are you going to get your satisfaction from something you know nothing about? Watching his career take off is nice, but that's about it!

"We finally have taken separate paths and separate interests. I never thought we would; we were high school sweethearts." Although Millie's ideal couple identity was disrupted as her husband turned more and more to his career, the fissuring of their togetherness allowed her the breathing space to rediscover an aspect of herself that she'd hidden away.

Resolutions differ just as the women differ and their particular time in history differs, but the journeys and the expectations have been strikingly similar, be it Roberta's marriage of the fifties, or Millie's of the sixties, or Erica's living together and marriage of the seventies. The asynchrony between what marriage and togetherness should be (the popular image) and what it is (the unique interactions of coupling) is jolting, moving some of us to reassess and question what we'd steadfastly believed. In many instances the hidden inner struggle—that unfinished business of connecting with ourselves—collides with the external struggles of coupling.

Having listened to the women, let's turn for a moment to those compilers of the human condition, the social and behavioral scientists. Pineo's follow-up study of 1,000 couples observed as newlyweds and then after twenty years of marriage is relevant.

He has reported a trend over the years which he's termed "disenchantment." [7] In subsequent studies, others, finding a similar phenomenon, have described it as a "cooling off."

Specifically, what is being observed seems to be a loss of fit, a mismatching within the couple. No longer are they the companions they'd been. With time there is a loss of intimacy, a cooling off sexually, and a lessening in sharing common activities. That finding is of particular note, since as newlyweds those couples were considered especially well matched. The direction and nature of the mismatching over the years, moreover, is revealing. The early disenchantments, those first jolts, were nearly predictable since they derived from an exaggerated image of the mate, a romantic, idealized image of the loved one. In the middle years, however, the reported mismatching had been unexpected and unpredictable, deriving from internal and external circumstances, such as changes in the personality and in the environment. Pineo observes that, with the passage of time, as each partner changed (or even if only one changed), their matching became no better than if they'd been brought together by chance. "Perfect matching," he states, "could only occur with some element of luck," since the grounds upon which we decide to marry diminish with time.

Over and again we'll discover those developmental disruptions and contradictions. Perfect matching, it seems, does not lead to perfect marriages. Still, differences can be disrupting, but disruption also provides the opportunity for growth.

"After seven years of marriage," one woman explained, "maybe I can begin to face the fact that I'd rather curl up with a good book than play golf with my husband. And that I'd rather see a Bergman movie than some escapist one. It's been too threatening even to *think* that way. You see, I had to be a better companion to my husband than his first wife. And I've been fed so much brouhaha about the ideal couples being those who have identical interests and tastes."

Paradoxically, separating from that earlier convergence can be the initiation of a genuine closeness. The added space of "cooling off" allows other aspects of ourselves to surface. When she found herself alone, Millie tells us, she was thrown

—thrown on her own resources, rediscovering her own serious interests.

As the tangles of merging unravel, so do the extravagant expectations of trying to fit the other person or oneself into another's image.

Every so often, we experience oceanic disillusionments, markers, that tell us it is a time for changing. For some, those "shocks" are met as challenges to be bridged; for others, they're ineluctable losses to be quickly, if thinly salved. So we talk him into having a baby, moving to a larger apartment, buying that house in the suburbs, or buying one in the country.

Chapter 3. / Two by Two: The Couple Identity

1. Douvan, E. and J. Adelson. *The Adolescent Experience.* New York: John Wiley & Sons, 1966.
2. Gross, A. "Marriage Counseling for Unwed Couples." *The New York Times Magazine,* April 24, 1977.
3. Broyard, A. "Reinvented Man." *The New York Times Book Review,* June 5, 1977.
4. Lowenthal, M., M. Thurnher, D. Chiriboga, *et al. Four Stages of Life: A Comparative Study of Women and Men Facing Transitions.* San Francisco: Jossey-Bass Behavioral Science Series, 1975.
5. Troll, L. *Early and Middle Adulthood: Life-span Developmental Series.* California: Brooks/Cole, 1975.
6. Ross, D. "The Story of the Top One Percent of the Women at Michigan State University." Unpublished study cited in L. Troll, *Early and Middle Adulthood.*
7. Pineo, P. "Disenchantment in the Later Years of Marriage." *Marriage and Family Living,* 1961, *23,* 3–11.

4

SHARED PROJECTS:
THE NEXT THINGS TO DO

WHEN THOSE FIRST ILLUSIONS BEGIN TO FADE, OR WHEN HE feels pinched for space—internal and external—and she feels an emptying space, what then?

It may take nine months, a year and a half, or seven years, but couples, wed and unwed, inevitably come to the point of Now What? In days past, we spoke of the honeymoon being over—a time when the difference and distance between a couple comes into sharper focus. We live together, wed or unwed; we sign that two-year lease and are anchored temporarily by the built-in bookcase, the color TV set, or the king-sized bed. But before we know it, it's time to renew that lease—and the relationship.* Once the honeymoon phase is over, the journey—pocked with expectations—is much the same for all couples. Two years, we discover, don't have much stretch. Women barrel ahead to commitments that will cement the union and only later (as contrasted to men) will they pause to question: Is this what I want for the rest of my life?

So what's next?

For those who decide to stay together, next is the renewal of the lease and a settling in of the relationship. With that we launch on the phase of "shared projects." It could be a bigger apartment, perhaps, or a house in the suburbs—more rooms to be filled by more things. It could be a baby—maybe. Or talk about whether to, or not.

Willy-nilly, openly or covertly, pre- or post-sixties, talk

* An intriguing observation. It's been reported that unwed couples experience a breakdown in their relationship after about a year and a half of living together—just about the time when the renewal of lease is approaching.

about babies sooner or later insinuates itself into most couple relationships. And having a baby, we'll discover, is a pivotal transition in every union—even more than getting married or living together! From the viewpoint of the human race, happily, it is one of the most common shared projects. From the individual woman's point of view, however, it often triggers feelings that are unsettling and totally unexpected. When they dared face those feelings, a good many women admitted pregnancy and motherhood floored them.

As in the decision to marry, it is often the man who gives the final nod, but it is the woman who initiates and wrestles with the *idea* of a baby. After all, it is she who experiences the pressure of time. It also is she who is oriented by the nature of her priorities toward cementing ties.

"Doesn't everybody?" Roberta asked, reflecting on those first years of marriage. "Having a baby just seemed like the next thing to do. I had no driving interest of my own. David and I planned on having four. Maybe the babies were to fill the growing space between us." Maybe.

The initiation of a new life cycle, however planned or unplanned, is the ultimate dialectic contradiction. When a couple become parents, the intimacy of the two is disrupted by a third,[1] and what was meant to bond frequently shocks and fissures. Once more women are faced with antagonisms: We wed to settle in and "unexpectedly" are unsettled. We live together, unwed, to keep our freedom, and "unexpectedly" seek our cages.

NESTING

Paul and Me, Paul and Me. We've encountered Ellen briefly as a newlywed. She's told us that despite her focus on a career—and a brief college interlude with a romantic rebel bent on revolution—she pushed for marriage at the age of twenty-two to Paul, a young man made of more familiar cloth. He was then in the throes of completing his training in oral surgery.

We pick up her story six years later. Now twenty-eight, she is an editor in a small publishing house and she has also decided it's time for a baby. Paul goes along with the idea. As we listen to Ellen, we'll hear the replay in her life and her marriage of those contradictory pulls in women between high adventure and "security," between that unsettling quest for a separate self and "settling down," between cementing and disrupting the couple identity.

"Until the past few weeks," Ellen explained, "it's always been Paul and me, Paul and me, Paul and me. My relationship to Paul is really important. We've always talked a lot with each other. He reads and comments on all my manuscripts. And I even learned to scuba dive for him. Still, lately, we've been floored. We're not the way we were."

When Ellen and I met, I thought we'd met before. She could have been a look-alike for Goldie Hawn, with melting pools of chocolate-brown eyes and long blond hair. Although the baby was "planned" for a vague time in the near future, the actual pregnancy threw them into a profusion of unexpecteds.

"I can't believe it. I can't believe it," she continued. "I was very upset when I thought for sure that I was pregnant. At first Paul didn't react and then he got upset too. He said, 'Well, it was *your* idea!' When I phoned my gynecologist and told the nurse I was pregnant, she said very quickly, 'Is this a wanted pregnancy or do you want to arrange an abortion?' That floored me too. If we decide on an abortion, I've got to let them know in three weeks!"

She jumped up to open a window. "I keep thinking what a baby could do to my life. Then, I think it's crazy our going ahead. Think of all the parts of me I'll have to give up. And then there's Paul and me. It's scary. We've already started to quarrel. That's because Paul is beginning to feel trapped. I've already been limited. I've a bad back so the doctor said to give up those long weekends away for a while. Paul's already letting me know that the open spaces are necessary for him, and that scuba diving is one of the important things in his life. He'll be there for the practical things, but I'll be carrying the main responsibility for the baby. I feel hurt. Abandoned almost.

"I guess we expected things to stay the same," she said, trying to reassure herself. "Or we expected to be *prepared* by knowing what to expect. I didn't expect to have such feelings. I always want everything under control. But how can you? We've hit snags before. Paul was thrown the first time I brought work home from the office—when we both realized I'd rather curl up with a manuscript than go jogging after dinner. That threw him. And we had to talk about it. And I was upset when I flipped over Jane Howard's *A Different Woman*, and he said Jane Howard didn't turn *him* on. I thought we should be the perfect match! And we *are* different. Once when we were daydreaming, he said, if he had his wish, he'd end up in the North Woods, and I said, I'd be on the Left Bank of Paris."

The distancing that took place between them as she heightened her nurturing, even in this early phase of mothering, was experienced as a loss to them both. Paul felt not only the loss of his freedom but also the loss of a companion. Ellen was thrown not only into reflecting on her relationship to Paul but also on her own image of being a mother.

Becoming Mother. As Ellen began thinking of herself as a mother, she also began comparing herself to other women—some of whom she'd held up as models of "freedom." Her efforts at rehearsing the different possible "mother" roles paid off. Slowly, she discovered that becoming a mother didn't mean becoming *her* mother. Her fear was common enough. After all, when we're disrupted, what do we fall back on but the familiar parental and cultural values and images.

"I think I can adjust to a baby in my life. I'm beginning to see that every mother is her own kind of mother. What I can't seem to adjust to is the picture of becoming a mother," Ellen explained. "What's really scaring me is that when I think mother, I think I'll be giving up a lot that is Ellen, and taking on a lot that is *my* mother. Like my mother saying she had a kid to fulfill the things she never did. I even had this fantasy that if I don't pursue my career, and get that book of poetry out, I'll be like my *father*. I'll be buying my kid a typewriter at the age of three and saying, 'Now kid, write!' " We laughed, knowing full well the truth of those fears.

"Right now I'm thinking that if I want an abortion, I'll have to decide soon," Ellen continued, tracing her hand in the air, going up one finger and down the next. "It's a roller-coaster. One minute I think you don't have to give up that much like my parents, and I can have help. Next minute, I'm thinking, I'll be giving up too much that's me. But that could be a copout in my own head. If you're disciplined and committed to your work, it can be done. Some women have; most women cop out. Which kind am I? I know the commitment has to come from the inside. The muses aren't always sitting on your shoulder. I know that. I'm afraid, because inside I'm not where I want to be yet. If I have an abortion . . .

"How do I picture my life five years from now? Probably with an executive position as an editor for a small quality house. I see Paul as a junior partner in his practice. He will come to terms with his work, even though he's not delighted. We have a little child in kindergarten. A cute little kid. It's nice. I'll have my space in about four, five years, because he'll be in school. Now we'll have enough money to do what we want. My dream is to be into projects that I want to be working on, discovering new authors, writing my own poetry. . . .

"Ten years from now? My dream? Maybe we'll own a brownstone in the Village. I'll have a nice big office where I'll be editor-in-chief. My child will be in school all day and for Christmas we'll all go south, scuba diving. He'll just swim. And in March, we'll be able to go without him. It will be more or less the way it was with Paul and me—ten years from now. I won't have to nurture that much. I might even have a book of poetry. Paul will be pretty much into his work. It'll be pretty good. I can see that picture with one child. But I'm afraid of those first months with a new baby."

Despite the fact that Ellen was on a merry-go-round of indecision, her trajectory of their future made room for a baby. With some trepidation, she saw herself transcending the traditional images of wife and mother. Her projection of her husband's role, however, is revealing. It falls pretty much within the traditional track. And why not? By and large, her husband is an unknown; therefore, she reverts to those images of masculinity of an earlier generation.

In her projection of their future, she gives voice to a dream common to many women. Threatened by the possible intrusion of the baby, she imagines a time in ten years when they will return to an undivided companionship. In fantasy, their relationship will be uninterrupted by the presence of a child, and more important, uninterrupted by the reality of their separate development, divergent interests, and perhaps even different rates of changing and growing.

Since Ellen wasn't certain what her engagements were for the next few weeks, she left promising to phone about another meeting. I'd been left with a cliff-hanger. Would they or wouldn't they go through with an abortion? And why was *I* so involved? I was torn. I thought it would be nice to have couples like Ellen and Paul people this world. But another part of me felt she had every right to opt for. . . . Still, wasn't I falling into that old either/or trap. Can't women manage both?

It was two weeks before I saw Ellen again. She laughed: "I've already booked a nurse for our scuba diving next winter. I've been doing a lot of thinking. I realize I really like Paul because he has created a personal space for himself that no one invades and that's what I want to create for myself. But I still feel there's a big difference between how men and women look at a relationship. Last night I said to Paul, 'If I work my whole life to get *the* book of poems out, and I was called to win a Pulitzer Prize, and you were laid up,

I would look first to be with you! I somewhere really feel that. Maybe I feel that *now*, maybe I won't feel that way later. I somehow wouldn't leave you lying there even to go get my most important thing.' Paul said: 'But I'd insist you go.' I said: 'I'd insist you go too, but it's just the difference in attitude.' I think men's 'I'm going anyway' is a very selfish attitude."

Shades of that feeling of abandonment. What's selfish and what's self? It's characteristic of the early years of coupling as we move from being all wrapped up in each other to being all wrapped up in the baby, to experience any distance as "selfish." Reflecting on her first few months of pregnancy, Ellen eloquently summarized the labor pains of growing up. "It's required a lot of work, and a lot of anguish. But when we've talked it out, it's been fine. I've never worked on our relationship before; it just went along with little snags here and there. Part of the work was all those expectations that came crashing down. But we're really and truly growing. And it's definitely a challenge. And next year is going to be hard too.

"But I realize I'm further along than women like my mother thirty years ago. I can recognize Paul's need for a personal space, a personal identity, because I recognize *my* need too. Women like my mother didn't, and couldn't. They never took their own place. I'm creating my own." Her mouth turned to a wide grin. "There's no doubt about it."

The Pre- and Post-Sixties. Ellen blueprints those post-sixties contradictions of "liberation." What of the pre-sixties women, those of us who were faced with the paradoxes of repression?

If there is a central difference between older and younger women, it is *not* in the process and expectations of coupling, but in openly facing their ambivalences, and facing them sooner. We of the past generation had our doubts, but we weren't supposed to.

Earlier, most women married with the expectation of

having children. One woman recalled: " 'I want a baby, I want a baby,' I used to tell my husband. I don't know why I said it. Maybe it was those *Saturday Evening Post* covers!" "In a way," another observed, "I was fulfilling my feelings about myself as a creative woman. That was what I had to give my husband."

The first baby usually came within the first year, and not a small number married because they were pregnant. (According to one statistic, one fifth of the women conceived before marriage.) In retrospect, however, many of the older women also admit feelings of ambivalence, especially if the leap into motherhood was precipitous. Their resentments centered not only on the fact that they felt unprepared and overwhelmed by the sudden responsibility, but they also felt cheated of the "honeymoon" phase. "I didn't have time to get myself together, to know my husband," one woman explained, "when this little creature came to live with us."

Prepared? Another illusion. An intriguing discovery in speaking with women of different generations was that whether the honeymoon lasted a thin eight months, or a full eight years, whether pregnancy was experienced as creative fulfillment or with ambivalence, whether it was something we drifted into as in the fifties or "prepared" for, often with an overdose of rationality, as in the seventies, most women confirmed that "having a baby was a tremendous shock"— for which they weren't nor could they have been prepared. How can one prepare for the unsettling emotions that are triggered? The more I listened, the more convinced I became that our lives are not shaped by finding the "right" answers, like whether to have a baby or not. Rather, we shape our journey by the attitudes and postures we assume in the face of disruption. Since the younger woman is "floored" sooner, she also realizes sooner that husband and babies don't resolve those Who am I? confusions—something the past generation took longer to discover. And she may even have an inkling earlier that there are no fixed resolutions, because growth requires a measure of disequilibrium.

She learns, in short, to look upon her life *not* in terms of polarities, but paradoxes.

Ellen and I decided to have our last meeting over·lunch. Sipping at her milk, she said: "I read someplace that if you don't have contradictory thoughts in the space of an hour, you're a simpleton. Yesterday, one minute I was daydreaming of Paul and me and the baby, and the very next minute I drifted off to someone I dated in college. When that happens, I can't believe myself! Then again, most people don't admit those feelings, so they're not bothered by them." Aren't we?

Sex and Babies. The first years of marriage are pivotal in the couple's sexual pattern of relating to each other, especially so for the woman whose first sexual experience has been with her spouse. Obviously, the number of babies a couple has is no index of their sexual activity or satisfaction. In fact, there is some suggestion that women who are dissatisfied with their marital relationship have a greater number of children. Being surrounded with children makes them feel personally more satisfied, for a time, while paradoxically placing still greater strain on the coupling.[2]

Since the first years of marriage are generally a time of greater sexual activity, those women who cemented their union immediately with children also seem to have precluded the playful aspects of sex. Their sexual relationship became another routine of living together—and, in some instances, serious business.

"We were hardly married," one woman, now fifty, reflected, "when I started dragging around, looking like a sack of potatoes. I was only twenty-one, got pregnant immediately, and out the window went all my expectations of passionate, romantic nights with my new husband. And even after the baby came, we just never got around to those passionate, romantic nights. We just kept getting less and less sexually free with each other, as we became more and more responsible for a family, a household, and my husband's career."

The women of the seventies, on the other hand, suffer a jolt of another kind. They fully expect that their sexual and emotional intimacy will remain unchanged. As the time grew close for her to deliver, one woman described the subtle changes between her and her husband. Once exuberant and confident, she looked at her protruding figure and was inundated with self-doubt.

"I tried on some maternity bathing suits," she explained, "and I wanted to cry. Last summer I had a bikini figure. This summer I look like my mother! I felt angry and alone."

Once eager for intercourse, she now recoiled from physical contact, while at the same time fearing the loss of their sexual intimacy. Yet, despite the fact that she withdrew, she also believed that her husband had lost interest in her. "It's frightening," she observed. "I used to think that my breasts were his; now I feel they belong to the baby. And I don't understand that he doesn't understand. When he's sick, *I* know exactly how *he* feels! I'm afraid about what will happen to our sexual relationship after the baby. I'm afraid that I'll be too tired for sex, and so will he."

Subtly, a wall of conflict and angers is erected. *He,* she feels, has failed to meet her expectations; *she,* he feels, has failed to meet his. Often, there is a mutual decrease in sexual interest and enthusiasm at this point in the relationship—which can be a snag, or a permanent state of affairs.

Women, be they in their late twenties or early fifties, expect a total sharing of all their experiences. And why not? Women not only share, they give away. Her breasts, like her vagina, her orgasm, and her uterus, rather than belonging to her, are out on perpetual loan. But paradoxically, that attitude doesn't bring the couple closer—it only weights the partner with greater expectations and more pressure to perform according to an ideal image, an idea.

The Baby Arrives. Unlike Ellen, Tracey was a woman who had been in pursuit of an idea—an *idea* of herself. When troubled, she'd bury her feelings and fall back on what she was supposed to feel. She described the years before the baby arrived as six and a half "fabulous" years with her husband in which they lived for each other with the freedom of two incomes, vacations to Porto Ercole, and winter skiing weekends. They had the freedom, she explained, to be alone.

Actually, I hadn't thought of Tracey as "free." Most of her life she'd been called on to perform—for her parents as the "good" daughter, in school as the "good" student, on her newspaper job as the "good" sport, and later for her husband as the *House Beautiful* "good" hostess. When we met she'd quit her job—tired of performing—and wanted to free-lance, doing more than the slim reporting that had been her lot on the woman's page. She skimmed the surface of things too easily, and resented it. She was ready to risk meatier stuff. But she also was frightened of the freedom. "I'm not sure that I'll be able to perform except under orders," she admitted. "It's second nature to me now. I seem to need an assignment, like doing homework, to force me to achieve. I feel this is a weakness, my having to lean on authority." Still, she'd taken the plunge and even enrolled in some refresher courses, hoping to give her sagging psyche an alcohol rub. That's how we first met.

Although Tracey was in her late twenties, she experienced a singular helplessness in effecting any change in her relationships. "I can't seem to make people listen to me," she lamented, "even when I shout!" Somehow she'd managed to bypass those teenage confrontations that pull us away from the familiar parental perceptions of the world. She'd really never left home.

The first thing one responded to in Tracey was her beauty. She possessed those natural good looks that every soap ad tells us we should have—the kind with hair blowing in the gentle breezes and all the tangled ends of our lives hidden away. She gave the impression of an unruffled, furbished, rubbed and scrubbed fragility. Her appearance, however, had been a mixed blessing; it just hadn't required her to labor.

She married in the early sixties, soon after college, to the boy next door (where next door was corporate country)

who was making his way in advertising, and had the traditional bride-wore-white dream wedding. They settled in Short
Hills, a wealthy community in New Jersey. However, un-
typically, she waited six years before becoming pregnant.

"I used to think that some things were meant to be." Her
eyes brimmed with tears. "I used to think that I was going
to have a beautiful marriage—which I do—and that I was
going to be an important print journalist. Now I'm beginning to see that *nothing* is ever meant to be. What works is
only what you *make* happen. Talent is 10 percent; work is
90 percent."

Troubled about her lack of focus, Tracey recalled a dream.
"I fell into a restless sleep one night. I was pitching, dis-
connected for hours. I was floating—my head was all of me—
floating like a balloon with a dangling string. The feeling
was that I, the balloon, wanted to become attached to something, hoping to find an idea that fit, but I was told that it
is better to be a free agent. But the floating wasn't satisfying
because I didn't feel I belonged anywhere. Before I was
completely awake I was conscious of being settled, just softly,
in a nest. I was aware of the pleasant rumpled gentleness of
my husband, who was in the nest and also was the nest."

In her dream she voices a common conflict: her longing
for anchoring, for attachments, and her deep-down knowing
that it is better to be a free agent. Her questing, however,
like that of most women, was still a head trip in which she
looks for an "idea" to fit the waking reality. The idea was
to make of her husband a nesting ground.

For Tracey, those contradictory pulls were temporarily
resolved. She became pregnant. Nevertheless, her pregnancy
was not without its doubts. She feared the loss of her "glorious one-to-one relationship" with her husband. She also
feared the loss of her "youth." Becoming a mother, like her
mother, meant becoming an "adult." Nevertheless, she made
of her pregnancy her own experience, tenaciously avoiding
all the cliché things one was supposed to do and feel.

The baby arrived, a boy, and she was precipitously plunged

into those old ambivalences which had been hidden away like an old broom. During her pregnancy she'd been bathed in the approval of family and friends. Abruptly, with a third presence in their one-to-one household, she was bolted into a profusion of "unexpecteds," bouncing from being all wrapped up in Kevin to being all wrapped up in the baby.

Although she had wanted to be the "best" mother and be totally immersed in her infant—there wasn't to be any help—she was anxious and weary. And to make matters worse, she felt guilty, because, after all, she wasn't supposed to have those feelings. Her sense of entrapment was acute. Feeling helpless and depressed, journalist that she was, she kept a journal from which I've abstracted some of the entries.

September 28

Little Andy. When I first held him, swaddled in white, he was light as air, just a cotton ball with a dark fuzzy head. My hospital stay was bliss—every need provided—like a week at Elizabeth Arden. Now we're home, to the breathtaking reality of parenthood.

And work? I really don't want to go back. I know that soon I can be organized and productive beyond Spock's *Baby and Child Care*. I'm sure I can keep working, write articles from home with Andy tucked happily beside me. The most important thing is that now I'm a mother, and Kevin is a father—our pride in each other increases, our mutual scope broadens.

October 4

A quiet time begins. In a way this is like having been a bride. Months of preparation, every friend and relative all involved and concerned, clustering around you at the event, and then they're gone. Last week friends bringing casseroles, sending flowers, cards, and presents, coming to sit and have tea, to help make formula, to give pointers on better-fitting diapers. Silently now, they settle back into their routines, and I'm all alone with my sweet boy. Who really is good. Well, okay, at two in the morning I could do without him. . . . Am I sorry we didn't have a nurse come? I don't know. It would be nice to sleep through the night, and I'm not so hung up now on proving that I can handle it alone. Amazonian me. I'm tired. Kevin says he's tired too. . . .

October 16

I stood at the kitchen door this morning, holding Andy and waving good-bye to Kevin. When he turned and waved back to us, warm in our cocoon, I realized for the first time that I'm jealous of him. He in his club tie and Brooks Brothers coat, me in my crummy robe and slippers. His world hasn't changed at all. His day involves talking to people, solving adult problems, sitting down to a white tablecloth at lunch. But my warm cocoon has become my whole world.

Maybe it's just that I'm tired. Maybe! I can hardly *see*. The Pablum and Similac, even Andy's delicate face are all seen through gauze. The house is full of dustballs and there's egg yolk on the refrigerator door. Oh, stop bitching. Can't you see you have everything? A fabulous husband, a beautiful baby, and days ahead that will be perfect.

Grow up.

December 22

I'm in the middle of a whirlpool. We've accepted (over Kevin's concerned protests) every Christmas invitation. I'm starved for activity! Fun! The problem: It's not really fun. By the time we get home at midnight I'm oblivious to the fact that I'm on duty at 2:00. This is the eighth week of round-the-clock feeding, and I'm beginning to feel like a tortured P.O.W. And the nightmares: I keep having this terrible dream that I've rolled over on Andy. Poor Kevin, the other night I tried to yank his head out of the covers; I was sure it was the baby.

January 17

We spent a lovely long weekend at the Reeds' Vermont farm. Number one sitter, Jill, came with us and took over for four full days and nights. Hallelujah, Andy now sleeps from seven at night to six in the morning. (He'd do it for Jill, but not for me.) So I feel better physically. Mentally someone has tied lead weights to my brain. I know I should settle down to work, to try to get some assignments, but I don't have the mental energy. Am I afraid of failing?

With Andy asleep in his basket, I drove down to the beach. Not a boat in sight. Has the world fallen asleep around me? Is the world dead? *It's as though I'm waiting for something. But what?*

January 27

It's following me around like a shadow. It's so inescapably true: We are going to die. All of us. I told Kevin about this. His brow knit a little, and I could see that he was saying to himself, "How she rants." He didn't say, "Oh yeah, wow, I see what you mean." I feel like I'm behind glass, even when I talk to Kevin. He's a taxi driver and I'm the fare behind the closed window. Why doesn't he turn around when I knock?

February 20

If no one can see what you see, why bother communicating? It would be lovely to relax and let an automatic pilot take over. I could function perfectly that way, be lucid and efficient, a loving wife, tender mother, brilliant partygoer, without participating at all. No one would suspect that the real me had folded up shop and gone away. Not even Kevin. He'd think I'm terrific. How delightful I'd seem. How I'd hate myself.

March 30

I took an hour and planned a whole life. I divided our possessions, and was quite generous. Kevin got the car, the house, and the hi-fi. In London I wouldn't need a car. . . . I got an apple-cheeked nanny. . . . What am I really trying to escape from?

April 4

It occurs to me that this mental indulgence has got to stop. How can I face Kevin at night when I've spent the day skiing in Sun Valley with an old college romance? I've got to do something. But what?

Tracey did do something. She phoned me. She'd kept those feelings tucked away long enough. It was time they got aired.

She later admitted her greatest fear in speaking about them was that she'd be told to fall in line and accept her role.

She also explained that all the reading she'd done about young motherhood was of little help. "Take this list of remedies from one of our well-meaning magazine doctors:

" 'Forget about being a good housekeeper.' (He's kidding.)

" 'Spend time with other young mothers to learn techniques.' (I may throw up.)

" 'Go to the movies with your husband.' (I get it, he *is* kidding.) There I was, in an existential void, and this yo-yo doctor tells me to go to the movies!

"Why doesn't women's lib comfort me either? The feminists make it sound too easy. Throw the kid in a day-care center and go back to work. I don't want to get rid of him. I'm not that kind of person. *But what kind am I?*"

That was the real dilemma. It wasn't a matter of going to the movies with her husband, *or* of putting Andy in a day-care center, but of finding her own way as she became more sensitive to who she was. Tracey was forced into facing unfinished business, the business of giving birth to herself. She was gripped in feelings of loss: loss of the early relationship with Kevin; loss of self in becoming mostly Andy's mother; loss of those images of what she should be, a "picture-book" mother or a gung-ho journalist. Since she was unable to fit herself into either image, she continued to ask: "What am I?"

In her journals, she sensitively sketches the often laborious and seemingly contradictory path women take to come round to themselves. The "fabulous" husband, unable to provide the nesting ground, experiencing his own feelings of loss and resentment, triggered in her feelings of jealousy and anger. How was it that this terrific partner couldn't understand her desperate fear that she may die without having been born? How was it that all he could say was to "get out a bit with friends" and their babies!

The ideal relationship splintered. She could no longer be totally contained in him. He'd been unable to supply her with answers or even to listen to her questions. She was left stranded, moving to her own currents, listening to her own rhythms.

The We of the early coupling unravels into an Us and a Him. The daydreaming begins. That old college romance. London and an apple-cheeked nanny. Just the baby and she. The incongruities multiply. She refuses to share her "sweet little one," threatened by her competitiveness with the efficient babysitter (an all-too-common dilemma). After all, wasn't she meant to be as good a mother as her mother? So she has nightmares of smothering the infant! She berates herself for daydreaming of another rescuer and is gripped by guilt, fearing that those dreams will erode her sanity and her relationship with Kevin.

Stranded, she struggled to thresh out who *she* was. She and Kevin decided on a major move. They sold their house in Short Hills and took an apartment in the city. Interestingly, their move was in the opposite direction from that of most couples. She also sold her first free-lance article since Andy's birth. At the same time, she rented office space—a small room of her own—to write part-time, and hired a sitter part-time. In modified version, she put her London daydream to work.

The last entry in her journal reads:

July 8

I'm a professional! I've a six-week deadline for a story. Today, home at 2:30, I packed Andy in the car and drove off to the beach. I took him in the water, holding tight to his slippery little body as he squealed and giggled. Then I realized: For the first time in ages, I was giggling too.

Is it happily ever after? Hardly. She'll choose and choose again, and through those choices she will define who and what she is.

The Suburbia-and-Chocolate-Mousse Syndrome. Tracey's exodus from suburbia sparked me. Whenever it was feasible, I had made a point of holding one of the interviews in the woman's home. It now dawned on me that I could recapture her person simply by recalling where she lived and how. I became fascinated, in particular, with the younger woman's use of living space as compared to those of us married in the fifties.

This is the way it was to be done: It was typical of the bride of the fifties to set out in marriage with a one-bedroom apartment in a community not too different from the one in which she was raised—frequently, that meant the suburbs. On special occasions she'd make the trip into the city, to "keep in touch," get her hair cut, or take a course in gourmet cooking. If she worked, it was a temporary affair; she looked forward to quitting and having her first baby. When the baby arrived, they began their Sunday morning circuit of model houses. The House became the open expression, for all the world to see, of settling down and spreading their roots.

The traditional living space had its country kitchen, formal living room (which was used only for company occasions), a separate dining room (also reserved for company occasions), two or three bedrooms, a "finished" basement—the children's stomping ground—and a family room. And, of course, the garden.

Where we build our nest and how we feather it becomes a piercing symbol of our personal meanings and values. And symbols are important. In fact, they sometimes take on more reality than so-called reality itself. A woman in her middle years summed it up. She was speaking of her daughter, who abruptly had to relocate, because her executive husband had been sent out to stake another territory. She explained: "Ken's already located a beautiful home with a swimming pool, and he'll get her a Mercedes. It does make a difference, he'll make it up to her." Just as the flowers, or the shining bauble, or even another baby—that women put so much stock in—are meant to make up for the wrenching loneliness when the largest part of the "I" has been given over to a "We" and an "All of Us."

Too often, especially in the fifties and sixties the House

became a substitute for meanings and values that were yet
to be personally derived. How we split and share our living
space, I discovered, reflects our priorities, our self-image, our
self-esteem, and sometimes even our changing.

Have you ever thought about *your* nesting instincts? Can
you picture the homes you've set up since you've left home?
Think about it. Have you *left* home? One woman, who'd just
moved into a rambling ranch-type house, was startled when
a friend dropped in and casually observed: "This house is
just like your mother's!" Reflecting on the homes of women
I'd seen at different periods of their lives, I became acutely
aware of my own evolution in space.

As I hail from a meld of Italian and French parentage,
not so strangely, the radical change in my living space has
been in the dining area. Since my husband and I were
engaged in a professional practice, we first set up house in
a one-bedroom apartment in the city—the kind with a tiny
dining nook off the windowless kitchen. Buffets were the
order of the day. I remember rehearsing chocolate mousses
and avocado ice cream until my partner turned alternately
brown and green. Then, in due course, the baby arrived, and
so did the time for the big move to an apartment large
enough to contain the infant child, his nurse, and a poodle.
The dining room was long and narrow, stiffly and oblongly
seating twelve. The chocolate mousses graduated to *crêpes
flambées* and *filet mignon en croûte*—not unlike mother's.

Now that the middle years stretch ahead, we've come full
circle. Our apartment, still in the city, is a two-bedroom
affair with little room for dead spaces in my life. We dine,
read, listen to music, and look at *Upstairs, Downstairs* and
the *Eleven O'clock News* in a space walled by books and
sparsely furnished with a refectory table that both is a desk
and seats six, and a small round table, seating four for
family dinner. I took a circuitous path to discover that books
feed me quite a bit more than mousses and that a dining
area is a dining area is a personal place with a personal
purpose where one eats and is also nourished.

We become a small chip in a large mosaic as the projects spread. A baby. Then another. And another. It structures our time and keeps us distracted, for a while. A larger apartment. A new wing to the house. Or a house in the country, perhaps. Anchored and secured, we collect prints, or antiques. We buy real estate. That's what euphemistically is labeled "common interests." We have so much in common, we tell ourselves. We love the same things. And as it sometimes happens, we're divorced! With an element of facetiousness, perhaps, I'm convinced that one couple has stayed together because of their brownstones. And another separated shortly after they ran out of contemporary American painters to buy. The paintings were a bigger bone of contention in court than their children.

What was the bricks and mortar of women's security—the house of the fifties—is the sound of the death knell for the younger woman, unless it's a brownstone in the city. The younger woman of the seventies seems much more in touch with her living space as an externalization of her inner life.

Ellen, in her inimitable fashion, traces the significance of feathering her nest. With the baby due, she and Paul planned their next move. To remain in the city, where they lived, was costly. Larger quarters, plus some help, would double their expenses. Still, determined to be more than parents, conflicted, they agreed to look for a larger apartment in the city. They were fully aware that how they set up house for the next several years would foreshadow the kind of limits they were placing on their own development. But suburbia, they soon discovered, didn't necessarily mean moving to the suburbs. Because they wanted to keep their expenses down, they were forced to look at more reasonable rentals, and those were usually complexes designed to accommodate young families.

Dejected, she'd resigned herself, or so she thought, to leasing in an apartment complex with baby-sitting co-ops, playgrounds, and a nearby park. In a dream, however, Ellen replays her doubts as she turns to one of her "liberated" friends for direction. She dreamed she was trying to convince her friend it was fine to move into the apartment complex. Awakening with a start, she realized that she was hard put to convince herself. She felt trapped. Paradoxically, although she disapproved of the "playground crowd," she also wanted very much to be approved and accepted by them. She'd boxed herself in both by the fear of being different and the fear of being swallowed up in a way of life that didn't define her. She feared "being snubbed" by the other young women—who might even "snub her little offspring"—and at the same time, she feared becoming all "park talk."

Struggling with the clichés of young motherhood, she again rehearsed the possible kinds of mothering and life-styles, and eventually found a large apartment that fit more easily into their life—one that wasn't too far from a public library.

Childless and Childfree. Obviously, shared projects run the gamut. I've devoted considerable space to a common one, having babies, because it's still the woman's priority. But what of those couples who, by choice or force of circumstance, remain childless? Or, as some think of it, childfree? What are the unexpected transitions of those women? What projects do they share? Has the childless woman found "the better way"? Indeed, one survey of women from Anchorage to San Antonio, in which 70 percent answered with a resounding "No" to the question: "If you had it all to do over again, would you have children?" causes one to question.[3]

Consider these two women: Betty Gilbert and Carol Anderson Salant. Betty and Fred Gilbert have been married seventeen years. Both teach in the history department of a city university. When they married, he was an associate professor and she, for the usual female reason, held the rank of assistant professor. From all external appearances, they seemed eminently well suited—they come from a similar background and they have common interests. Despite the fact that they were both professionals, however, they fell into the traditional division of labor. Since he earned more than she, he was the self-appointed "breadwinner," delegated to devote his energies to his work. She, on the other hand, was to manage all the nitty-gritty of running a home, and when the babies came along, to rear them. She felt defenseless against such cold logic.

From the beginning, this "perfect" couple coagulated into one, until it became increasingly difficult to determine where one began and the other ended. Neither really felt they could make it on their own; neither could really tolerate difference; it threatened their merger. But then, they'd both been reared with the same givens. She learned early in life to cultivate only those ways in which she was like her parents and to mask any difference. Being male, he'd been taught that he had the ruling edge. Tradition was on his side. Their *modus vivendi* had been: This is the way it's done— *his* way. For her to even imagine saying: This is the way *I* do things caused considerable guilt.

Betty was thirty-one when they married. Pressured by her age, she talked often about having a baby. Lukewarm to the idea at first, he eventually agreed. It was then that she discovered she would be unable to bring a baby to term, and a hysterectomy followed. She felt diminished, a second-class citizen, and even more worthless in his eyes. If she couldn't give him a child, what would she give him?

In the absence of motherhood, she turned to her husband, devoting most of her energies to "mothering" him. Once the "honeymoon" was over, they launched on a project common to many childless couples—the "parenting" of each other by turns. Now one, now the other. She was as emotionally committed to her spouse's needs and fleeting moods as any new mother can be. He was as "tyrannical" as any favored son would be. A seemingly perfect fit.

She took care to prepare him well-balanced meals, saw to it that his clothes were impeccable, sorted his mail, listened to his articles, accepted his tantrums, and made certain that he put on his galoshes. She nurtured him, but *not* without expectations. She'd groom him for "success" so that he, in turn, would nurture her. Her "selfless" joy was to have been in his achievement; her reward, in his adoration and paternal support.

The closeted achievers, the wives of the late forties, the fifties, and even the early sixties, learned to siphon their competitiveness and aggression through their husbands, and later, if they had children, their children. They constructed their personal gods who were to cherish them and achieve for them.

And so Betty waited. Waited for him to complete her. Waited for him to give her the parenting she'd yearned for. Her world filled up with more and more waiting. Her life calcified into patterns that both stripped her and gave rise to extravagant expectations and insecurities.

He, in turn, grew increasingly dependent on her for his world to run smoothly. Childless, they had the freedom for trips to the Orient (which she arranged, although she preferred Europe), to spend weekends on a farm (which she arranged, although she preferred the seashore) and to join an anti-pollution group (which she initiated)—yet she felt helpless and crowded out by his insistent dependency on her.

Still occupying a one-bedroom apartment, she thought a house with more room, with a study for Fred, perhaps, would ease the strain. She convinced him to invest in a small brownstone near the university.

Betty was forty-eight when we met. In our first meeting her talk centered on Fred and the house. My efforts to sound her out about herself and her professional interest—medieval history—were systematically sidetracked. The following time we met at her home.

The house had a musty air of things past, despite the fact that it was furnished in glass and chrome. Old newspapers, journals, books spilled out from every corner. Fred's small study, she explained, had proliferated and insinuated itself everywhere. Downstairs, where we went for coffee and cake,

Fred's presence was again in evidence. The kitchen floor was tracked with mud. It had been snowing.

Her blue eyes skimmed my face. Apologizing, she explained that the housekeeper had the flu, and she'd been overwhelmed; everything felt as if it were rushing in at her. She was obsessed with the tyrannical presence of the House, with never-ending Things to Do. Even their talk, she explained, had dwindled down to the plumbing that needed repair, the study that needed painting, the walk that needed shoveling. The House shackled and distanced them.

As if a fatherless child, the house became *her* house—something to structure *her* time—splitting them into an Us and a Him. Their Togetherness wore thin. She felt choked by the connections that had sustained her, and was forced to admit that his dependency, which had provided her with a sense of purpose and power, now was suffocating. She'd failed as the "perfect" wife-mother, she told herself, just as Fred had failed to provide the perfect support. At first disrupted and upset, she gradually began to feel as if some weight had been lifted. Perfection, she grudgingly conceded, was not part of the human condition. But perhaps, just perhaps, she thought, she could relinquish the fringe benefits of their merger, and try to allow both of them breathing space. Perhaps she could salvage herself. That, she decided, would be her next project—one she'd work on alone.

Although the kinds of projects the childless couple undertakes may differ—trips to exotic islands, the farm upstate, the brownstone, the political causes, or the joint career—the process of change in the couple identity, with its conflicts and contradictions, is ultimately similar.

Unlike Betty, Carol Anderson Salant is childless by choice. At the age of thirty-four, she married Brian Salant, a noted scientist in cancer research. It was her first marriage and his second.

Just out of college, some thirteen years before, Carol had begun working for Brian as a lowly lab assistant. Today, she's earned a Ph.D. in physics and a reputation in her own field of expertise. (Carol has several stories to tell—see Chapters 9 and 12; for the time being we'll pick up the threads of her life as a newlywed.)

Brian was estranged from his former wife, a woman who spent years in and out of hospitals, and their one daughter, who'd been left pretty much with her mother. Carol explained that as the years passed, Brian spent less and less time at home. "His wife couldn't carry on even the minimal routines, like preparing him dinner. She provided a roof and that was about it. So we ate together and worked together and eventually drifted into a brief affair. I was in my early twenties, so that didn't last very long. I was curious about the world. Besides, he was determined to stick by his wife until his daughter was grown. It's been only in the past few years that we resumed our affair with any commitment."

For those past few years Carol had lived in the negative aura of being the "other" woman. She was determined, however, to "keep an ostrich approach" to her relationship, although she was all too aware of the gossip surrounding them. But that was over now. They'd been married for eight months.

Since they worked at some distance from Washington, D.C., we agreed to meet in the circular high-rise complex of Watergate, where they lived. Carol, I subsequently learned, had selected the apartment in preference to the usual suburban house—which would have been more convenient to their labs—because a house seemed to demand more time than she intended to devote to housekeeping.

A cleaning woman answered the door and led me to a sparsely furnished octagonal room with a sweeping view of the city. The room itself looked as if it had yet to decide what shape it was going to take. After a few moments, breathless, Carol arrived, took my hand in a solid grip, and explained: "One of the computers broke down, and I'm the trouble shooter. I got so absorbed, I lost track of time." Her speech was clipped.

Where to begin? What better place, I thought, with a

newlywed, than her new marriage—prestigious scientist or not, affair or not.

"Does a research scientist have the same bruises that the average newlywed suffers?" I asked. "For instance, discovering that he's taciturn in the morning and it really isn't within your power to make him ravishingly happy?"

A frown spread across her face and then she laughed self-consciously: "You know, you grow up and it's drummed into you that you must be the best mother, the best cook, the best housewife, the best this, that, and the next thing. There comes a point where you know you can't be that! And you've got to give it up somehow. In the space of a few months I got my Ph.D., got married, moved to a new apartment, a new bed, started running a house, and running home every night to get supper on the table. I had to do all sorts of things that I didn't bother with, living alone."

With a sweep of her hand, she continued: "Look at this place. I haven't got the *dreamtime* to decide what I want to do with it. How much we'll entertain. Exactly what our needs will be. And besides all that, I also want to be with Brian. You can't be all things to all people. I know that. But I don't think I've reached the point yet where I know it emotionally."

Although she'd recently celebrated her thirty-fifth birthday, she generated a verve and vitality that gave the impression of a much younger woman. But she was thirty-five, and her childbearing years were numbered.

"Do you plan on having children?" I asked. She answered almost too quickly: "I'm equivocal. I had a miscarriage three months ago, and I realized something—I wasn't that unhappy about it. And I know I'm not getting any younger. It made me think. It's Brian who wants children. One of the big disappointments in his life is that he's always wanted a large family, and he really hasn't had a family."

Carol had tread the common route; she wanted to please; she wanted to give her husband all he'd missed out on, especially all that his former wife had been unable to provide. She'd set out to be the "better wife." But an unswerving integrity, lodged straight in the center of her psyche, rejected the idea and the fetus.

"I feel a bit badly about it," she explained. "But a child needs a mother, and frankly I'm beginning to realize that I'm not ready yet—nor may I *ever* be—to be the sole nurturer. I won't give up my career; I've a huge emotional commitment to my work. And my work and being Brian's wife overlap. They're mixed together."

Difficult as it is to face, babies often are not a genuine choice with a genuine desire for nurturing children. Frequently, they seem to be the woman's need to be doing something. Something that will please him and/or something that will identify and embrace her. Isn't that what it means to be a complete woman? Frequently they are the choice and values of parents and society, and not necessarily ours. Unhappily, that kind of choice often serves only to whittle the woman to one dimension—a hand-me-down, threadbare image of wife-and-mother, which may or may not fit her.

Carol eloquently described the interlarding of the woman's need to please and the man's "dream" of parenting. Admittedly, she had an advantage. Since Brian already had a daughter, she was able to see him as a father and a family person. And the more she saw, the more her doubts increased. She quickly understood that any children would soon become *her* project. Besides, they'd already set out on a project that linked them together—their work. Brian had been the spinner of dreams, and Carol, as his assistant, had found a way to make them work. She'd lit the match to the tallow.

Pregnant, she found herself in a similar position, with a difference. She had no investment in mothering, and she didn't want to become a mother, if it wasn't going to be a fully shared project. She explained, "I think Brian's got a lot of dreams that are unfulfilled, not the least of which is to have a large family. I've been luckier than most. This is my husband's second marriage. My eyes have been opened. I can see what happens when his daughter comes to stay with us for the weekends. We have a weekend house in Virginia; we love to play tennis. But I've been the one to forgo tennis, to make lunch, or to go to the movies with·her, or whatever. He isn't even aware of it. He leaves early in the morning and doesn't come back until late in the afternoon, relaxed and distracted. If she's angry or has something on her mind, it's me she tells."

The Executive Syndrome. "His commitments to a family and running a house," she continued, "are small. Brian is a successful man and he's obviously built a tremendous organization. The head of any research project has. Over the last twenty years he's become accustomed to getting other people to do things for him. That's the executive syndrome. He'll have the dream and I'd have total responsibility for carrying it out—raising the children and running the home. But before we will decide to have children, I see it clearly, he will have to face up to what being a father means. I'm not willing to take 100 percent responsibility for a dream that is 80 percent his."

Jolted for the moment, her thoughts churning, with one miscarriage behind her, Carol possessed a remarkable capacity for landing on target. The project they now shared was their work. However, having experienced her measure of unexpecteds in her youth, she was sufficiently sober to realize that that, too, could change. And then what?

She laughed, a dry laugh, less of amusement than of embarrassment. "I like Brian because he has a successful career, and he works hard at it. That's one of the reasons it took me so long to get married—I like winners. I frankly haven't much patience with unsuccessful people. It may be arrogant of me. But that's the way I am. By 'success' I mean hard work and mastery of your field. Scientific success. I don't mean the money, the publicity, or the travel. I came from poverty. If I went back to poverty, it would be tough but I could manage it. Public acclaim I don't like. I'm reserved about my feelings. I don't need lots and lots of people and great hurrahs. The public exposure, the amount of travel, constant dinner engagements, I don't like that at all. They're hard work for me.

"It worries me a bit, though. I think if Brian were less successful, less capable, I'd like him less. It crosses my mind occasionally that we all get older and as you do another star shines. He brings it up too. There's an eleven-year difference in age. In research you reach your peak in your forties. I just hope that that doesn't alter my attitude toward him. But then, I think I'll have grown some too."

Despite their separate expertise, and the fact that Brian supports her efforts toward establishing herself as a professional in her own right, Carol sees their fate as one. She has already set in mind that time in their growth when the asynchronies take place, the "cooling off," when they're likely to run out of the project they share. In her intelligent, open questing, Carol dramatizes the inevitability of those "shocks" that move and change us, deepening our identity and increasing our autonomy. Again and again, it becomes clear that there is no final resolution, no doing of the right or wrong thing. Rather, it is the attitude with which we face those contradictions, and the way we meet them, that defines us.

Carol described those shocks of changing—the disequilibrium, the disruption and the synthesis—in a way that merits our attention: "I've gone through phases in my life when there's been turmoil inside of me. It doesn't make you unhappy, it's just that you don't know quite who you are, or what you are. You know changes are going on. And then in a while it settles down. And you know yourself a little bit better. Right now there is so much that's new. In my work, we've come in for a new recognition. Then after living for years alone, all of a sudden I'm living with a man, and a part-time step-daughter. I'm taking care of a home. My entire social life has changed. I have to entertain in a way that, when I think of it, last year would have gotten me absolutely unglued. But I'm slipping into it. At the moment, I don't know who I am. You need time to absorb all the changes. When I think of my being a little bit like a computer, I understand myself better. It's like learning to play golf. That takes probably an integration of several hundred signals. You've got to put them all together but there's *no way* you can absorb them all at once. I've got a theory that you can jam your personal computer. I know it. I can try so hard, get everything worked out in advance, analyzed to shreds, that it won't work! You've just got to let it happen. And it does. You've got to let it synthesize."

Shocks of change—those unanticipated gaps between what we expect and what happens—are often experiences of loss. Frequently they're emotional losses—a dark knowledge, a "flaw" in the couple identity, an irretrievable loss of innocence. And at times they're experiences of physical loss as well. Those are the losses that disrupt our self-image, and often our means of identifying ourselves. They are also the contradictions, seminal to our development, that trigger those central transitions and even those turning points in our lives. They are the jolts that set us apart and initiate a lifelong process of stock-taking.

We share one of the more common projects—for example, of parenting—to cement the coupling, and we lose the uninterrupted companionship of the twosome. We feel the pinch of privacy and of intimacy. And for many women the dream of a personal development "folds up shop and goes away." And so begins her wait. We have children, a house, a garden to anchor our Togetherness, and imperceptibly our center gravitates from him to them as the I reshapes itself around the children, the house, the garden. Those are the dialectical antagonisms of "settling." We lose some freedoms and gain some rooting.

But transitions are also times of changing, when our image of who we are and what we're supposed to be is blurred and in flux. They are times when our coupling, dislodged from "the way we were," is jolted into sharper focus and reassessment. The mosaic of our lives no longer neatly fits.

Is it the insinuating presence of a third, an odd number, that breaks the symmetry of the two? Is it like that third roommate in college that distances the pair?

We're beset by polarities. At one time parenting was the glorification of womanhood and the next thing to do. Currently, we torture ourselves whether to, or not. But those are plastic choices that shred and sidetrack us. Motherhood, per se, neither defines nor diminishes the woman or the couple. What can and does diminish her is a total closeting in nurturing—whether she chooses to become a mother or not—precluding the development of other dimensions of the self. Our developmental journey, paradoxically, is not defined by the next things that couples do, but by those contradictory unanticipated feelings and events surrounding those shared projects.

Women have discovered that their relationships change as the seasons change, whether we're anchored by a baby, a career, or a brownstone. Relationships change despite our efforts to remain the same, or our efforts to "prepare" for those changes. The only "preparation" is in learning to face the inevitability of change and to meet it as a challenge. Too many women have preferred an "ostrich approach" to their lives, reluctantly facing the fact that even long-term projects come to an end.

Before we go on to what happens when we run out of shared projects, try this: Picture yourself five years from now. Close your eyes if it helps. What's the picture like? Where are you? Have you budged from where you've been? What are you being and doing? What kinds of projects do you see yourself in? Are they *all* shared? What's different about you? Is there a glimmer of a dream yet? A personal dream?

Chapter 4. / Shared Projects: The Next Things to Do

1. Datan, N. "We Get Too Soon Old and Too Late Smart: Dialectical Dilemmas in Life-span Developmental Theory." Invited address: American Psychological Association, September, 1975
2. Blood, R. D. and D. M. Wolfe. *Husbands and Wives: The Dynamics of Married Living.* New York: The Free Press, 1960.
3. Landers, A. "If You Had to Do It Over Again Would You Have Children? A Survey." *Good Housekeeping Magazine,* June, 1976.

5

MRS. GOODWIFE: RUNNING OUT OF PROJECTS

So you're skirting forty or fifty and those expectations of marriage and babies didn't come through. You didn't get what you dreamed of. Or you did—and there's still a black pit centered in your gut.

So you got your equity—the house in the suburbs. And you've built that extra wing. You got your garden, and the strawberries and lettuce have come and gone. Or you got the brownstone in the heart of the city. Or, mechanically, every three years the lease is renewed. And you've seen your husband through his schooling. You've supported him on his way. And you've raised your children. You even took that Caribbean cruise. You got most of what you'd wanted. And some of what you expected. And lots that you hadn't. So what now?

Now most women tell themselves it's their turn. Remember, they had said, *after* I marry, *after* his career is set, *after* the babies are born, *after* the children are in school, *after* the children are away at college, *then* I can start thinking about myself. Maybe go back to school. Maybe take up interior decorating. Maybe go back to writing. Maybe go back to substitute teaching. Maybe get a job.

We've cushioned ourselves in the illusion that time has frozen over for the world as well. Those *after* fictions are the way we've coded our lives.

Well, now it's *after*. Once again we're forced to face change, in another pivotal beginning. Once again we question: What do we do for an encore? Only this time it's a bit different. We feel we're running out of time, running out of projects, and even running out of dreams.

After is no specific age. It is being thirty-six, or forty-six, or fifty-six. *After* is a state of mind. It is an inner feeling that lies cheek to jowl with changes in our social and biological clocks. It is a sudden sense of impending change—a sense of widening distances and differences.

If anything can be said about the middle years, paradoxically, it is that they are *not* age-related, but events-related. They're characterized, not by the passage of time, but by the events—biological, psychological, and social—that have filled that time. And perhaps at no other period is there such a coalescing of events that prod us to face endings and propel us to new beginnings.

Contrary to the popular image, After is not necessarily a time of gradual decline. Rather it's a time of unique reassessments. It is a time when we begin to question: What's it been all about? In social psychologist Bernice Neugarten's words, it is a time when our lives become "time-left-to-live" rather than "time-since-birth," bringing an awareness of death as a reality—not so much ours, as our mate's. It is a time for the rehearsal of widowhood.[1] But, as we'll discover, the loss of a mate takes many shapes—in fact as well as in our feelings.

After is the beginning realization, for one reason or another, that we may have to stand alone. It is a time when our meanings and priorities must change, if we're to change. A time when the urgency of generating our *own* meanings is heightened. But it is difficult to discover our meanings and our priorities, when for years that's not been what we've been concerned with.

Still, as we'll learn, the middle years can bring dramatic turnarounds for women. Beginning in our mid-thirties and peaking in our mid-fifties, women have undergone a string of transitions that begin to identify them apart from their relationships with their men or their children. For most women, these "shocks" register a profound breakdown in their symbiotic mergers, furnishing a breakthrough in their sense of a personal self.

Those shocks, sharper now, fall when our experience of time itself is narrowing. Old dreams—those dreams of romance and high adventure—are slipping through our fingers like tiny fish. Foreshadowed in our thirties, the experience of a single, solitary self reemerges, moving us from the splintered "We" to the many-faceted "I."

Indeed, there are different ways that women have dealt with their middle years. We can't, therefore, speak of them with any accuracy as a time of *predictable crises*, in terms of an inevitable, invariant sequence. So much depends on how effectively we've met the challenges of transition and change all along, and how practiced we are in changing.

Unhappily, some women have lived their lives through denial, and this is never more evident than in mid-life.[2] They become busier and busier. They plunge into more parties—Tupperware and otherwise. They join more clubs, do more volunteer work, go to Weight Watchers, or join the Y for exercises.

Others have learned to hide in other ways. They withdraw. They become depressed, apathetic, and rageful.[3] They immobilize. But many more, as we'll learn, keep to their promise. For them, *after* is a time when they tell themselves: "I've earned the right to part of my life for myself!" It's been one of those psychological truisms, now borne out by research, that the sexes move in opposite directions with age. As women age, they change from a passive to a more active posture in the world; this difference has been found to hold true even in primitive cultures! Middle-aged women, it's been reported, seem more at ease with their aggressive impulses.[4] *After* is a time when women can move from a narrow to an ever-widening life.

What are those events that launch us into mid-life and jolt some of us into making our present and our future different from our past? What are the events that prod us to think: This time will be different!

Have you ever stopped to wonder, as many women do, what will happen when inevitably the children grow and leave? Or, as some women have discovered, when they repudiate us, in adolescent rebellion, seeking their own autonomy? Or, when our spouse, also in mid-life, searching the bare bones of self, ambivalent about *his* future, cloaks himself in higher and higher achievements, or in another woman, or both?

What happens when we encounter that profoundest contradiction of them all? When we discover that despite our postponements of self, we haven't been, nor can we ever be, the perfect wife or the perfect mother? What happens when we discover those meanings that we held sacrosanct melting and dissolving, when we discover that we really don't know what a perfect wife or a perfect mother is? And worse still, what happens when we don't know who or what *we* are?

With a few deft strokes, one woman, married twenty-two years, summarized those mid-life contradictions that jolted her to sit up and take notice. Her words poured out as if she'd rehearsed them: "I think it's dreadful, this business of the middle years where the kids are rebelling or leaving— mine accused me of being so protective that I deprived them of a father—and your husband is looking at twenty-year-olds in miniskirts. And the goddamn house is there all the time! It's hard to find meaning if what you've done is express yourself through other people."

Consistent with our thesis, but startling nevertheless, the woman in her forties and fifties is more likely to *act* upon her heightened feminine consciousness than is the younger woman who has still to suffer those yearnings for selfhood through a man. After years establishing the bonds of intimacy and after experiencing the jolts of merging and distancing, women in their middle years feel freer to get on with achieving a separate identity. At long last, identity takes precedence over her concern with union and intimacy.

Let's consider two women who've met the challenge: Katherine Butler and Maureen Cleary. The stories they have to tell of changing would have been unexpected and unpredictable had we met them, say, ten years before.

THE DARK SHADOW OF THE OTHER WOMAN

I phoned Kate because I'd learned that her fabric designs were being featured in a fashion show, and that her career had begun a slim ten years before. Just fifty, she has been married twenty-seven years to George Butler. If I'd wanted to invent a story about a woman who was a perfect "victim," and how she stopped being a victim, I could do no better than to conjure up Kate.

Kate had been raised in a religious family by a mother, harassed and demanding, who alternated between an all-encompassing love and histrionic fits of temper. She soon became a barometer of others' moods, developing an expertise for pleasing. She described herself as a "joy" to her parents, teachers, and classmates. In fact, in junior college she was voted the most popular, the best natured, and the sweetheart of the class. In retrospect these were dubious honors; at the time, they caused her to run home, brimming with happiness, exclaiming: "Everybody loves me!"

At the age of twenty-two, she met George Butler and it was "zap" at first sight. He'd returned from military service and was going back to college to complete his degree in physics. She recalled the lost look in his eyes; she felt for his vulnerability. He seemed unlocated, and she, she thought, could heal him.

The passage from her parents' house to that of her husband was turbulent. She married, she explained, because she "was getting older" and she was "expected" to marry. But her mother disapproved of George—*she* didn't like the look in his eyes. Kate's effort to separate from her family plunged her into another bind. No longer pleasing her mother, she now set out to please her young husband.

They moved to Connecticut, where he taught at a small college and continued his studies. The next ten years of her life she lived as if painting in numbers. Color 1, The Couple Identity. Color 2, Support Husband's Schooling and Career. (She explained: "Because he was still in school when we married, I always was more protective and supportive of him than I should have been.) Color 3, The Arrival of a Baby Girl—and the unraveling into an Us and a Him. Color 4, The House in the Suburbs. Color 5, Another Baby—a son. Color 6, A Vegetable Garden. Canning tomatoes. Thrifty spending. And a house bulging with diapers, playpens, and highchairs spattered with oatmeal. Color 7, A Bad Case of Ulcers. . . .

Those were unexamined years in which she tried hard to please, fulfilling that image of the best wife and mother. Unlike her mother, she would take the "lesser role" because she wanted her husband to be the "stronger one."

The tone of the marriage was soon set. In a way, he became her tyrannical conscience. Each morning he'd leave her with a list of things to do, like bringing the suit to the cleaners, phoning the garage man about the muffler, phoning the insurance man about renewing the fire coverage, making sure to balance the checkbook. Each evening, she'd face her failings with a glacial evaluation of her performance. Twisting herself into a "We," her own identity was submerged, and she desperately relied on his approval as an intrinsic sign of her worth.

The first "shock" in their union occurred with the birth of their baby, when Kate's dream of being the perfect helpmate collapsed in ashes. A buoyant redhead with sparkling blueberry eyes, she seemed to wilt when she spoke of that time. "When I came home with the baby I discovered that my husband had the worst temper I've ever seen. I don't remember what about, but he got very angry with me.

I was standing in the bedroom and he picked up a bud vase and smashed it against the wall. For years after, he was the sensitive one, and I learned to do circles around his temper! And his temper was always on the surface. Every frustration he had at work, he took out at home by breaking dishes, pencils, chairs, and once he even threatened me."

That first fissuring in their relationship, however, only prodded her to try harder. A year and a half later another baby was born and Kate's center shifted from being the perfect wife to being the perfect mother. Since George was disinterested and possibly even resentful of the children, she doubled her efforts at childrearing. She became the children's constant companion, taking them to swimming lessons, ice skating, fishing. "All the things a father should do," she explained. "I got so involved with the children that I became even more dependent on my husband. I couldn't go anywhere socially without him. I couldn't even carry on a conversation except about the babies and the house."

One year blurred into the next; Kate cocooned herself in her marriage. "I don't think being a housewife is a bad thing to be; in fact, it can be very rewarding raising children," she explained. "But I seemed to lose all interest in myself. I gained weight and even though I liked being well dressed, we got so used to living on a budget, even when we didn't have to anymore, that I saved all our money. There always seemed to be something more important to spend it on than clothes. I got caught up in an image of what I thought a wife should be, a Mrs. Goodwife, and what I thought he wanted. He watched his money very carefully. I played out my role to the extreme, I guess."

Like litmus paper, Kate registered the change in his every mood. Still, it all turned out so different from what she'd been led to expect. And before she knew it she was thirty-four and faced with, perhaps, the most profound contradiction of them all.

"Do you want to hear Shock Number Two?" she asked. A long shadow fell across her face. "I never talk about it. I developed a persistent cough. I went to our family doctor and he said it was nothing. But the cough didn't go away. Finally, he X-rayed and I had to face cancer."

Still protective of her husband, Kate withheld the doctor's diagnosis. She explained that her husband was taking the last of his exams for a graduate degree and she didn't want to disrupt him. It was a full week later when a malignant tumor was removed. Alive and energetic one day, she was faced with dying the next.

If that was *Shock* Number 2, in Kate's words, it also turned out to be *Miracle* Number 2 because it changed the direction of her life. (Miracle Number 1 was her survival in the battle with cancer.)

"For a while, I wasn't sure how it would turn out," she said. "Then, gradually, as I grew stronger, a funny thing happened. I suddenly became conscious of time. Not so much my-whole-life kind of time, but everyday time—the way I was spending my time. I don't mean that I consciously sat myself down and thought about it. It just happened. All I knew was that life suddenly became very sweet. The air smelled sweeter. People's faces looked different. Color. Color became more intense. Everything was turned around. My children looked more beautiful. *It was as if I'd been planted in a new direction!* Everything took on a brilliant light and everything that had been invisible became visible. And you know, that was sixteen years ago, and I still haven't gotten over it.

"I was given the gift of life," she said, barely audibly.

Indeed, she discovered the gift of *her* life—a life that slowly was to disentangle itself from being exclusively a wife-and-mother. She learned that our lives are lived, not in great sweeps of cosmic time, but in the small graspable everyday time.

But how often do we take time out to think about that? What if *you* did? Could you list your priorities in terms of the actual amount of hours you spend on the everyday routines, like chauffeuring the children, cleaning, washing, marketing, preparing meals, or even on the telephone?

Kate's life had been laced with more than the average dose of self-abnegation. The suspension of her everyday living, disrupting the common routines, forced her to experience another aspect of herself.

Without conscious intent concerning long-term goals or a career, she set out on a small palpable goal—to change the direction of her everyday living. Without fanfare, one afternoon she wandered into an artist's supply shop and bought some brushes, watercolors, and sketch pads. That's how Miracle Number 2 began.

"Here in Westport," Kate was saying, "there is a community of ladies who go to the beach and spend the day with their children, gossiping, playing duplicate bridge, knitting —that sort of thing. Well, life became too precious suddenly. So I told myself, I don't want to be one of those women. In order to have a little privacy, and be with my children—they were pre-teens—I needed to find something to do, something quiet that would get me out of those gossiping sessions. So I went into town and bought some artist's supplies. I thought: Why not? I can be on the beach with my children and also paint! That would isolate me from the ladies and their talk. And very important, I'd changed. I didn't care anymore that they'd say, 'Isn't she peculiar? She's *painting*.'

"How did I happen to pick painting? Well, my mother taught art at home, and there were always students streaming in and out. Without thinking, that's what I began doing. Watercolors. The kids loved it. Then I showed my work to an art-gallery owner nearby, and that started me off to what eventually became my fabric designs. But I didn't take it seriously at first. Of course, George laughed. That wasn't his idea of a housewife, but it hadn't been mine either."

Most miracles, like everything else, are firmly rooted in who we are. Under stress, Kate fell back on her early resources. Painting, which later evolved into fabric designing, was for her a return to her childhood, a time when she'd felt special. As she began to take herself more seriously, it separated her from a willing martyrdom—but the more involved she became with her interests, the more her husband's anger flared. Yet, despite their chaotic relationship, Kate considered his rages evidence of his involvement; and they kept her very much concerned with his life. It is noteworthy in terms of women's ways that she changed in the relationship only after *he* withdrew from her.

Over the years, she'd put herself on ice, and slowly she'd begun to thaw. However, not until Kate faced those dark, hard cores of pain, injuries to what she'd been led to believe —like *everybody* will love me, because I work so hard at it— did she come into her own. She commented: "My illness taught me that you've got to face the hurt, so that the healing can take place." Perhaps for women, there is no greater injury as the one that challenges our very worth as persons and as women. Especially if that's the aspect of ourselves that we've systematically denied.

Only with that kind of conflict and blow to her self-esteem —what Kate describes as Shock Number 3 and Miracle Number 3—did she gather herself and overcome her masochism. She changed in fundamental ways, not because she was forty-six, but because those unexpected events—social, biological, and psychological—propelled her changing. She'd labored much of her life; she'd arduously been inching her way, when abruptly she was catapulted.

How does a "victim" recast her image and stop being victim? Kate answered my question slowly; her voice was fluid and warm. "I was shocked, really shocked when I discovered George had been having an affair. It wasn't only for the obvious reasons—I'd been such an innocent!—but *she* became the concrete evidence of our relationship. The deception. Mine and his. It forced me to face it. It also forced me to face myself. I was shocked out of my dream world."

The Saturday Affair. "One evening I picked up his briefcase to take it into the den. It's funny now," she reflected. "I was still being the perfect wife. It was open and I dropped it. I'd been so oblivious. His love letters spilled out, flying all over. They weren't even sealed! And I read them. I was devastated; I thought it was the end of my world.

"I realized how much we'd grown apart. I confronted him and he denied it at first. Then, I told him I saw the letters. And he said, 'I'm never going to discuss it with you.' I offered him a divorce, but that's not what he wanted. I don't know what he wants, but it doesn't matter anymore. For the past five years there's been this silence between us, but I wouldn't demean myself and play watchdog.

"It was his Saturday Affair—those are the suburbanites' affairs. Every Saturday he'd say he was going shopping, even though I knew he detested shopping. He'd leave at one and get back at six.

"Those letters were so beautiful. So romantic. One of them was even a rough draft. A draft that he'd kept. The thought that he could express himself to another woman tormented me."

The Other Woman. Could she ever piece this patchwork of a life together again? she wondered. Every morning for three months she vomited—just as she had years before when she was told her chances for surviving the cancer were slim. She felt sick in body and in spirit. She'd been betrayed. She vomited the final bits of an illusion.

That image of the other woman sliced through her and became a nagging obsession. What did she look like? Was she tall? Slender? Young? She imagined her as someone he worked with at the college—someone intelligent, informed, and involved in the world. Saturday afternoons were probably the only times she was free so they could meet.

Where did they go? To a motel? She tried to picture them together—how they made love. Did he *love* her? What were the things they talked about? Science? World affairs? How long had they known each other? Were they *still* together? What really were his plans for the future? She entertained thoughts of running into them accidentally, or even meeting her at a faculty tea. She would talk to her so she could know what she was like—what her strong points were, and her weaknesses.

She summoned a leaden resolve to face up to him and, more important, to face herself. Suddenly, she knew no fear. She stared in the mirror, and a stranger stared back. She heard the strength in her voice as she told herself: I exist too. I think I've earned the right. Slowly, she began shedding the sackcloth and ashes of the perennial victim. Slowly, what she'd thought of as her competition—that "other" woman— became a beacon to the other woman in her that she'd hidden away. She began to fight free of those strangling images of the perfect wife and mother, loosening those last vestiges of guilt and doubt.

"I know this must sound funny," Kate observed, "but the woman my husband was involved with changed my image of myself—of what a woman should be. That old image of me was pretty much destroyed. I felt worthless; my pride hurt and my ego sagged. I went out and bought a completely new wardrobe. Don't misunderstand, I don't mean that as a sur- face thing. I suddenly really *cared enough about myself* to want to take care of myself. No more skimping. No more tattered sweaters. I'd lost fifteen pounds because I'd been up- set, but it was becoming. I didn't want to be a gray-haired lady anymore either. So I went red!

"I got shocked out of my complacency in many ways. She did me a service. I wanted to be the woman I imagined him with. An involved, independent woman. Maybe it was the kind of woman I wanted to be all along, but never dared be. But now I knew that I might be standing alone. It motivated me. I became more serious about my work—which led to my being picked up by a fashion designer, and the fashion show of my fabrics. And craziest of all, now he really wants me. But I've got so used to the feeling of freedom that it doesn't matter.

"And it's never changed. It was like looking in the mirror and finding me. It was the real turning point in my life because I was freed; I was a person. And you know what? As that happened, he also began seeing me as a separate person, and not as an extension of him. He can actually approve of some of the things I do now.

"But it isn't important anymore. I look back now and can feel my innocence! The way I looked, the impression I made, *was* important to him. And then, for a while, my life seemed to completely center around the children. I can justify that now by saying that I was trying to compensate for the fact that he spent so little time with them. George is a cold scientist, I'm afraid. He was bored with children; he couldn't talk to them on any level. But that's not really the point; I see that now. It's not a matter of making my husband or my children the center. Either way, I was leaving myself out. I'm not sure where our marriage is headed. But that isn't important anymore either. Not now that I've got me."

Perfect matching in so many marriages, unhappily, is not the intertwining of strengths but rather of our felt lacks. The urge toward coupling seems to be more in that spirit than in any other. Kate's consuming wish to please—more accurately, to be loved—and her readiness to shape herself in the other's image fueled and stoked her husband's irrational demands. George became adroit at communicating double messages. He paradoxically expected Kate to be the perfect homemaker while he also expected her to be the perfect companion and mistress. She was to be frugal, obedient, and docile, and also fashionable, independent, and worldly!

Whatever the mutual disillusionments and rancors in a marriage, they're more sharply experienced and acted upon in the middle years. Mid-life has been variously tagged as the time of disenchantment, a time of cooling off, and a time of diminishing male fervor—in short, a time when a good many women scavenge the libraries and bookshops for books on sexual impotence.

"Why is it," one bookshop owner asked, only half in jest, "that so many middle-aged women ask for books on male impotence?"

"Only middle-aged *wives*," I parried.

So much of male impotence, as one researcher observed, is related to what goes on above the belt rather than below. The passage of time does bring with it a certain complacency and some measure of indifference. And what better arena to express that indifference than in the conjugal bed? And what perfect timing for the "other" woman!

No soap opera worthy of its name has neglected to include the Other Woman in its cast of characters. In fiction and in life, when women have been forthright in acknowledging the presence of the other woman, she has played a pivotal role in prompting their growth.

Still, many women ask where have we, one of the most enlightened generations of wives, gone wrong? In Kate's words, in our innocence—our several innocences, to be precise.

One day, after fifteen or so years of marriage, we look across the table and innocently happen on a stranger. For Kate it was inconceivable that her husband could write passionate love letters. It was inconceivable that part of him had been closeted from her and had gone unshared. Or possibly he had changed through the years and it had escaped her. She looked at him and no longer saw the person she thought she knew.

Where had she gone wrong? She'd been all she thought *he*'d wanted, a Mrs. Goodwife, and yet she'd failed. The contradictions deepen as the transitions unfold. It seemed to her that the very reason he'd been enchanted with her—her docility—was now the reason for his disenchantment.

The "Saturday Affair," however, served its function. It caused Kate to look at her husband with new eyes. The support and nurturance he'd demanded at one stage was no longer welcomed or respected. And, more important, it pressed her to look at herself. The "I" turned inward and took stock. What she saw was a woman quicksanded in a timeworn image of what a good wife is supposed to be.

The shattering of one set of illusions, moreover, made

room for a reassessment. She looked to her past as well as to her future. She no longer saw her mother as only a domineering woman. She now also understood that her mother was a woman who had struggled to maintain her own identity. With a resurgence of vague gropings for freedom, her work, once a hobby, now took on the full measure of its worth. And although her marriage was up for grabs, there followed a greater appreciation and respect for one another. Caught in another seeming contradiction, she discovered that a genuine intimacy could flourish only with an increasing sense of self. And in a similar vein, the increasing disenchantment didn't necessarily lead to a greater dissatisfaction. If anything, the quality of her life improved.

As I was getting ready to leave the weatherbeaten house in Westport with its gently sloping lawns, Kate reached for my hand. "I think it's so important," she began hesitantly, "for women to be let into other women's lives. What I'd like to share with others is that fifty is a great age to be. Despite all my downs and ups, my life has been joyous. I've been able to put things in their right slot. Age has helped me. I see that the problems I've had aren't *all* of who I am. I've reached the point in my life where everything is finally coming together. From forty-nine to your mid-fifties can be a glorious time for a woman. It's a time for reaping."

She tugged self-consciously at the chic plum-colored scarf knotted around her neck and smiled. It was definitely the smile of a woman pleased with herself.

Just as the "other" woman freed the other woman in Kate, the adolescent's bolt for freedom frees some women. One such woman is Maureen Cleary, whom we're about to encounter.

Like Kate, Maureen discovered in her middle years, in the words of poet Marge Piercy, that:

> Loss is also clearance.
> Emptiness is also receptivity.

Chapter 5. / Mrs. Goodwife: Running Out of Projects

1. Neugarten, B. L. "The Psychology of the Aging: An Overview." *American Psychological Association, Master Lectures on Developmental Psychology.* JSAS Catalog of Selected Documents in Psychology, 1976, 6(4).
2. Marmor, J. *Psychiatry in Transition.* New York: Brunner/Mazel, 1974.
3. McCranie, E. J. "Neurotic Problems in Middle Age." *The Family in Distress,* 1976, 2, 1–3.
4. Gutman, D. L. "The Cross-cultural Perspective: Notes Toward a Comparative Psychology of Aging." In *Handbook of the Psychology of Aging,* edited by J. E. Birren. New York: Van Nostrand Reinhold. In press.

6

SUPERMOTHER:
RUNNING OUT
OF PROJECTS

WE'VE BEEN WRAPPED UP IN OUR MEN, WRAPPED UP IN OUR house, wrapped up in mothering—our children and our men. And so we pass through still another jolt: the emptying nest, a concept I'd like to broaden to include not only the ending of nurturing our children but also the ending of nurturing our spouse. This is something that the childless couple may become acutely aware of.

Despite the measure of relief that some women experience in relinquishing responsibilities, particularly those of child-rearing, this phase is another pivotal transition—as critical a time, if not more so, as that decision to become a mother. It is a phase in which we restructure our meanings, our time, our emotional investments, and our self-image. Sooner for some, later for others, we face the reality that neither our spouse nor our children are created in our image—nor we in theirs—and we're thrown, imageless.

In the whirling blender of "middlescence," filled to the brim with our husbands' complacency, dissatisfaction, or wandering eyes, add still another ingredient for those of us who also are mothers—our children's rebellions, recriminations, or departures. Those wrenchings, the proverbial straw piled on already fraying relationships, have moved women like Maureen Cleary to reassess their lives and to reorder their priorities.

What's a Nice Girl Like You Doing in a Place Like This?

I met Maureen at a NOW meeting for the older woman—older being thirty-five and over! She was one of four speakers. She'd swept up to the microphone, her shimmering dark hair flowing down to her shoulders. She looked vital and self-possessed. "I'm a forty-four-year-old woman, going on twenty-one," she laughed. She'd been married for twenty-two years, she announced, and had five children—the three oldest now in their own apartments and self-supporting, one away, and one readying to leave.

One morning, she explained, on her knees scrubbing the kitchen floor, elbow high in soapsuds, she heard herself asking: "What's a nice girl like you doing in a place like this?" Armed with a fifteen-year-old *summa cum laude* B.A., she went looking for a job. At the time, her teenage daughter was hospitalized for a drug-induced breakdown; her husband, angry, refused to pay the $17,000 for the hospital care. Maureen took a job and paid for her daughter's treatment. Shortly after, she discovered her husband was living with a twenty-year-old! At this juncture in her story, Maureen pointed to the Exit door with a grand gesture and swept off the stage to a burst of thunderous applause.

That night I phoned Maureen to ask for a meeting. She'd recently moved into her own apartment, which she shared with another woman. Maureen was a runaway of sorts.

She sat opposite me with her long legs crossed. A colorful scarf, wrapped around her head, hid her long hair. She said the word that best characterized her life at the moment was "rocky."

"Rocky" characterized her past as well. Maureen came from working-class parents who had separated when she was ten. Her father, an alcoholic, was at best a misty memory. She'd worked hard to put herself through college, and had graduated with honors. She married Douglas Cleary, at present the managing editor for a national magazine, immediately after graduation to get away from a mother who'd become controlling and resentful.

Her marriage, however, proved a poor escape. Maureen

became the nagging cliché of a harried housewife; Douglas began to drink. For the first fifteen years of their marriage, she spent all her time with the children—the first four babies came in as many years; the fifth came along because she saw herself as "Superwoman." And as she tells us, she was "starving to death." As a family, they were set in a familiar pattern. Maureen explained: "Even though they outnumbered me, and they had more hands than I did, and were stronger, I did all the work. And my husband was fond of making big speeches like: 'Mother is the disciple of the gospel of work. She thinks cleanliness is next to godliness.'" Motherhood and homemaking were both venerated and denigrated. "My husband," Maureen continued, "always acted as if cleaning, cooking, ironing—none of those things were important. As a life's career there's nothing much to be said for scrubbing floors, but it's one of those necessary, crummy things that has to be done."

Maureen was starving to death both intellectually and emotionally. As the economic pressures of supporting a large family mounted, her husband became increasingly distant. Acutely lonely, she felt as if her brain and her heart were rusting; Douglas found more and more comfort in alcohol. A meticulous homemaker, she buried herself in the house and in the children. Her days crept by.

With the birth of her last child, she became seriously depressed. "He didn't understand," she explained. "And I think he drank more and more to get out of the turmoil of all those kids. I realize now that if I'd gone back to work I probably could have alleviated some of the pressure on me and on him. If I had known at twenty-one what I discovered at forty! I was overworked at home and in a rage. I became more and more demanding."

Still, each was fulfilling the image they had of their role; each was carrying out the original contract. It was for her to work and see him through his graduate studies. When the babies arrived, it was for him to support them as best he could, and for her to devote her energies to raising them.

"If I weren't with them every minute," she explained, "I thought they'd be deprived of mothering."

Perhaps the babies were meant to fill the emptiness between and within—but they too failed. And shortly after her youngest son was born, she took to bed. A doctor was summoned; he filled her with tranquilizers. With some bitterness, she recalls: "The doctor wasn't my friend. He drugged me up so that they could put me back in harness again. He put me right back where I was to begin with, and said: 'Yes, you can!' Well, I did. But it was all wrong. What I needed was to take a look at my life, not to go on gritting my teeth with a dogged determination to carry on."

Unhappily, the social structures supported her roles. That experience is all too common with too many women who become Valium poppers. Rather than face and meet our rancors, we're supported in swallowing them down. Rather than being permitted her grieving, as her years of childbearing came to a close, Maureen was given tranquilizers to douse her feelings. Regretfully, the only newness in an otherwise bleak existence had been the newness of a newborn: She'd invested far too much in being a Superwoman mother. She'd overplayed her role, as many women do, to justify the maintenance of her marriage, which gave structure and meaning to her life.

Maureen felt trapped; she was depressed and she also was guilty about being depressed. Her head spun in a familiar female litany. Why wasn't she happy? she thought, berating herself. She had a handsome professional husband. Yes, her house was falling apart, but it was on a beautiful tree-lined street in the suburbs. And she had five beautiful children. Why *wasn't* she happy?

Why had she gotten up every morning in a paroxysm of fear? Sit up, she'd tell herself. Put your feet on the floor. Stand up. Robot-like, she gave herself orders. "I couldn't take it out on the children," she explained. "It wasn't their fault. So I'd wait until they were asleep and would fall on the kitchen floor and cry."

She looked down at her strong, lean hands. "It just didn't have to be that way," she protested. The next six years were a waking nightmare in which Maureen struggled with feelings of super-responsibility. A great sadness seemed to engulf her as she remembered that period. "I kept demanding from him but in a self-defeating way. In a querulous, attacking way. He tried but he wasn't used to taking responsibility and he was unhappy at work. I drove him out.

"It was a lot of grief, those years. I was thirty-seven, the youngest was three, and the other four were in their teens. Can you imagine four teenagers under one roof, acting up?"

She turned to face me, and with her usual disarming candor, explained: "Well, my husband found himself a twenty-year-old vine-ripened tomato who looked at him with adoring eyes. He rented an apartment and they were living together. I was annihilated. And would you believe it, I didn't know he'd moved out! I couldn't tell the difference. He was home so seldom. A 'friend' told me. When I confronted him, he told me he wanted a divorce. I said, 'Fine. Go get it!' But I couldn't stand on my anger. It had been a good, healthy response, but it didn't last. I wanted to die; I felt abandoned. I chased and pursued him. With no self-esteem and little dignity, I coaxed him back. I was determined to carry on my home and hold the kids together. At thirty-seven, I felt very old and very miserable. Of course, it didn't work."

Compromises seldom do. They're like applying a Band-aid to an injury that requires radical treatment. Once again, Maureen postponed herself, ostensibly, for that much-abused "children's sake." In reality, her husband's threat to leave her reawakened an old injury—her abandonment by her father. We replay old tapes.

"Things just went downhill," she was saying. "That's when a friend asked me to join him in a psychodrama group. I went, supposedly to help him out. The first time, I looked around and saw a bunch of kids in their twenties. I thought, they have young problems, and I have old problems—this is *not* for me. But I learned so much from those young people that night that I returned. There was this twenty-five-year-old who adopted me. He said, 'Maureen, I want you to go home and look in the mirror and say over and over, I am entitled. I am entitled.' That was a twenty-five-year-old kid!

"My children thought it was really far out that their mother was doing something as fantastic as psychodrama. And one by one they asked if they could come along. So I let them come. All but the youngest, I think, were there. Well, that night it was Cleary night. My kids did a job on me. I ended sitting on the floor in a fetal position against the wall. I was ready for a psychological iron lung.

"They tore into me. They said I should have done something about my marriage. After all, I was the sober one and he was the sick one. Why hadn't I done anything about it? Because I couldn't get along with their father, they said, I deprived *them* of a father. They said I was super-responsible, compulsive, overprotective, and took up too much space! They went on and on, blaming and accusing. I'd been trying to keep the kids from going under, and they told me I really was keeping them from their father.

"But later I realized it was the most beneficent thing that could have happened to me! I was unglued, devastated. I went home that night and lay awake: *What had all the blood, sweat, and tears been for?* All those sacrifices? I'd been the low one on the totem pole. Everybody was first and I was left with the crumbs. I was starving. And I thought, I wasn't happy. My husband wasn't happy. And the kids weren't happy. What was it all about?

"I kept looking at the door with such longing. I thought I'd just like to walk out and keep going into the horizon. But I was trapped in the fear that my husband wouldn't be responsible. It was really the boy I was worried about because the others were more or less on their own. I was also aware, though, that I was holding on to that little boy because he was all I had. And if anyone, he was the one that was being deprived of a father—just so long as I was around.

It was the worst night of my life. And then I had a dream—that's what pushed me out the door."

She leaned forward with the air of someone about to reveal something quite extraordinary. And it was. "The dream was so vivid, I'll never forget it. I was in an apartment and it was a dingy, dingy place. The living room was narrow and dark. There was only one window, looking out on an airshaft. The whole place was furnished in early mother-in-law hand-me-down furniture. So the only thing you could do was throw it out or burn it, because there was dirt in the very molecules of the fibers. The whole place was like that, the walls, everything. That's the shape this place was in. *And I'm working here and I'm working there and nothing is showing. I'm getting so very tired.* Off the living room was a windowless room and inside were cribs, *babies' cribs, lots of them. They were all pulled apart*—headboards, rails, springs, helter-skelter. *I started trying to organize those too.* I'm working like crazy, when I'm called into an equally dingy kitchen.

"There I see two of my children. I start to clean up—first on top of the refrigerator—when I saw what I took to be a family pet, a little monkey. He had a collar on. He was chained to the door. He sat there, almost mummified. He was so shriveled, skeletal. Like those pictures of the Bangla Desh, starving to death.

"I looked at the monkey and felt awful. Oh my God, I forgot he was there. I had neglected him. I hadn't fed him. I didn't remember the last time I'd even given him water. I had this horrible sinking guilty feeling that I had forgotten. I said to my daughter: 'I didn't feed the monkey!' She had a little gerbil she was feeding and she said, *'I'll help you.'* The poor animal just fell on the food. How could I have forgotten?

"When I awoke I realized that I was that mummified monkey, and that I was starving, and that it had been going on for twenty years! What *have* I been doing for twenty years? What has it been all about?"

Tears streamed down her cheeks. She tapped her cigarette against the table, swallowed hard, and lit it. I felt touched, but she seemed unconcerned with me or the effect she was having. Maureen had changed, even before my very eyes.

What Has It Been All About? About growing into our own skins!

At thirty-seven Maureen had thought of herself as old. She felt her youth fading, her childbearing coming to an end, her children separating, and her husband indifferent. The end of childbearing? I'm acutely aware that I've made no reference to menopause as a significant event in the life of the middle-aged woman. That's because she didn't either. The beginning and ending of the menses, events that most of us anticipate, have not been experienced as the critical transitions we may have supposed. To be sure, menopause marks the end of childbearing and signals a tangible fact of aging, but it's one of those expected transitions that's discounted much before the actual physiological event. Interestingly, in one study, the loss of reproductive capacity was not as important a concern as not knowing what to expect.[1] Like Maureen, most women face an end to their childbearing and feelings about aging well before menopause per se.

It wasn't the empty womb, the emptying nest, or even the empty bed that escalated Maureen's panic, but the emptying image of herself. It became more and more difficult to continue identifying herself through the reflected image of her professional husband—when she felt so stifled intellectually— or through her children, who were seeking their own independence.

Those meanings that she'd sought outside herself had emptied out, and she'd generated no new ones to replace them. A revealing postscript in terms of the adolescent developmental process: Left with the children, Douglas Cleary took charge. And being in charge, *he,* then, became the target of their rebellions.

Looking back, Maureen discovered that their confrontation proved her liberation. At age forty-four she felt younger than she had in her thirties. Often we think, Oh, those terrible adolescent years! Just as we thought, Oh, those terrible twos! But that's only one side of the picture. Those "terrible" years are also shocks of freedom and liberation, dissolving the symbiotic knots, forcing us to stand apart.

It is noteworthy that in Maureen's dream the cribs are pulled apart, signaling the end of childbearing, and that it is her teenage daughter, feeding her growing self, who helps her. Paradoxically, a number of women have admitted that they've looked to their daughters as their role models! Striking out for her own autonomy, Maureen's daughter illuminated the way.

Currently an active member of the National Organization for Women, Maureen hopes to reach other "older" women and give them the support she found in the women's movement. I've referred to Maureen as a runaway of sorts. She is typical of an increasing number of women who, rather than disappearing into the night, separate from their household with a responsible decision. Maureen did leave her home, but she also saw to it that she was available when her children needed her.

I asked Maureen what it was she'd want most, if she could be granted any wish in the world. She took a deep breath, stretched her arms toward the sky and replied: "I'm slowly working myself out of my chains. What I really and truly would like, as long as I'm reaching for the moon, is to achieve autonomy in intimacy. To have a loving relationship without giving myself up."

Where Have We Gone Wrong? Maureen purportedly held the family together for the "children's sake," and then suffered what was, for her, the ultimate betrayal. She'd cloaked herself in motherhood, and when the time came for her brood to separate, she felt stripped.

If her spouse and offspring were able to sort themselves out only in anger or in withdrawal, then Maureen seemed to separate from them only with raging feelings of betrayal, or abandonment, or worse still, of failure. But whom have we really failed? Who has betrayed or abandoned whom—if not ourselves? Over the years, we've ignored and displaced our center. It seemed easier that way.

Where have we, one of the most enlightened generations of mothers, gone wrong? Again, in our innocence! Our innocence concerning the process of development, autonomy, and identity.

I'm afraid, however, that we aren't the only culprits. The social climate in which we live has contributed substantially, if innocently, in keeping us mouseholed. Until recently, much of the literature concerning mothering, even in our scientific annals, has been written from the viewpoint of the developmental changes in the child. Little has been inferred about the concomitant developmental changes in the *mother* as she's thrust into relinquishing a familiar role.

Like Kate's "other" woman, who disrupted her image of a wife, the increasing autonomy of our adolescents disrupts our image of a mother. Mostly, it disrupts the familiar meanings that have structured our years—the relationships and routines by which we have measured our time. How often do we still hear ourselves say: "Put on your wool scarf—it's ten degrees out!" "You've barely touched your vegetables!" "What time will you be home; you have an early class." And how often do we also hear the bristling angers of the recipients of all that "mothering." So we begin to question.

Hurt and angry, one woman confided: "I'm trying to get it all together myself, and when Nancy stays out so late, and is so defiant about it—even if she is nineteen—I resent her. I can't get on with it. She becomes an intrusion."

What intrudes, really, is the "mothering" relevant to an earlier stage, short-circuiting the attempts of both teenager and mother to give each other living space. That image of the *best* mother, like the one of the *best* wife, is ever present to sandbag us. We seem innocent of the fact that whatever our image of the perfect mother might be, it is in the nature of growth to disrupt it.

We can be the most understanding, loving, "friend-type" mother, who is into the latest jargon, marches for ERA, supports the decriminalization of grass, strums punk rock, and wears punk fashions. Or we may be of a traditional bent, bake the best cheesecake, knit sweaters and gloves, and listen to Puccini. Either way, we're all in the same boat—a rocking one.

Under an oppressive cloud of doubt, we gradually discover that we haven't been perfect mothers, but we may discover as well that we haven't failed *them*. It may be comforting for some of us to recall the biblical story of Jesus in the Temple. Even Mary, the prototype of the perfect mother to the perfect son, suffered the first pangs of separation. After searching for the young Jesus for three days, you may remember, she was told: How come you came looking for me? Don't you know I must be about my Father's business?

One of the many traps about being a perfect mother is that we must raise perfect children. With all the "blood, sweat, and tears" that Maureen put into raising her children, the least she could hope for, in return, was to be rewarded with their achievements. In her When They Grow Up dreams, she saw them grow to prominence. One child was to become a famous painter-sculptor. Another, a writer. Another . . .

So not only are we to be the *best* mother, but our children are to be the *best* children. When He grows up, we tell ourselves, he'll look like Robert Redford, have SAT scores in the 900s with Princetonharvardyale and every Smithradcliffeholyoke girl clamoring at his door. In addition, he'll admire our wisdom and appreciate our labors. (One can tell my own offspring is a son. With minor changes one can substitute She for He.)

Comes the day of reckoning and we may discover that our *best* son/daughter isn't that beautiful; in fact, our offspring is a bit frumpy, doesn't know what to major in, is thinking of dropping out of school, and thinks our concern with weight is ancient, our values are flaky, and our makeup is too much!

At the same time that we're checking out our fantasy of our *best* child, we're also checking out our fantasy of our *perfect* life. Is there no end to our wanting to shape reality to fit our fantasy molds?

In mid-life, more than ever, fantasy and reality collide, which takes us to the root of our innocence. We've slurred over the dialectics of transitions and separations. Merging, as we've seen again and again, bears the seeds of its own distancing. And distancing involves disruption, as a wife and as a mother. And disruption and change always involve the persons we're separating from.

Divorce As a Resolution? Maureen's bolt for freedom didn't come with the distancing between herself and her husband—concretized by his affair—but interestingly, it took place with the final fissuring between herself and her children, who for years had been the mainstay of her identity.

Is the thrust toward the development of a self inimical to the traditional marriage and childrearing? Does such a journey always end alone? Is divorce the ultimate resolution of the couple "identity" crisis?

Both Kate and Maureen face the possibility of divorce. They typify the extreme in fissuring. We should note, however, that they also typified the extreme in overplaying their roles, the one as a mothering wife, the other as a Supermother.[2] The traditional images of wife-and-mother, set in cement, *are* a burden to a separate self, leaving no room for the vicissitudes of changing.

Like any process, changing takes time and labor. Upset, one woman, fifty and childless, having mothered her spouse for years, reflected: "How can I change? That's the way he *knows* me." More precisely, that's the means she's used to making herself known and loved.

Most women pay a high price for that promise of love and approval. Indeed, that was the case for Kate and Maureen. Therefore, for their husbands' attitudes toward them to change, it was necessary for them to change. Certainly, the fact that we can relinquish those roles that have identified us is a measure of the fact that we're ready to stand apart.

But we'll find that divorcing, per se, like living together, is not the solution to all our problems. Women who've divorced and remarried and haven't developed their own identity enter the new union with the old expectations and assumptions. Although divorce rates have been on a steady increase, that doesn't mean that our expectations have changed; more likely, it points up the change in our level of tolerance. In the early twentieth century, widowhood was frequent and tolerance levels were high; the divorce rate was low. Couples who have smaller expectations and greater tolerance don't divorce, marital dissatisfaction or no.

In the chapter that follows we'll encounter women in their middle years who've experienced an abrupt turnaround in their lives, and are still married, as well as some others who have changed, and have divorced, and remarried.

Our children, and sometimes our men, unwittingly free us, but we don't know what to do with freedom. We've misplaced our center and we've clearly worked ourselves out of a job. Still, the loss—the fact that we're not permitted to continue in our familiar self-image—clears the way.

For some women the departure of their last child is a relief, and some couples even report that they get along better, freed from the restrictions of child rearing.[3] That, however, isn't the point. The distress in mid-life is not the launching of our last child, but the rupturing of those mergers that defined us. Women are betrayed not by the emptying nest, a wastebasket term, but by the stultifying images that had been the centripetal force of their identity.

Before we examine how we can make use of those heightened moments of flux in our lives, we should pause, I think, and do some soul-searching about those issues of identity, wifedom, and motherhood. Have you ever stopped to listen to the way *you* identify yourself, say, to a new acquaintance? Or to your hairdresser, perhaps? Or to a friend? And have you ever stopped to consider that how you slice up your time also reflects how you identify yourself?

Chapter 6. / Supermother: Running Out of Projects

1. Neugarten, B. L., V. Wood, R. J. Kraines, and B. Loomis. "Women's Attitudes Toward the Menopause." In *Middle Age & Aging: A Reader in Social Psychology,* edited by B. L. Neugarten. Chicago: University of Chicago Press, 1968.
2. McCranie, E. J. "Neurotic Problems in Middle Age." *The Family in Distress,* 1976, 2, 1–3.
3. Deutscher, I. "The Quality of Postparental Life: Definitions of the Situation." *Journal of Marriage and Family,* 1964, 26, 52–59.

7

SLICING THE PIE

SINCE THE WOMEN I INTERVIEWED WERE UNKNOWN TO ME, MY initial contact over the phone entailed our identifying ourselves to one another. At first the purpose of the phone call was simply to set a date to meet. After a half dozen or so calls, however, I was struck by an interesting pattern that was emerging. The women fell back on one or two ways of identifying themselves, and also on one or two ways of quelling their anxieties and doubts about being interviewed. It made me pause.

They very quickly identified themselves as mainly wife, or mainly mother. Take Alice Brown, who warned me when I first approached her: "My husband is so unpredictable, I may have to change our appointment at the eleventh hour."

It was eight o'clock the morning before we were to meet when my phone rang. "It never dawned on me," she explained, "but when I told my husband about the interview, he felt strongly about my *not* doing it." There was a strained silence before she continued. "I'm sorry. I hope I haven't gummed up your schedule. Maybe you can use me as a footnote."

Her husband, Charles Jameson Brown, is one of those successful men whose name is familiar only to those in the know. I felt awkward. After all, Alice had been an executive who, at forty, had married her boss to become a homemaker and mother.

Not ready to let the matter drop, I asked: "What were his objections?" "That I'd be too frank," she replied. "Finally he said, 'Oh, go ahead and do it.' I almost was going to make a big deal about it. I almost never do anything on my own. But it wasn't worth it. It would be different if I felt strongly about it."

Why do women tell? I wondered. Why do they consult their husbands on issues that concern no one but themselves? In a similar situation, would Charles Jameson Brown have consulted Alice? Are women really telling, or are they *asking*? Asking for what? Permission? Approval? A resolution of their own doubts? Or are they avoiding the responsibility for their own wants?

"I didn't tell Frederick," Betty Gilbert began. "He'd only say, 'What do you want to do *that* for?' " Betty and Frederick, you may remember, are a professional couple.

"I did tell a friend, though," she explained. "And I told her not to tell Frederick. She said, 'That's nice. I've always wanted to be interviewed.' I must admit *I* felt two ways about it. Did I tell my friend and not my husband because I wanted the 'Yes, girl, you can do it' side to win?

"Take next weekend," she continued. "There's a conference in Vermont. I'll ask Frederick if I should go, knowing me." Her lips fell in a faint pout.

"Go ahead," I said. "Ask him!"

"Now? What do you mean? How?"

"Give yourself permission. Then, switch and disapprove of yourself, like Frederick. Give yourself all the pros and cons out loud as if you were really split in two—one part your husband's voice, and the other part your voice."

She grinned self-consciously, closed her eyes, and set her face in a frown.

"Why do you want to go? It's such a drag. How will you get there? The meeting is at some out-of-the-way place."

Her eyes still closed, she turned to the other side and smiled.

"Go ahead. You really should. It will help you in your work to know what's going on."

Frowning: "Who needs it? Last time they were a bunch of stuffed shirts. You felt left out, especially at mealtimes, when you couldn't hide away."

Smiling: "You'll meet new people. Maybe you'll find a

friend who has the same interests as you. They have marvelous walks. And a pool."

Frowning: "A pool! You'll never get into last summer's
bathing suit with the flab you've accumulated. Your thighs
are getting dimpled. Imagine you poolside?"

Her eyes shot open. "Who needs Frederick's disapproval?
I'm split down the middle."

Betty had spoken from both sides of her mouth—literally
and figuratively—with the ease of a pro gliding on ice. Like
too many clotted communications, telling is rarely just
telling. Try Betty's monologue the next time you feel an
urge to check with your husband on some decision that's
ultimately yours.

Some women, I discovered, *informed* their husbands that
they were being interviewed and others told, or didn't tell,
using the couple identity to avoid their own conflicts. For
some, telling is sharing information. For others, it's a means
of unloading conflicts. That kind of telling is really asking
the other to enter our personal battleground of doubts.
The husband's "unpredictable" demands, I learned, were
an easy blind for a woman to hide from those painful confrontations with herself that would identify who *she* is.

It was much the same state of affairs with the children's
"unpredictable" demands. Bettina had ended our phone
conversation with: "I'll keep our date—unless, of course, my
son is sick and home from school."

At a small gathering of as many "illustrious" wives as
husbands (after an interpretation of Ibsen's place in the modern drama and, inevitably, his and Strindberg's stand on
women), a curious discussion followed. We began talking
about ourselves as parents—mothers and fathers, but mostly
mothers. Curious, because there we were, "advantaged" men
and women, "be-ers" and "do-ers," questioning.

"It's fine to talk about having your pie and eating it too,
but leaving the office drained some nights and being a mother
to two preschoolers isn't easy. And too many feminists make

it sound too easy." More than a fistful of noted and notorious authors owe their beginnings to the intense young woman who was speaking. A gourmet of the literary world, she has set in motion—discovered, nurtured, and marketed—the works of writers who otherwise might have remained un-feathered and unsung.

"No, it isn't easy," I said. "But then what is? Would chang-ing diapers, cooking, and cleaning be easy as a lifetime career?"

Despite my ready answer, her genuine concern unsettled me. Were women exchanging one set of myths for another? It would be Pollyanna-ish to deny the fact that the profes-sional who is a mother, unlike the professional who is a father, carries the greater burden of demand as the repository of that elusive something known as mothering. No doubt about it, mothers and fathers are faced with different expecta-tions—even from their children. Can we, as women, have our lives and have our children too? I began worrying the ques-tion like a dog worrying a bone. Perhaps changing diapers and doing dishes was easier—easier on that damnable con-science!

At the dinner table the next evening with our then-sixteen-year-old son, who was on his latest extravagance, not eating, I felt an "irrational" upsurge of anger. What was I so angry about? It wasn't about the steak, string beans, and baked potato ignored on his dish. Nor about the cherry pie, *his* favorite. It wasn't even that I'd interrupted a paper due the next day to make certain to get a hot meal on the table. I was angry at the wasted time and energy that would go into my ranting: "See here, if you lose one more ounce you'll look like the Pillar saints!" And if that didn't work: "Listen, your brain will shrivel to the size of a pea . . . if that hasn't hap-pened already!"

Our eyes locked; my ravings bounced off him like feathers. Ignored, I felt like that sliced pie: one portion a raving writer, one portion an understanding mother, one portion a no-nonsense psychotherapist, one portion. . . . I thought of

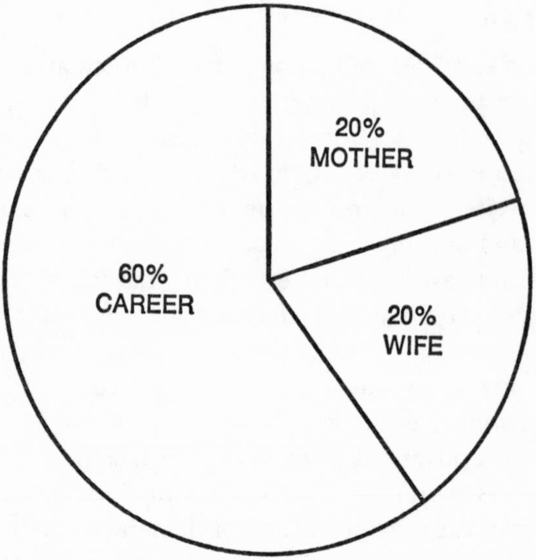

FIGURE 6 / Son's Current Perception of His Mother

the woman I'd interviewed who'd said: "There just isn't enough of me to go around."

"Lucian," I began, reaching for a pencil and pad and tracing a circle, "if this circle is a pie, and that pie is me, slice it up into portions according to how much of me you feel is a mother, a wife, and all the other things I'm into. And then label the pieces."

Observing the results, I got carried away and asked him to slice another pie, this time according to how it was when he was a little boy. Soon my husband and I were slicing up pies of our own.

Two of Lucian's pies have been faithfully reproduced as striking examples of the "facts" and "fictions" of one's life.

From the viewpoint of "facts," Figure 7 is inaccurate. The portion of my life in a structured career was far greater when our son was small than it is today. That was a time in my life when I was beginning a profession and was investing time and energy in learning my craft well, writing articles,

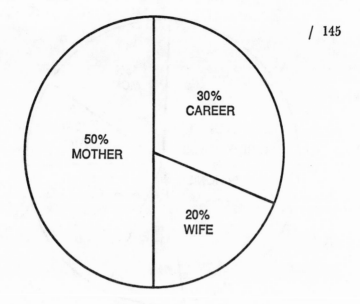

FIGURE 7 / Son's Perception of the Way It Was

co-authoring two textbooks, and building a private practice. Perhaps because I was actively aware of being away from home, when I was home, I was *really* home. What a child experiences is not clock-time togetherness, but the emotional availability of the parent.

Many "good mothers" put in twenty-four hours a day, quilting themselves in the reassurance that they are "good mothers" while emotionally unavailable to their children. One can be occupying the same room and be light years away emotionally.

Before we explore how some women have seen themselves, try slicing some pies of your own. Try, as one woman did, a Before pie of the first years of marriage, and a Now pie. Or, as another did, slice a How It Is pie, and a How You Would Like to Be pie. Or ask your youngsters to slice a pie according to how they see you. The results can be enlightening.

Bettina, who is the mother of a fourteen-year-old daughter

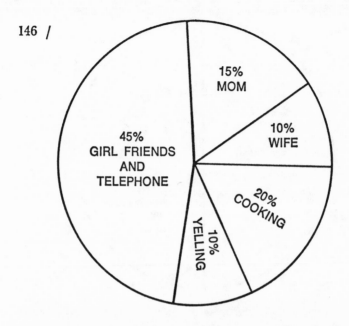

FIGURE 8 / Bettina's Son's Perception of His Mother

and an eleven-year-old son, said to me: "I can't imagine myself working. I don't approve of it. Even if I were widowed tomorrow, I can't picture myself picking myself up and going to work. At least not while my children are at home. It would be unfair to them. Once my children are grown and married, I might go back to work."

Dropping in on Bettina one afternoon, I asked her son to play "Slice a Mother Pie."

Despite Bettina's omnipresence in the home and her good intentions, her son seemed eager for an emotional energy that he experienced as being siphoned off elsewhere.

And then there were the pies of Roberta and her son, Tim. Roberta is forty-five, so she suggested doing a Before pie and a Now pie, since, she explained, the first ten years of her marriage were quite different. She has four children; the eldest is married, two are away at school, and Tim is at home.

With the passing years, Roberta's changing relationships to her husband, her children, and herself are graphically por-

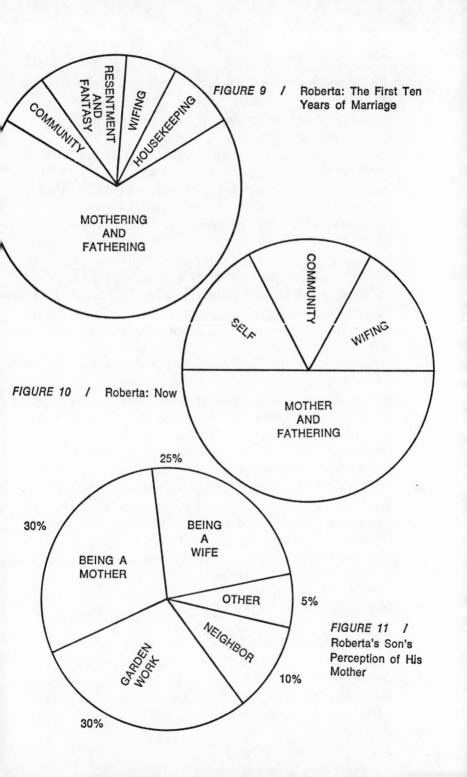

FIGURE 9 / Roberta: The First Ten Years of Marriage

FIGURE 10 / Roberta: Now

FIGURE 11 / Roberta's Son's Perception of His Mother

trayed. Since her husband is an international banker and travels much of the time, Roberta's role of mothering—encompassing fathering as well—is a large part of her life (Figure 9), even now (Figure 10). One can't help wonder, however, since only Tim remains at home, whether the still considerable space occupied by "mothering and fathering" doesn't reflect an emotional overinvestment, rather than a reality. With time, as those first "shocks" of coupling and parenting faded, and her resentments and fantasizing occupied less of her energies, there appeared a growing sense of self, a growing interest in the community, and a growing role in her husband's life (Figure 10). For all that, however, "mothering and fathering" remain a crucial identification—despite the fact that Tim's meticulous perception of his mother defines her as being as much a gardener as a mother (Figure 11)!

Certainly, mothers and pies unsettle the serious issue of just what is a "good" mother. Is "good" a quantitative or a qualitative measure? A rash of research studies by sociologists, psychologists, demographers, and so on support the fact that maternal absence, per se, doesn't foster a feeling of deprivation in the child. Indeed, some studies suggest that the working mother may even be spending more time in "positive interaction" with her child than the nonworking mother.[1] Working, in itself, doesn't bear a one-to-one correlation with either how "good" a mother, how "good" a wife, or how defined a person you are. Any good baker knows that a pie is a subtle blend of many ingredients, and to isolate any one and say, "That's it!" wouldn't even produce a decent pie.

Physical presence has been confused with emotional presence—a maternal energy, openness, and availability that transcends the common notions of clock time and body space.

The sliced pies had spun me off. Just as I earlier had collected women's Life Lines, I now started to accumulate Pies, and what I'd suspected became graphically visible. How we spend our time identifies us—it is the way that we make ourselves visible and known. The growing sense of self that

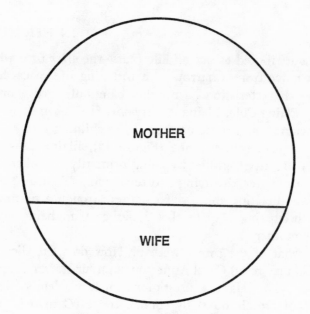

FIGURE 12 / Elaine: Early Years
of First Marriage

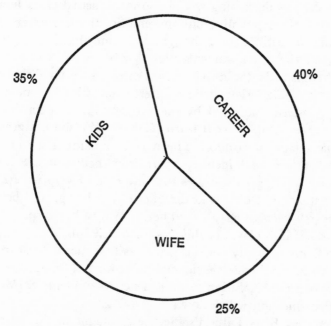

35%

40%

KIDS

CAREER

WIFE

25%

FIGURE 13 / Elaine: After
Remarriage. Now

Roberta attributed to her middle years—the *after* time when women move from a narrow to a widening life space—happily was characteristic of a number of middle-aged women.

Take Elaine Cole. Elaine is forty-one. She's been divorced, has remarried, and is the mother of five children.

With a feather-like stroke (Figure 12), Elaine described an early identity engulfed by being primarily a mother, and also a wife. Later, divorcing and remarrying (Figure 13), she added another line and a self emerges through a newfound career, occupying a space that is larger than being either wife or mother.

And what of the career woman? How does she slice her life? You may recall Carol Anderson, a physicist, who recently married Brian Salant, a prestigious nuclear scientist. Carol and Brian are childless, by choice. It was Carol who said after one miscarriage that she was "equivocal" about having children.

As Carol traced her Pie (Figure 14), she explained that what she was describing was not so much actual clock hours in her various pursuits, but the emotional commitment. A significant distinction, I thought, and one that held, I was sure, for the other women's Pies as well.

There is little doubt that Carol's career is a Shared Project and that being Brian's wife is intertwined with her identity as a physicist, indicated by the broken line between Wife and Career. But, as we'll learn (Chapter 12), she has grown in that relationship, and has been able to maintain an autonomy, mastery, and identity apart from being Mrs. Salant.

Carol strikingly illustrates that the core of who we are is in what we do. Doing is in the fiber of her being. And being a research scientist has allowed her to bring a broad spectrum of the self into play, not the least of which is being a wife, a friend, and a family person. But does that mean that career women define themselves through their work? More precisely, is a career the resolution to women's crises of identity? (More on that question will follow.)

Consider Betty Gilbert's Pie. Betty taught in the history

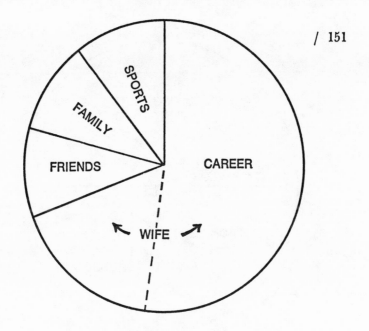

FIGURE 14 / Carol: Career-and-Wife

department of a city university. She and Frederick, both in their middle years, are childless. Betty was unable to carry a baby to term. Earlier in this chapter we listened to her inner monologue. Betty has sliced two Pies, one according to how she is (Figure 15) and the other according to how she'd like to be (Figure 16).

Although Betty, like Carol, is a professional woman, she clearly identifies herself with "mothering"—even though she's childless! That, she'd explained, is how she's known. And it is largely how she defines herself. The amount of space given to the self in contrast to that occupied by "taking care of . . ." is limited (Figure 15). In describing the person she'd like to be (Figure 16), although the professional aspect carries more weight, she still defines herself through a relationship to a man—be it in a fantasized relationship to a rescuer, or in a changing relationship to her husband.

At first, coupling and parenting serve the woman as a

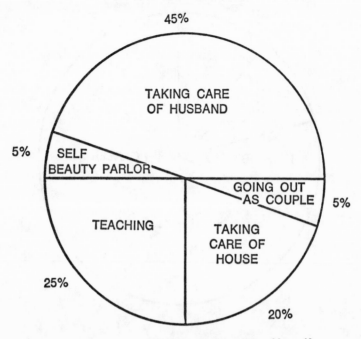

FIGURE 15 / Betty: How She Sees Herself

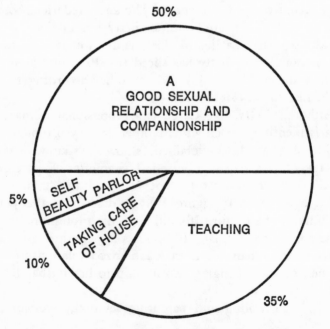

FIGURE 16 / Betty: How She Would Like to Be

career serves the man. It channels our energies, gives us a focus, and crystallizes our roles. In short, it sets our social and biological clocks in motion. But roles with gravitational pulls centered in others have a way of running out. Pauline Bart of the University of Illinois School of Medicine writes: "If one were to design a depressogenic role, a role with a strong potential for causing depression, one could not do better than the traditional female role." Mothering, especially, becomes the great burial ground of "planned obsolescence." [2]

A word about women and depression. A higher incidence of depression has been consistently reported for women as contrasted to men. Depression, according to some researchers, is an outgrowth of feelings of helplessness.[3] And what more fertile ground to develop a feeling of helplessness than the dependent role in which women are reared? If we stop to think, most women are totally dependent on someone else to provide their basic needs—such as food and shelter. We haven't been expected to develop the palpable relationship between actions and the consequences of our actions. We haven't cultivated the sense that we have a measure of control over our fate—a control based on feelings of mastery and autonomy. Too many of us live as if caught in the vortex of a whirlpool, helpless to control our direction or in a bottomless pit with no way out.

Despite our "planned obsolescence," however, it strikes me that women can and do grow by the "unplanned" obsolescence of roles that cause us to shed one skin after another until, slowly, we come to our own tender center.

A role may be the visible witness of aspects of a woman's femaleness, but it is not the sharp limit of who she is. The process of self-definition is an active, evolving response to critical events—by no means a rigid orderly progression—that leads us to changing.

Indeed, the cultural climate—what has been expected of us as women—has made its inroads. It has radically affected how we go about defining ourselves, and in so doing, it has radically changed our defining selves. I'm reminded of a trenchant passage in Joan Didion's *The Book of Common Prayer,* in which she describes the passport of her protagonist, Charlotte Douglas—the passport as a symbol of her passage and identity through the life journey. The document reads: Nationality—NORTEAMERICANA; Type of Visa—TURISTA; Occupation—MADRE.

Our roles are not *performed* as if so many actors were donning fictional characters that could be thrown off at the play's end. We do, and as we do, we are.

In the chapters that follow, we'll explore how some women have developed that sense of being and doing, of autonomy and mastery. And we'll look into some of the tools that have assisted them on that journey.

Chapter 7. / Slicing the Pie

1. Hoffman, L. W. and F. I. Nye. *Working Mothers.* San Francisco: The Jossey-Bass Behavioral Science Series, 1974.
2. Bart, P. "Depression in Middle-aged Women." In *Women in Sexist Society,* edited by V. Gornick and B. Moran. New York: The New American Library, 1971.
3. Bernard, J. "Homosociality and Female Depression." *Journal of Social Issues,* 1976, *32,* 213–238.

III

STRATEGIES

I learned to make my mind large, as the universe is large, so that there is room for paradoxes.

—MAXINE HONG KINGSTON,
The Woman Warrior

8

STARTING WITH EVE: LOSS OF INNOCENCE

IT ALL BEGAN WITH EVE, THAT MOTHER OF US ALL. EVERYTHING did, I suppose. With me it began at age five when I swallowed the story of the Garden of Eden whole, then in my teens rejected it, and now, thanks to Nancy Datan, a gifted developmental psychologist, I subscribe to it for quite other reasons.

How many of us even remember the story? According to Dr. Datan, very few. Oh, we may remember that there was a Garden of Eden and in that garden was a tree whose fruit gave knowledge of good and evil, and this tree was forbidden to Adam and Eve, and that along came a serpent who tempted Eve, and she took the fruit and shared it with Adam, and as a result they were cast out of the Garden, and Eve was punished with the pain of childbirth and Adam with laboring for his bread.

That's all I remembered until my memory was refreshed. The real reason for the expulsion was to prevent them from tasting of the fruit of a second tree, the Tree of Life. To that Dr. Datan adds, "I am prepared to conclude that if we were given a second chance in the Garden of Eden, we would make straight for the Tree of the Knowledge of Good and Evil once more—knowledge, however dangerous, is evidently a more powerful temptation than immortality." [1]

What does all that have to do with women and their development? Along with Datan and others, I believe Eve is indeed an elegant model of the pattern of adult development, particularly female adult development. In the story of the Garden of Eden we have, to be sure, the stereotyped division of labor: Adam was to know the pain of labor in the field,

Eve in birth. But birthing, I've come to discover, is not only laboring to bring forth the other but also oneself.

Eve is a marker in pointing the way for the developmental route from innocence to self-awareness, from dependency to self-reliance.[1] In the story we have, perhaps, the first recorded human paradox. We're told about the loss and pain of expulsion—leaving home, as it were, where all is provided—and at the same time about the achievement of self-knowledge and self-reliance in having to be sustained by the fruits of one's own labors. A major transition, indeed.

What, then, can we derive as the seminal characteristics of major transitions in women's lives? I'll have to begin with a few hundred words of theory. I don't mean to overwhelm with theory for the sake of theory. Rather, I hope that the theory will moor us in a knowledge and attitude that may frame our lives, lessen our innocence, and perhaps even loosen some of those barnacled expectations.

Major transitions are almost always accompanied by ambivalence. Understandably, we're torn between being provided for on the one hand and having to rely on our own resources on the other. Admittedly, too, major change also involves a loss—the destructuring necessary to any creative act. More precisely, in this instance it is a loss of innocence. In the women's words, they were "shocked" as one expectation after another was disrupted. These are firsts in their lives that women speak of as jolting and also propelling them into a chain of changing.

What are these firsts? Usually they're ushered in by some pivotal event. Menstruation? Graduation? Sexual intercourse? Marriage? Motherhood? Divorce? Illness? Death? Widowhood? Those could be critical events. Maybe. What makes an event critical is that it contains an element of the *unexpected*, contradicting what we've been led to believe. Like the fluctuating stock market, human nature has a way of discounting even catastrophes, if they're anticipated or familiar. In round-robin fashion, we've learned that an event is critical if it involves a loss of innocence and the achievement of some new knowledge—a gut knowing—knowing in a way that we've never known before. Thus, the anticipated death of a moribund parent may not be as critical an event in our life as the loss of a child that stops us short, confronting us with the fleeting nature of life.

Too often we feel trapped in irreconcilable contradictions, until we see our lives not as we've been taught to expect them to be, but as they actually unfold. The woman's life course is a series of alternating developments—contradictory pulls of enchantments and disenchantments, centers of darkness and flashes of illumination—one the underside of the other.

Too often we ask ourselves questions like: When should I start having intercourse? When should I marry? Have a baby? Go back to work? What's the right age? As women tell it, it's neither a matter of right age nor specific event. Instead, it is the disruption of deeply ingrained attitudes and expectations about sex, marriage, motherhood, and work that causes major upheavals and transitions. In short, unless we disrupt the old and the familiar and suffer the disenchantments, there's no room for the new.

Contemplating marriage to Paul, Stephanie, the protagonist in Francine du Plessix Gray's jolting *Lovers and Tyrants*, reflects: "But I already know that I do not like myself, that I need to be reborn, and that in order to go on living I must break myself apart in order to put myself together again and Paul will never let me break apart." And so she writes him: "But in wanting to give me so much aren't you cornering me, aren't you protecting me from those encounters with fate which women are so brutally deprived of?" Despite her protestations, Stephanie marries Paul soon after, and therein lies every woman's conflict.

Our attitudes and expectations, burrowed in our psyches, strung out over a lifetime, strongly influence whether and how we meet the challenge of adult development. How we perceive the distance between what our life is, and what we've been taught it ought to be, and how we cope with that contradition, clearly defines the shape of our transitions, of our changing and of our life course. Those women who've met the challenge of passage had to clear their way from a child-like innocence and dependence to an enthusiastic, youthful self-awareness and independence, and ultimately to a new responsibility for the new freedom and new knowledge. Those briefly are aspects of the dynamics of the major transitions in women's lives. The life course is a sometimes painful labor.

From all we've heard and learned, we may well ask why women haven't settled for the stability and security of coupling. Perhaps that's a little like asking why Eve didn't settle for the security of paradise?

Like it or not, the mere act of living doesn't allow for settling. Transitions are in the nature of living things, just as summer follows spring, and winter, autumn. Stability and upheaval, merging and distancing, illusions and disillusionments are the contrasts we embrace to encounter our own meanings.

Still, what triggers our changing? We may have heard enough from theorists of adult development, but I don't think we can afford to neglect the work of just one other: Klaus Riegel.[2, 3] As I listened to the women, hour after hour, each unique and special, it was the work of Riegel that returned to my thoughts, keeping me moored. Stressing a dialectical approach to human development, Riegel seemed to speak more to the center of women's concerns than the frequently quoted works of Erikson.[4]

According to Riegel, it is the contradictory, the paradoxical, the unpredictable that triggers the conflict that disrupts the status quo that jolts us into taking note of our lives. Adult development, he explains, takes place in the simultaneous movement along four dimensions: (1) inner-biological (2) individual-psychological (3) cultural-sociological (4) outer-physical. Whenever progression within or between those dimensions is out of step, a crisis ensues.[3]

Simply stated, those are the life events which, psychologically and emotionally, we hadn't anticipated or allowed for in our lives. We are "shocked"—as, for example, when we're confronted with a life-threatening illness (inner-biological). It was Kate who observed: "There was such a contradiction between my feeling fine and alive one day, and being told I had cancer the next, with maybe only months to live."

We're shocked as well when we confront the contradiction of merger and the distancing necessary for development (individual-psychological). There is a fundamental disharmony when the personal development of the wife is traditionally subordinate to the personal development of her husband. For women, the almost total absorption in coupling, unfortunately, has emphasized the reconciliation of gender differences, rather than the recognition and enhancement of those differences.

There are also those shocks of discovering that we're out of step with our social environs (cultural-sociological). Maggie, whom we're about to meet, explained that her husband had joined a back-to-the-earth movement. She said: "We found this farm and moved. All our new neighbors were baking bread and making sausages. They were held up as models for me by my husband. But I enjoyed books and had just discovered photography. I wasn't for pulling the plow and stomping on grapes. I was looked on as the oddball."

Happily, we're less likely to be subject to those harsh jolts or life catastrophes that Riegel refers to as the outer-physical —war, famines, floods, and pestilence. Dialogues within ourselves and between us and our world that contradict, that dislocate who we've been, or who we're supposed to be, de-structure the familiar order of our lives—a first step in re-structuring a new synthesis.[5,6,7] We cling to "bedrocks" of security only to discover that it is shocks to our stability that dislodge us from a faded past and move us toward a fresh present and future.

In replaying the women's taped interviews, I was struck by the use of certain images that came up with an uncommon

regularity. Like: "His love was the *bedrock* of my identity."
Or, "Suddenly I was *shocked* out of myself." Or, "I became
aware of a growing *chasm* between us." Unwittingly, their
images reflected the female experience of change. With a
dramatic unanimity they described the shocks of change that
registered the fissures in their coupling, much like the Richter
scale registers the seismic changes in the earth's crust. It was
clear that fundamental change in women followed the loosening in their significant relationships. Those are the dishar-
monies that trigger the journey for a separate identity.

To flesh out the theory, consider Evelyn. (Remember her
Life Line—only the positives are important!) Divorced, single,
and dreading those first signs of aging, she confided: "I'm
terrified of growing old, of losing my sex appeal, and I'm
embarrassed to admit it. I'm suddenly unsure about *everything*. I won't know who I am. What am I supposed to do?
Do I relax, let go, and let my ex-husband support me? Do
I let my lover take care of me? He wants to. Do I take my
work seriously, ask for that raise and support myself?"

Not really expecting any answers, she paused for a breath,
and then abruptly continued: "Listen to me. Just listen.
My mother put in her weekly call from St. Petersburg last
night. She didn't say, 'Hello dear, how are you? How's work?'
She said, 'Has your skin cleared yet? Are you still seeing the
skin doctor? Are you seeing Steve? Are you dating anyone
else?' Any wonder I'm terrified of growing old? And of everything? I'm in the same spot she is. We're both coming from
the same place. The same place I've always been. I'm asking
myself the same questions she asks me. The questions she's
asked me since I was a teenager."

It was clear that those values she'd swallowed as an adolescent had settled in a lump, causing her mental indigestion.
Despite all the living she'd done—a divorce, rearing a daughter on her own, and a subsequent love affair—she'd failed to
shape her own values or to derive her own meanings. As yet.

If we listen to her questions, however, we'll detect the
first signals of change: conflict and ambivalence. "Do I let

my lover take care of me? Or do I support myself?" That, in brief, is the nature of transitions. They are times when the old is outworn and the new is still not within our grasp. We find ourselves with one foot in the past, and the other uncertain where to set down. As our stability is disrupted, we feel off balance. However, even though the transitions in our lives, aging for one, aren't within our control, the *meanings* we give them are. The fundamental difference between women who eventually stretch their boundaries and those who wither on the vine is a dialectical attitude to impending change that propels them to meet the challenge. Woman's development is better grasped by embracing the contradictions—the top and the underside of her meanings and priorities—than by trying to explain them away. Too much of our energy is spent figuring out *why* we are the way we are, rather than *how* we can meet the challenge of transitions.

Too many women are trapped by polarities, splitting themselves into either/ors, narrowing all they might become. Thus, they look upon themselves as either masculine or feminine, aggressive or passive, sexual or intellectual, a homemaker or a career woman. Let's look, then, to the strategies for coping and for changing.

Chapter 8.   /   Starting with Eve: Loss of Innocence

1. Datan, N. "Forbidden Fruits and Sorrow: Aspects of Adult Development Dynamics." Paper presented at the American Psychological Association. Chicago, 1975.
2. Riegel, K. "Adult Life Crises: A Dialectical Interpretation of Development." *Life-Span Developmental Psychology*. Ed. N. Datan and L. Ginsberg. New York: Academic Press, 1975.
3. Riegel, K. "The Dialectics of Human Development." *American Psychologist*, 1976, *31*, 689–700.

4. Erikson, E. H. *Childhood and Society.* New York: Norton, 1950.
5. Gordon, W. *Synectics: The Development of Creative Capacity.* New York: Collier Books, 1961.
6. McLuhan, M. and H. Parker. *Through the Vanishing Point: Space in Poetry and Painting.* New York: Harper & Row, 1968.
7. Carpenter, E. *They Became What They Beheld.* New York: Outerbridge & Dienstfrey/Ballantine, 1970.

9

THE QUEST FOR
THE POSTPONED SELF

ACCORDING TO ONE OF THOSE SEEMINGLY OBSCURE STUDIES, adults consistently overestimate the size of their heads and underestimate the reach of their arms.[1] I don't know whether that finding shows a gender difference, but I do know that the psychological analogy in terms of women's self-evaluation and self-image is striking. Too much of what happens to women happens in the head and too little in the doing.

In this chapter we'll explore the woman's journey for a separate identity, not in theory or in philosophy, but in practice and in strategy. We'll listen to what happens to women and their relationships as they strive to define that postponed self. In the closing chapters that follow we'll also examine how, with a heightened awareness of self, women come to know what they want. We'll learn that for most women the struggle is not so much getting what they want as it is knowing what they want.

How do women achieve a personal identity? How do we begin to sort ourselves out? How do we create a fresh future? An immediate future? With a few deft strokes, as only a perceptive writer can, Doris Lessing gives the experience of most women over the stretch of years. In the short story "To Room Nineteen," she writes: "What it amounted to was that Susan saw herself as she had been at twenty-eight, unmarried; and then again somewhere about fifty, blossoming from the root of what she had been twenty years before. As if the essential Susan were in abeyance, as if she were in cold storage. . . . What then, was this essential Susan? She did not know." [2]

Women, unhappily, have not been reared to know. And, by and large, women do not know. Lessing's protagonist identifies the lacunae, the gaping void, which women describe between the time of their singleness—unmarried and yearning for coupling—and the time when that couple identity has leaked away.

As we shall learn, the "essential" self—a personal identity —is neither a psychological abstraction nor a weighty philosophical inquiry. One woman, a homemaker for many years, describing a newfound talent, summed it all up with as succinct a description of a separate self in action as any: "Painting was the only thing I did," she explained, "that was *only* mine."

How many of us, if we took the time to think about our lives, could find a single thing that is singly ours? Those of us who are middle-aged, reared with expectations and postures that are no longer functional, have been especially whiplashed in this matter of a separate identity. A vocational counselor of women, Patricia Thom, observes: "Identity has not been such a pressing problem for women when they were not part of the larger world outside of home and family, but a woman today needs to know who she is, what her skills are, what she wants, and what she thinks is important." [3]

Can you flesh out that bill of particulars? If I were to ask: "Who are you" would you mechanically reply, as so many women do, "I'm a wife and mother"? What would you reply if I were to ask: "Who are you apart from being a wife? Apart from being a mother, who are you? Who are you apart from being a reflection or an absence of those central relationships?" Some women, for example, persist forever and unalterably in being the widow of, or the ex-wife of. . . . Can you define your special skills with the sharpness of a pen sketch? Can you make a list of your priorities? Do you know what you want—not in vague, misty terms, but in concrete specifics?

If you're like most women, you'll be hard put to answer those questions. But there seems to come a time in the lives of women when they begin to wonder about all that. Just about the time that men look ahead toward that "after I retire," women experience the uneasy squeeze that, for them, After is Now. And now it is their turn to come out of retirement.

If women in their middle years have asked: What's it been all about? they've also exclaimed: Whatever happened to——? She used to be So-and-So's wife. Those women who've lacked a personal focus and direction, who didn't know what they wanted for themselves, suddenly seem to find their own voice. Not because they've abruptly hit forty, but because they encounter a number of coalescing jolts—social, biological, and psychological—that press them outward, away from centering on their relationship to a man, away from nurturing and cultivating the other.

To begin. We're suddenly and subtly facing the first signs of aging, whether it is that we've come to the end of our child-bearing or of our child rearing, or that we're beginning to fight that middle-age spread, or those crow's-feet around our eyes, muting our wide-eyed wondrous look. Subtly and suddenly we know that we can no longer lean on our good looks, or our good nature, or our sex appeal, or our popularity, or even our helplessness to get us what we believe we're supposed to have. Moreover, most of our relationships—those we should have—are changing. In Erikson's words, there is a feeling of stagnation.[4] If we've chosen the traditional path of marriage and a family, we awake one morning, bored or depressed, to find that we've worked ourselves out of a job. But, happily, we've also worked ourselves out of those faded images that have been the fulcrum of our identity.

Certainly the break with those central roles, which have occupied and bolstered us, or even the rehearsal in our minds of such breaks, propels us to think singly. The wellspring of our identity in our twenties and thirties is drying up. The priority that we've given marriage and/or the rearing of children has led to the submergence of whole aspects of the Self—the me that's been tucked away—which in mid-life, with an urgent consciousness of time-left-to-live, pushes for airing.

In speaking of men's mid-life crises, Levinson describes the resurgence of the abandoned dream,[5] a concept that also is relevant for women. One of the startling ways women have expressed the thrust for a separate identity has been in the abrupt blossoming of a hidden talent or a skill, something of which they'd seemed hardly aware, a mysterious manifestation. Only there really isn't any mystery about it as we begin to probe those mildewed dreams.

The burgeoning of an abandoned dream is noteworthy since it often follows on the heels of the death of another dream. Mid-life is a time when the woman's expectation of fulfillment and achievement through another is rudely interrupted. As one woman tearfully explained: "I hoped my daughter would go into law. She was a straight-A student at Smith. And all she talks about is getting married." And still another: "My husband and I had such hopes for our son. Well, he came home this summer and announced that he wasn't going back to college next fall." In short, we haven't made that much difference. The life cycle follows its own paradoxical path.

The resurgence of the dream, for women, is not only expressed in a work choice. It often involves a sexual reawakening as well. That, as we'll see, is particularly so for those who've married young and whose sexual self has been defined exclusively through their marriage.

Because so many women use the marital relationship to hide in, whole aspects of the self, intellectual and sexual, as well as whole efforts toward the development of a personal autonomy go underground. The resurgence of the one, however, is intimately related to the achievement of the other. As women become increasingly aware of wants apart from their marital and family relationships, they're also confronted with the unfinished business of their youth—their considerable dependency.

We've been wide-eyed long enough; I've no intention to mislead. There is no magic transformation and no easy resolution. As a matter of fact, the attitude with which we launch our newfound talents is frequently more crucial than the particular goal or its achievement. If work, for example, or even a new sexual awakening, is used to "get us out of ourselves," a kind of occupational therapy, or to enhance us in our husbands' eyes, it's unlikely that much will accrue to our self-esteem, self-image, or self-definition.

Growing up isn't easy; it's necessary. Or so the actuarial tables tell us. Did you know that currently one fifth of all women between fifty-five and sixty-four are widowed? And that one out of every six women over twenty-one has been a widow? [6] Social scientist Helena Lopata, tracing the life plan of the average middle-class woman, put it even more tersely: marriage at twenty, followed by the first child at twenty-two, and motherhood stretching until the last child leaves home. Then, at age forty-six, the woman can look forward to fifteen years of marriage with her husband, followed by fifteen years of widowhood. [7]

Still, easy or not, with changing attitudes and values women have launched on some remarkable journeys. Despite the concentration of research on men and their mid-life, mid-career crises, on closer observation we'll find that women face perhaps an even larger percentage of those mid-life, mid-career crises as they abruptly awaken to the fact that their job as homemaker is running out. And women seem to be awakening to that fact earlier and earlier. The life-span profile of women is changing, even though the social and emotional expectations are lagging behind. In terms of actual fact, the mothering role is shrinking.

Families have been steadily decreasing in size. In 1974 43 percent of the married women expected to have no more than two children. Women also are living longer. The life expectancy of women in 1974 was seventy-six years of age, as contrasted with the life expectancy in 1920, when it was under fifty-five. Those factors, coupled with the unprecedented high percentage of women in the labor force cause Lois Wladis Hoffman, who has reported extensively on her studies of the lives of working mothers, to comment: "Over the life span, many women already are spending more of their lives in employment than in mothering. . . . Technological advances have streamlined housekeeping and cooking to the point that the housewife role is not a full-time job and does not seem an essential or adequate contribution as a sole commitment. . . . Several studies have indicated that the full-time housewife whose children are all in school is generally low in self-esteem and high in psychological symtoms." [8]

Traditionally, the acceptable role for a woman has been homemaking. The woman who defined herself in broader terms, more often than not, was put on the defensive. (Currently, the situation is becoming somewhat reversed.) Traditionally, the life course of the woman and the life course of the family have been one and the same. Thus, we thought of only two kinds of women: those who had families and those who had careers.[9]

The inclination to continue to think in terms of polarities has had its unfortunate spin-off. If women have careers, does that mean that men must be the homemakers? Or, if women are aggressive and ambitious, does that mean that they can't be warm and loving mates and mothers? Are self-definition, self-expression, and autonomy antithetical to marriage and childbearing? I hardly think so. The fact is that such polarities don't exist in reality. Women have always been ambitious and aggressive. But when their ambitions have been siphoned off through their mates and their children, it's been considered acceptable and even admirable.

It behooves us to look at our lives with a fresh eye. Let's consider the challenge of that postponed self. Let's examine how some women have faced the mounting urgency to sift out their own identity, renewing "the quality of their lives." [10] As we've seen again and again, women are motivated to new beginnings with the heightened consciousness of endings, knowing in a way they hadn't known before that life is indeed fleeting.

ANATOMY OF CHANGING

For the first twenty-two years of her marriage, Maggie Fuller had been a devoted wife and a nurturing mother of two daughters and a son. At the age of forty-two, her life took still another turn. That was a complete turnaround. When we met, Maggie had celebrated her seventieth birthday.

Maggie Fuller, Photographer. "Yoo-hoo, who's there?"
"Yoo-hoo, Maggie, it's me, Iris."
The watermelon-green door swung open and I was greeted by a striking woman. She wore large red hoop earrings and a flowing red gown of batik. Her hair, like silvery spun silk, was coiled round and round in a smart twist on the back of her head. I looked past Maggie into the stretched-out studio that was now her home. I'd entered a Cocteau fantasy, even though Maggie herself seemed firmly planted on this earth. Every inch of wall space was covered with her work —blow-ups of photographs. These were photographs of discarded objects, like old pots, broken broom handles, broken dolls, all somehow stripped of personal investment and reassembled in a composition that gave them a new life and a new meaning. It seemed to me that her photography was a sharp metaphor for the little that I'd already been told about her life.

At the age of forty-two, Maggie first discovered her talent for photography. At the age of sixty, she listened to her husband announce: "I don't love you the way a man should love a woman anymore. I want a few years' happiness . . ." Numbed, Maggie packed a suitcase and asked him to drive her to the station; she left the small community that had

sheltered her for forty years and headed for a large Mid-
western city.

The Final Scene of a Marriage. "Was it another woman
that precipitated the break?" I'd asked Maggie.

"It really started when I was forty-two. It was then that
his jealousy and possessiveness of me began to evaporate.
And so did his sexual and emotional interest in me. Before
that, our sex life was good. After that, I became a recep-
tacle. But it wasn't until he was in his late fifties that he
had an affair with a woman his daughter's age. I had no
idea that he was seeing this woman. That went on for three
years.

"One afternoon my oldest daughter came to visit, and she
said, 'You know, I think Daddy's seeing Rose.' 'Oh, what
makes you think so?' I asked. She gave me a few hints. I
called my husband at the office and said, 'Annie just told
me that you've been seeing Rose for some time; I think
you'd better come home.'

"My daughter and I were in the living room. He told me,
'I don't love you the way a man should love a woman anymore. I want a few years' happiness with Rose. It was you
who said you wanted part of your life for yourself. Remember? You can now get a divorce on the charge . . .' I turned
to stone. My daughter, my thirty-nine-year-old daughter,
went into hysterics. She's crying hysterically and saying to
her father, 'I've adored you all my life.' And I'm just sitting
there, stone. She's crying, 'Your feet have turned to clay.'
That cliché thing. I went upstairs and packed a suitcase and
said to my husband, 'Take me to the train. I'm going to
Chicago.' "

Maggie agreed to speak with me largely because she'd
liked an article I'd written on creativity. She said she'd
hoped that I might be the vehicle to other women, although
she knew that illusions die hard. She placed her hope for a
different future between women and men on the young.
She'd been dismayed by the older women who, when they

heard of her separation, showed no grasp of the woman's situation. Instead, all they suggested was that she make herself over. "I got so many letters," she explained, "saying, 'cut your hair, bleach it blond, and re-do yourself.'" As she talked, she rolled her eyes and shook her head.

The assumption was, of course, that only in winning back her husband or in finding another man could Maggie regain her self-esteem. "It escapes me," Maggie said, "that women didn't seem to understand that we are really alone. Prisoners in our own skin."

She motioned me to a large overstuffed chair as she settled in her favorite spot, a couch by day, a bed by night. "I walked out of two completely furnished houses," she said. "My career at the age of forty-two made me an oddball in the small Virginia community where I lived. But I cared for the home and would have sat there until rigor mortis set in. You see, I thought I was secure in my old life with the two homes, and the oriental rugs and the books from floor to ceiling. And I posed very becomingly in front of those bookcases for the local newspaper, as the wife of Ralph Fuller. I think I've finally learned that I don't have to prove my worth anymore."

Material things held a special significance for Maggie. She'd been raised by an impoverished widowed mother who'd worked hard to keep the family together. With only an elementary-school diploma, Maggie dropped out of school in tenth grade. Possessing no skills, but with an intelligence and an enthusiasm for learning, she went to work in an office at the age of fifteen. "I didn't have enough education to do the office work." She laughed, a trifle sadly. "But I faked it, until I made up my own shorthand and crazy typing."

Ralph and Maggie met when they were still in their teens. He was a lifeguard at the local swimming pool during the day and attended college, majoring in business administration, at night. By reputation, he was aloof and different from the other boys.

Maggie set out to engage him. She also set out to make

herself engaging. As a young girl she'd felt ugly and awkward. She told herself that since she was so ugly, she would have to cultivate other talents to get beaux. To her own surprise, she became Queen of the Moonglow Ballroom, an outstanding swimmer, and "great at bullshitting the boyfriends."

For Better or for Worse. They married with Maggie's money, since Ralph was still going to school. She became pregnant almost immediately, continued to work except for a short period, and "paid for the baby." They also made a small down payment on a house. When her husband finished his studies, he was fearful of giving up his job, with its lean but steady paycheck, in order to launch his career.

"I was the driving force behind him," Maggie explained. "And that bastard could never acknowledge it. With my encouragement and financial support, he finally struck out on his own.

"I should have known better. I was getting signals all along, even before we got married, but I ignored them, or told myself they were signs of great love. I didn't see his tremendous possessiveness and insecurity. Before we were married, my swimming coach wanted me to try out for the team. Ralph objected. 'I will not walk behind you carrying a towel,' he said, 'and having everybody call me Mr. Margaret Hoffman.' So I didn't try out."

After the first child was born, Maggie returned to work. "All through the years, though," she recalled, "he was terribly jealous of my relationships on the job. Finally he said he wanted me to stay home and have more children. He was terribly disappointed when the first baby was a girl. He'd wanted a son to carry on his name, be an athlete and a business magnate."

Motherhood was smothered in dreams. "I wanted children," Maggie told me. "I used to scream 'I want a baby, I want a baby.' I don't know why, Iris. I used to talk about the joys of being a complete woman, and of giving birth.

I don't know whether it was the *Saturday Evening Post* covers or what. . . . How do you know reality from illusion while you're living through it? As I look back, I can see that most of it was an illusion."

Maggie seemed to have attained her goals and then some. In her early forties, she lived in a well-to-do suburb—"the kind of restricted neighborhood that had no Jews, no niggers, and only one pet." It was a far cry from the squalid alley of her childhood. Her daughters had graduated from college and were already married; her son was about to leave for college. Her marriage was set in its patterns—Ralph made the decisions, and she, willy-nilly, carried them out. His possessiveness was still the barometer of great love.

Like a good many women of her generation, hers had been a heliocentric existence. After years of orbiting around her husband and family, she found herself without the pulls that both had anchored her and, sadly, had distanced her from herself. As the nest emptied and the family routines slipped away, Maggie began to ponder her life. She seemed to be floating in a world devoid of the familiar meanings. But perhaps, she thought, now was *her* time.

Her husband and children had been out in the world, acquiring that education she'd yearned for, accomplishing things, fulfilling their dreams. And she had had to fight for everything. Maggie explained: "Any change in the family that was my idea was immediately put down. I fought. But that was held against me by the whole family. At the end, my daughters called me Hitler, and my son said I had to be the star of the family, and women with egos like mine had to live alone in one room, because nobody can stand them."

Her eyes glistened as she threw back her handsome head. "And Iris, I'm sure that if I had sat in a corner of my living room, raising African violets and picking my nose, the family would have said: 'What are we going to do about that old woman? There she sits. Why isn't she doing something?' Another of my illusions. You know what I thought? I thought, here my family all have degrees, and they would be proud of me if I had something of my own. My one daughter had a B.S., my other daughter had a B.A., my son was going into graduate studies, my husband had an advanced degree in business administration. And I just had an eighth-grade diploma. I thought, I'm the only dum-dum in the middle of so much brains, so I'll get myself a little education. And they'll be proud of me. And oh . . .'" Maggie's voice broke, but she forced a gravelly laugh, punctuating the irony.

"I've Earned the Right to Part of My Life!" Maggie was forty-two, Ralph a year older when they ran out of their last project: raising a family. The glue that had kept them together dried out.

"My husband and I were left facing each other with 'What's new?' Nothing. And he began to get restless about the restricted neighborhood. It discriminated against animals! He wanted a country estate with lots of animals. And he started going around with a copy of *Two Acres and Independence* tucked under his arm.

"Every Sunday we would go to look at the most god-awful, broken-down tenant farms, farms where the house was down in the valley, and all you could see was sky. I felt sick every Sunday. Finally he took me to see this house, sitting on a hillside, surrounded by ten acres. It was truly beautiful country. So we moved. My husband went back to the earth and he expected me to follow. With my husband there was no asking, ever. There was just telling. And I wasn't interested in pulling the plow and stomping the grapes. I liked books and I had just discovered photography.

"There were other women in the community who were making sausages and milking cows, and my husband held them up as models. But I refused. And that's where the trouble began. I said to him, 'I think I've earned the right to part of my life for myself.' Well, that's what he threw back at me when he made his farewell speech. He saved it all that time. Eighteen years."

From the Roots of the Youthful Self. We can't help wondering, how does a talent spring forth? After years of focusing on her family's needs, how did Maggie find her own focus? And her professionalism?

As we unraveled the threads of Maggie's life, it all seemed to follow so simply. All her life a doer and a hard worker, Maggie discovered her dream and went after it with the same enthusiasm, commitment, and unswerving sense of direction that she'd shown earlier in caring for her family. Dilettantism, we'll discover, is a life attitude. And creativity is merely a way of being in the world.

We discover our strengths, our skills, and our talents in the everyday being and doing. Maggie explained: "All my life I did *partially* creative things—sewing, knitting, crocheting. I made every stitch of clothes. My daughters were voted the best-dressed girls in school. I won dressmaking prizes. But it was only *partially* satisfying. And I felt guilty that I didn't feel fulfilled, even though I had what was supposed to make every woman complete: family, husband, and a beautiful home. I didn't understand it.

"So why didn't I stay in the kitchen and grit my teeth? I didn't know about photography or art. When I started, I knew absolutely nothing. I started because my husband had been into photography and there were some odds and ends of paints I used to color his photographs. So at first I started to paint from odds and ends—abstract designs. Then, since we had so many cameras around, I began photographing ordinary things and making them into compositions."

And being Maggie, she was determined to learn it all. She went to every show she could and decided to take a correspondence course in photography. For the first time in her life she came in contact with kindred spirits. "Little by little, I became part of the art world, met photographers, and talked about things that meant something to me.

"I remember my very first composition. It was awful, amateurish, but I looked at it. 'My God, it's permanent!' It isn't washing dishes three times a day, it isn't changing beds every morning, it isn't spitting and polishing the same thing over and over. It's only done *once*. Here it is! Finished! A composition! How it contrasted to my day-in-and-day-out life. I was drunk with power.

"I realize now that I had to come to something of my own to fill that inner emptiness. I had not been a whole person." But there are no simple paths to glory. Nor, for that matter, is there any one path. Although those were exciting, fulfilling days of learning a new craft for Maggie, they also were days of ambivalence, conflict, and guilts.

"Do you want to hear the biggest laugh?" she asked, rolling forward. "I couldn't imagine my husband breaking up our home, because I thought I was indispensable. Can you imagine anybody really and truly thinking they were indispensable?

"What I'd been doing at home was bending over backwards with cooking and housekeeping. I was very organized and efficient. So in the old life, to allay my guilt about doing something myself, I had to compensate for the time spent on photography. First thing in the morning before I went into the studio, I'd clean, make the beds, and plan dinner. I'd come back in the afternoon in time to make the Manhattan—my husband used to drink Manhattans with a cherry in it—and dinner. Then my conscience was clear. I'd lecture all over the place, telling women how easy it was to handle a career and a home—if you're organized.

"The trouble began when my work, which had been amateurish, suddenly became more than a hobby, was regarded seriously, and got recognition. It threw them. My husband and my kids felt that they were appendages of *me* —instead of the other way around like it had been. My husband would come home in a fury and take it out on me."

The struggle, moreover, was not only with her marriage and her career, but also with her own self-doubts and anxieties as she attempted to fulfill her dream. Maggie worked hard for three years. Finally, when she felt she was ready, she wrote to a noted photographer whom she'd admired and asked him to evaluate the body of her work. At his prompting, she submitted her photographs to a museum jury. They were accepted! The following year she won a prize. Maggie recalled: "That was the beginning. People started asking, 'Who is Maggie Fuller? Who is she?' "

"Who is she now?" I asked.

"I still don't know," Maggie replied. "Now I can say what I am, an artist, without faltering and suffering guilt. But I'm still working on the *who*. That's a forever thing. I'll go to the incinerator with that one.

"The attacks of anxiety, really!" Maggie continued. "I suffered every time there'd be a letter from a jury. Was I accepted? The intense fear in opening that envelope. Well, I *accomplished* all that. I've been exhibited as far as Texas. When I left home, I came here and started on the same treadmill. I ran around looking for galleries to represent me, looking for exhibits. My work has been shown in Chicago, but, Iris, I'm tired. In the past few years, I've grown desireless of art-world recognition. And I don't know if I can continue to live fairly contentedly without continuing to accumulate accomplishments." Such are the labors, conflicts, and contradictions of achieving, propelling Maggie deeper and deeper into honing herself.

A Woman of the Seventies. When she boarded the train for Chicago that fateful afternoon, Maggie had intended to visit her son, who was getting a divorce. She explained: "I thought, well, maybe he'll let me come and sit in a corner of his kitchen. It was the Lord's blessing he didn't." Her son checked her into a residential hotel known for its arty but indigent clientele.

At the age of sixty, Maggie was to spend the night alone, harbored in strange surroundings for the first time in her life. Cocooned in marriage for forty years, she now felt stripped. Everything seemed to have slipped away. She felt terror—such terror that she couldn't even remember how to let the water drain out of the tub. She began clawing at the porcelain. Each step out of her room proved another obstacle. She didn't know how to run the automatic elevator; how to tip; how to handle money.

The real turning point for women, it seems to me, can only come with a loss of an essential innocence. Maggie tells us that with her separation, the unthinkable happened. She knew in a way she couldn't have known before that she wasn't indispensable and that she was really on her own. There is no forever and ever. Those critical "first times" have been referred to as "shocks of recognition," ushering, as they do, genuine turning points in our lives. They're neither predictable, nor do they follow an orderly sequence of events. Rather, they seem to be a sudden, abrupt kind of knowledge, a knowledge that life will never be quite the same.[11]

Maggie faced that crisis as she'd faced the many other critical transitions in her life—with intelligence and determination.

What to *do*? "Kid," she told herself, "you're on your own now. Take it one step at a time." She took her own good advice. It grew dark. She lay on the bed, floating on its surface. The room closed in on her like the lid of a coffin. She thought of other sleepless nights nursing children's colds, finishing party dresses, or waiting for Annie's key to turn in the lock. Waves of rage and guilt washed over her. She felt betrayed and abandoned, while at the same time she blamed herself for wanting more from life.

What to do? She mapped out a strategy for getting herself out of the hotel room and into the streets of what seemed a forbidding and friendless city. Never had the winter seemed more bitter or more gray. Her old life had blown away like the wind-tossed newspapers.

"First, I got to know my street," Maggie said. "I would stop at the smaller shops, stay away from the supermarkets, and patronize the same shop every day. That way I got to know the shopkeeper. I also learned how to manage money. It turned out to have been the best approach I could have made."

Soon Maggie became absorbed in the playful coming and going from her hotel room to the local five-and-dime. She began to move in rhythm with the cars, trucks, and bustling crowds. And Woolworth's was turned into a playground of invention. She discovered the automatic picture booth buried in its basement, and photographer that she was, she began taking miles of snapshots. "I'd make faces at myself," she recalled. Those excursions ignited her inventiveness. With scissors and paste, she transformed the self-portraits into whimsical composites that spilled over into her work. One, the body of a nude with a lute hiding her crotch, was topped with Maggie's black-wigged head.

Now that there were no more circles on the calendar, marking Bill's visit, or Beth's new dress, or Ralph's dinner party, encircling and structuring her life, she began to find her own routines for survival. Her urgent attempts to adapt to her new life, however, weren't meant to deny or mask her situation. Her need to know herself continued to nag at her. At her son's suggestion, she launched on another journey, an inner quest. At the age of sixty, she began a brief period of psychotherapy.

"If you had to do it over, Maggie, would you?"

Her eyes turned a hot blue. "The whole trip? No matter how Pitiful Pearl I sound, I don't go into attacks of regret. What's done is done. But I wouldn't want the *whole* trip. There is one thing I wish had been different. I wish I had been prepared to be alone. Women should be prepared to be alone, because we are.

"I feel that every creative person pays a heavy price in her relationships. Of course, if I'd been married to a man who had security in his career and in his masculinity, then it would have been different.

"The woman that my husband is living with is a duplicate of me as a young wife. But I also know that if I had remained as I was, invisible, he would have left me for being a dull old woman."

"What are you looking forward to?"

"In my old life I used to say, 'I'm marking time until death comes along.' I'm looking forward to accepting myself completely, without having to defend or *prove* anything. I've still got conflicts. And I'm working on them."

AFTERTHOUGHTS

For the first forty-two years of her life Maggie believed that all she needed to be fulfilled was "getting a good guy, getting married, and having children." What defines Maggie is not the usual dream of rescue, not the disillusionment of that dream, but how and what she did as her dream of the complete life closed in on her like a dense fog.

Her life has been awesome for its dramatic changes. If she confronts us with nothing else, it is that talents and skills that go unaired have a way of festering the spirit. And by the same token, airing them also labors the spirit, requiring us to relinquish those youthful dependencies.

She illustrates a fairly common female circumstance. A woman invents her life around a man because it is expected and because it also suits her, only to discover that "insufficiency of spirit." We learn that we must become more than what we've been, not because it is The Answer, or Nirvana, but because we really have no choice. There is no Happily Ever After. We grow, before and after, in paradox and in contradiction. But as we grow—if nothing else—whatever we may lose, we gain ourselves: a marvelous hedge against living alone. And a must in choosing someone with whom to live.

It would be imprecise, therefore, to say that in marriage Maggie lost her identity—a misguided notion, conjuring images of some precious bauble lost down the kitchen drain. More accurately, Maggie submerged and postponed those possibilities of defining a personal self. Her betrayal is not that her children grew, or that her husband went off with a younger woman. As Maggie readily acknowledges, her betrayal started early in all those seemingly insignificant compromises she made to get married and to stay married.

I've related Maggie's story in some detail because her life touches on several issues of considerable concern to women: separations—be they through divorce or widowhood; career and homemaking; society's and the family's role in supporting or subverting women in their quest for a personal identity—the issue of overloaded roles.

About Divorce and Widowhood. One of Maggie's observations made a particular impression. Looking back on her seventy years, she'd said the one thing she would have liked was to have been prepared for being alone. That statement on the heels of what I'd read gives us all pause for reflection: There are some 3.5 million women across the United States categorized as "displaced homemakers"— women who have worked inside the home and who suddenly find themselves divorcees or widows without any known marketable skills.

For women, divorce and widowhood is a devastating experience, slicing at the roots of their identity and security— emotional as well as financial. The loss of a mate, especially when marriage has been the fulcrum of our identity, whether through our or his choice or through the haphazard circumstance of widowhood, gives rise to feelings of grief, betrayal, and abandonment, of rage and guilt, of emptiness and the anxiety of a future alone.

The actual or emotional death of someone we've loved is a loss. Still, the deeper grieving frequently is for the self that's been tied to the couple identity, and the broken promise of a forever and ever. That clearly is the case with widowhood—even in women who'd seemingly been on their own. In her poignant autobiography, *Widow*, Lynn Caine observes: "My job? That had been running off to play! Now it was for *real*."

Even with women who see themselves as career women, their primary concern still seems to be men. Recently I conducted a workshop for professional women, all of whom had been or were married and had families. Interestingly, except for my insistence on heightening their consciousness, they would have spent all our time and emotional energy talking about the presence or absence of men in their lives rather than talking about themselves or their careers.

The anxieties of having to cope with the real world leave us particularly vulnerable. Isn't *anyone* better than living alone? The financial and emotional insecurity in not having a man often reignites those old rescue fantasies, plummeting us into replaying old scripts, picking up where we left off. Feeling that we've failed, or that we've been deprived of what every woman should have, we can pay a high price for recoupling. Frequently, we fall into unrewarding sexual encounters, hoping to quench those feelings that we're no longer sexually desirable either because our husbands no longer desire us, or because we bear that leaden image of "widow." And Maggie proved no exception.

Of Sixty, Sex, and the Single Woman. I wondered about Maggie's sex life after the separation. It seemed to me that at sixty she didn't have the same options in our society as, for instance, her husband, who was living with a woman twenty years his junior.

"I can't imagine having a sexual relationship without an emotional attachment," she explained. "In fact, I can't even 'throw' *myself*. The summer before we separated I was as hot as a firecracker, chasing my husband around, and he was covering himself, saying, 'I'm too tired,' or 'I'm too sleepy.' I didn't know what was going on. I spent a lot of time alone in the country. I tried to masturbate. And I didn't even 'throw' myself. I didn't have any luck at all.

"After I came to Chicago, my therapist said to me, 'Oh, you'll find a man who will love you for the very qualities for which your husband rejected you.' He had me so keyed up, I was picking up men at the Data Computer. I was looking at men's crotches and thinking, well, he looks pretty well hung. I was bringing all kinds of creepy old men home. They were all over sixty and they were apparently unable to have an erection without a so-called blow job. All they wanted was a blow job and there was no thought of me. Who needed that. So I said, 'Get out. Get out. Get out.' " Maggie flailed her arms, sweeping them out of her life.

"I'm glad I went through that period," she reflected, "because my therapist thought I was afraid of men. That proved I wasn't. They just weren't available. But, goddamnit, I resent it that an old man like my husband can be with a woman his daughter's age, and that's a sign of potency. If a woman has a lover her son's age, she's a pervert."

Maggie had fallen into proving her worth to still another man. After all, her therapist was a man. Unfortunately, too many divorced and widowed women feel that way too. In encouraging recoupling, what is the implicit message? That women can't or shouldn't make it on their own? That they're incomplete without recoupling? That their self-esteem can be regained only through another man?

The problem with that is that it perpetuates the woman's myth of helplessness and does little toward the development of her inner resources or autonomy. In counseling divorced and widowed women, interestingly, the current emphasis is not recoupling, but autonomy.

Divorce and widowhood are critical events that abruptly fissure the couple identity, and separations accepted as a challenge have propelled an increasing number of women to seek their own identity. It was Lynn Caine who observed: "I owe the person I am today to Martin's death. If he had not died, I am sure I would have lived happily ever after as a twentieth-century child-wife, never knowing what I was missing." [12] Perhaps. I'm more inclined to think that she would have come to that postponed self eventually, as many women do.

Recoupling is quite a different choice when two people come together out of a genuine need for intimacy rather than out of desperate feelings of financial insecurity or emotional incapacity. Such insecurities, paradoxically, cannot be assuaged by the simple fact of recoupling.

I continue to be dismayed at how much women are willing to pay for the "security" of coupling and how little they're willing to labor for the security of a personal definition. One woman in particular comes to mind. Unhappy in a mismatched love affair, she admitted that it had been far less anxiety-provoking to continue the affair, accepting the extras that she felt she would have been unable to provide for herself—like the fur coat, and weekends at the Hamptons—than to try to better her own career goals. She explained: "I was used to the constant pain of feeling like a second-class citizen. It became an old habit."

Personal autonomy, however, cannot be achieved unless we become increasingly aware of our old habits. We need to become inner- rather than outer-directed; our goals must change. Rather than focus on "getting and holding a man," we need to get to know ourselves, face our dependency, and get to know our skills, what we want, and what we consider important. In a financial or emotionally dependent state, we really aren't free to choose. More often than not, we wait to be chosen.

Dianne Carter, a counselor of divorced women, observes: "For many women this is the first time they've been without parents or a man on whom to lean. They are neither trained nor expected to take care of themselves. Suddenly becoming an adult would be difficult under any circumstances, but doing it while sustaining the loss of affection is, perhaps, the hardest thing many women will ever do." [13] I'm certain that is why women don't do. The fear of losing affection keeps us trapped—until we discover that we've lost it anyway. "Women must decide," continues Dianne Carter, "what they want from life and for themselves."

Career and Homemaking and Role Overload. But what price autonomy? Clearly that was a question Maggie faced and met. She tells us that her husband purportedly left her because she wanted something more for herself, but she also tells us that he would have left her for growing into a dull old woman. The friction began when she worked not to help support the family—as she'd done during the first years of marriage, and not as a kind of dabbling, a hobby—as when she'd started out in photography. The "trouble" started when her work identified her as a separate person apart from her marriage and family.

To speak of that friction as a conflict between a career and marriage is simplistic. The statement has been made, even by some professionals, that women cannot successfully manage work and marriage until after the age of thirty-five. (Can you imagine a lawyer, a physician, a nuclear scientist starting out on their careers after thirty-five?) That, of course, is pure fiction. Even as early as 1950, one fourth of the labor force were women. Currently there are some 38.8 million working women in every stage of the life cycle. But work is acceptable —if you *have* to. According to a 1976 Labor Department figure, 46 percent of children under eighteen have working mothers. This figure is believed to reflect the rising divorce rate. Women have always worked, if they've had to, and they've always managed. The oversimplified dictum of a family first and everything else second, unfortunately, has been one of those self-fulfilling and self-perpetuating prophecies that have kept women from reaching for a more responsible and rewarding work.

Women, however, have not combined careers and homemaking with ease, particularly when work has stemmed from a need for self-expression, something that was *only* theirs. Like so many women, Maggie suffered from tattered, timeworn images of what has been decreed as feminine. Her drive for achievement, mastery, recognition, and even her consummate curiosity—qualities that were the essential Maggie— when expressed for her own development, and not for the family's sake, suddenly were considered unfeminine.

Hers is not a simple conflict of career and homemaking,

but what has been referred to as a role overload. She had to fight not because she questioned her right to something all her own, but because her husband and her grown children were threatened by her new and larger role—and her immediate community also considered her an "oddball." There were too many others who had a stake in maintaining the status quo. But she fought.

Who was Maggie Fuller? More than the wife of Ralph Fuller and the mother of two married daughters and a son. Indeed, it is difficult for a family to be abruptly confronted with another image of the person who for years had been "the little woman and Mom." Indeed, it also is heady stuff for the wife and mother. . . . All the more reason, it seems to me, for us to be concerned with those central issues of identity, mastery, and autonomy *before* we choose a partner. Too often a woman is defined, by default, through her husband—through his interests, his work, his status in the community—and then abruptly uses that cushioning to support her venturing, something that marriage, set in fixed patterns, can't always do.

One woman succinctly summed it up when she observed: "In my first marriage I didn't know who I was so I played the role of little wife to the hilt. Then suddenly I woke up. My second marriage is different. My present husband knew who I was before we married." And women are waking up earlier, which, no doubt, explains the rise in divorce rates among the young.

Just as a myth has been perpetuated to plague the older woman, erecting a polarity between work and marriage, another myth is taking shape to plague the younger woman. The new fiction is that work, *any* work, willy-nilly, is the sure path to a personal autonomy and a separate identity. That sort of thinking shows little understanding of the kinds of risk, emotional commitment, or responsibility that cause us to stretch and grow. Work that is a hobby, or "going off to play," or without pay, for that matter, does little to change our self-image or build our self-confidence.

There is a whole subculture of women in volunteer work, for example, that should be questioned, especially since volunteering is considered so laudatory. The more I probed the motivations for working without pay, the more disenchanted I grew. I discovered that if a woman doesn't accept money for a job, there doesn't seem to be any limit to the kinds of jobs she's willing to undertake. Her feeling of worth, however, expressed in dollars and cents, is quite another matter. Despite the high-level functioning required in some volunteer work, unhappily it's undervalued both by the woman and by the prospective employer. Volunteering may serve a purpose to overcome those re-entry anxieties as women return to the work world, but it is clearly only a start. Women traditionally have been reluctant to be evaluated in dollars and cents. And in our society, like it or not, money is one measure of our worth and of our independence.

The next time you're considering volunteering for a job, I suggest some soul-searching. Would you have applied for such work if you were being paid? If not, why not? Is it really a choice? Are you fearful of openly admitting a want? An ambition? Are you afraid of not measuring up? Of the commitment? Of the success?

Too many women volunteer because they're afraid of openly competing, afraid of the emotional investment, and afraid of undergoing the training required for the more prestigious, power-laden jobs. Therefore, they take on those jobs, without pay, simply because they are the unpaid daughters of, or wife of. After all, you can't be fired if you haven't been hired.

Equally self-defeating is looking upon work as occupational therapy. Getting out of the house a little bit is acceptable to society and nonthreatening to her family. An editor and active volunteer in community services, Doris Gold, observed: "Several volunteer leaders themselves agree that voluntarism is pseudowork, with the focus frequently on the satisfaction of the volunteer rather than on the job to be accomplished." [14]

Voluntarism too readily plays into the woman's attitude

that she doesn't need to; it smacks of "going off to play." The reality is that we all need to grow up and need to learn that we're capable of taking care of ourselves. Volunteering—when it prevents us from developing that kind of self-confidence and personal responsibility—is self-defeating and perpetuates those manipulative and defensive postures women have hidden behind too long.

We've explored the life of Maggie, a turn-of-the-century woman who had only an elementary-school education and few of the supports that might have led her earlier to her own development. What of the contemporary woman? Are such concepts as role overload still relevant? Let's briefly consider Elaine Cole. Born in the thirties, forty-one years old, coming from a family of influence and means, Elaine possesses a bachelor's degree from a notable woman's college.

What Do You Do Besides Take Care of the Children? A frail, petite woman in a chic pants suit with black hair and eyes to match, Elaine was softspoken and somewhat hesitant. Although her parents saw to it that she had the "best" education and advised her not to marry young, that was really the only thing they'd groomed her for. She graduated Radcliffe in June with a job waiting for her in September on a national magazine that's spawned many a talented journalist. That summer she became pregnant, and shortly thereafter she married the young man, who'd merely been a "summer romance"—a not-so-unconscious choice. Marriage, she thought, was better than facing what would have been, for her, the ordeal of the threatening, competitive world of journalism.

A lean six years later, she found herself with three children, a marriage that was splintering, a large house in the suburbs, and blinding headaches. Her gifts and her dreams, whatever they'd been, were suspended. Her young husband, meanwhile, had begun his ambitious climb to success, dragging with him all the expected images of home, family, and "making it." Elaine was alone a lot. Her thoughts began to twist and knot inside her. She was sure she'd developed a brain tumor.

The internist studied her quietly and after a silence that seemed endless spoke. She never forgot his question. "What do you do besides take care of your children?" he asked. In a haze coated with fatigue, she couldn't think what to reply. His question, however, fell like a beacon light squarely on its target.

Alone that night, she lay in bed thinking. Her husband was on a trip and she had to face it. She was relieved. She was relieved and resentful and lonely. She had to face the fact that she'd made a questionable choice that fateful July. She'd thrown a dozen veils over her mind and now they'd started to peel away. It took a year before the decision formed itself. Just as he was about to leave on another trip, she asked him for a divorce. He was shocked and shattered; he'd had no inkling that she'd been unhappy.

She returned to her parents' house and "waited" out the next seven years. She'd gone from her parents to her husband and back to her disapproving parents, always cushioned financially, and still very much the child. And incredible as it all now seems, it hadn't bothered her one bit. Someone had to provide for the children; if not her husband, then her father.

Looking back on her life, she was quick to admit that those seven years were ones of hibernation. She couldn't fathom why she hadn't gotten her masters degree and a job, especially since she'd been provided for financially and all the children were in school. Except that it hadn't occurred to her; it just hadn't been expected. She was waiting, after all, to pick up the threads. She waited for what every girl is supposed to have—a man who would cause her to hear bells. She met him in the shape of Matt Cole, a confirmed bachelor.

Elaine remarried and took up her life where she'd left off. Eleven years after her divorce, she had five children—two daughters with Matt—a home in the suburbs, a herb garden, a station wagon, a sports car, and a marriage suffering from weighty expectations. The babies, the home, and the hearth were what she felt she had to give. They also were a way of cementing the bonds, staking her claim, and distancing herself from the world out there.

Dredging her past, Elaine looked grave as her dark eyes fixed me. Her hair, worn loosely, framed a pinched face. Her youngest child was born shortly before her fortieth birthday. "Something happened," she explained, "when I realized I wasn't going to have any more children. Something happened to me emotionally. I started thinking about my life differently. I realized I didn't know what to do, but I knew I had to find something that was all my own—something other than keeping house. I had to become someone besides Matt's wife." In the past, each time she'd felt free to begin a career, she'd decide instead on another baby. Now the seed that had been planted that year before her divorce was ready to take hold.

Uncertain where to begin, she consulted an institute for vocational and career planning and there she was given a battery of tests. That, she explained, was the beginning of an entirely new attitude toward life, a turning point.

Her changing self-image, moreover, resounded in all her relationships. The day she was to return for her test results was also her baby daughter's birthday. She felt torn, guilty about leaving her. To make matters more difficult, her housekeeper phoned that she was ill. Realizing what the meeting meant to her, Matt offered to stay home from the office. He'd become as interested as she in this new image of his wife. As she walked into the counselor's office, she was flooded with the old doubts. Had her brain turned to mush? she wondered. Reassured by the encouraging report, she returned to school and took up journalism, an abandoned dream. After a time she began free-lancing and sold several articles to magazines.

Elaine's path, however, continues to be a rocky one. Her efforts to carve out a personal identity are hampered by a past in which her sense of worth leaned heavily on being Matt Cole's wife. Although Matt consciously supports her efforts, he too has had to face some giant expectations and some giant steps both in his work and in the assumption of a family. His means of coping with the internal pressures has been through drinking, and whether he is conscious of it or not, Elaine is kept in a nurturing role.

Still, like Maggie's, Elaine's conflict cannot be flatly characterized as a struggle between marriage and homemaking. Hers has been a conflict common to a great many women who are overloaded in their roles, straddling the old and the new. Women are quick to point to their guilt as the great wall barring them from doing something for themselves. They are slower to acknowledge, however, the greater barrier, those entrapping feelings of wanting to be taken care of. It was Elaine's immobilizing fear of failing, and perhaps even of succeeding, that plunged her into a precipitous pregnancy and marriage. Masked behind every guilt about the other, I suggest that there is a more profound guilt about ourselves.

At the time I first spoke with Elaine, she was in the heady flush of learning and working at a new craft. She had taken her heart in hand, ignored her guilts regarding the family, and overcome the re-entry anxiety. The making of a professional, however, as Maggie has shown us, requires still another labor. Not only must we face and meet our own inclination to spin more cocoons, but we also must face the "givens" of most work: the competition; the rejections; the need to fight for what we want; the anxieties about failing and—equally as defeating—those about succeeding; and, perhaps the ultimate measure of the long-distance runner, perseverance.

Primarily, we battle our own dependency, and only secondarily others'. If we were as persevering and concerned with our identity as we have been with the couple identity, there is nothing that we wouldn't undertake. Neither competition, nor homework, nor long hours, nor boredom would daunt us. Rhetoric and enthusiasm are good for starters, but a realistic attitude about our skills and the real work world is better to keep us going.

Role Diversity. The mid-life crises seem unavoidable. The common myths of femininity and masculinity offer neither women nor men sufficient room to stretch beyond where they've been. For too many women, marriage has been not a viable relationship, but psychic networks of what we've been conditioned to expect and believe we should have.

The woman's dilemma is not, as it is popularly depicted, choosing between a career and homemaking. Nor is the current coinage that a career, *ipso facto*, defines the woman, a valid assessment. The real dilemma is one of role diversity—defrosting those facets of ourselves that have been in deep freeze. Rather than continue to belabor false choices, we would do better to turn our energies into knowing what we want and cultivating those wants, whatever talents or skills they may involve, so that they can accrue to our benefit and that of society.

How would you rate yourself in terms of role diversity? Do you feel that you've achieved most, some, or none of what you set out to do? Of what you set out to be? Do you feel that your goals as a girl had enough stretch to see you through the span of years? Those are the questions I've asked some women. Are you ready to take stock and to do something about you? I've also asked some of the women to do just that. Take stock. And what better way to take stock than by writing one's own obituary! It sounds morbid, but after the first shock, it isn't really.

Have you ever wondered what your obituary would say? It isn't the usual passing thought, I know. Think about it anyway. And while you're thinking, take a pencil in hand and . . .

"One last request," I said to Bettina, sheepish at my unfortunate choice of words. "Would you write your obituary? A final summary of your life. Something that could appear in your local newspaper, or even *The New York Times.*"

Bettina is in her mid-thirties. She dropped out of college during her last year to marry Peter Neal, an attorney who comes from a well-known family. They have two sons. After the birth of her second child, Bettina had a stillbirth. An Rh factor prevented her from having more children.

She leaned back, lit a cigarette, and then wrote:

Bettina Neal, b. 1942. Born and raised in Boston, Massachusetts. The daughter of the late Franco De Martino and Angela De Martino. She was married for sixteen years to Peter Neal. She also leaves two children, Peter Neal, Jr., 16, and Franco Neal, 11.

Bettina's identity clearly is imbedded in the We of daughter, wife, and mother—so much so that she neglected to mention any sibling relationships, and made no note of the considerable public recognition she has received for her volunteer work.

Like Bettina, have you defined yourself exclusively in terms of a "We" and an "All of Us"? If that is how you see yourself, take up your pencil again and project yourself into the future. This time write how you would like that final summary to read.

Elaine Cole phoned to tell me that for weeks since our meeting she's been editing and revising her obituary. "I know that sounds morbid," she said, "but it hasn't been. I've been adding all the things that I'm looking forward to doing by the time I'm eighty-five."

I pulled out her obituary and read:

Elaine Cole, age 85, of Westport, Connecticut died today after a short illness. Mrs. Cole, widow of Matt Cole, a well-known industrialist, was for many years a well-known journalist, contributing many articles to various newspapers and magazines. She was an innovator in initiating the now-popular weekly TV series with a magazine format and lectured widely.

Mrs. Cole graduated from Radcliffe, *cum laude,* in 1956. Nineteen years later she returned to school at The Columbia

School of Journalism and pursued a number of courses which launched her into a successful career.

She is survived by five children and nine grandchildren.

Elaine sees herself as surviving her husband—a statistically valid assumption—and as leading a full, creative life. Images, nevertheless, die hard. She still persists in thinking that *Mrs.* Cole graduated Radcliffe *cum laude*—a grammatical and factual error. It was Elaine Morris who graduated Radcliffe, or, at any rate, *Elaine* Cole.

Remember, we didn't say it was easy. We're saying that we can and do change; and as we do, we renew the quality of our lives.

Let's move to another facet of the woman's life: the sexual aspects of the self—another facet that, paradoxically, has been known to go underground in marriage.

Chapter 9. / The Quest for the Postponed Self

1. Report in *Practical Psychology Newsletter* of a study by Drs. Schlater, Baker, and Wapner, October, 1973.
2. Lessing, D. "To Room Nineteen." In *Women and Fiction,* edited by S. Cahill. New York: New American Library, 1975.
3. Thom, P., *et al.* "The Woman's Resource Center: An Educational Model for Counseling Women." *Adult Leadership,* 1975, *24,* 129–132.
4. Erikson, E. H. *Childhood and Society.* New York: Norton, 1950.
5. Levinson, D., C. Darrow, E. Klein, M. Levinson, and B. McKee. "The Psychological Development of Men in Early Adulthood and the Mid-life Transition." *Life-*

History Research in Psychopathology, 3, University of Minnesota Press, 1974.

6. Reports of the Bureau of the Census, March, 1976.

7. Report of a meeting of the Society for Life-Cycle Psychology and Aging. Address by Helena Z. Lopata reported in *Clinical Psychiatry News,* October, 1977.

8. Hoffman, L. Wladis. "Changes in Family Roles, Society, and Sex Differences." *American Psychologist,* 1977, *32,* 644–657.

9. Van Dusen, R., and E. Sheldon. "The Changing Status of American Women: A Life-cycle Perspective." *American Psychologist,* 1976, *31,* 106–116.

10. Vriend, T. H. "The Case for Women." *Vocational Guidance Quarterly,* 1977, *25,* 329–331.

11. Schneidman, E. S. "Aspects of the Dying Process." *Psychiatric Annals,* 1977, *7,* 25–40.

12. Caine, L. *Widow.* New York: William Morrow & Co., 1974.

13. Carter, D. "Counseling Divorced Women." *The Personnel and Guidance Journal,* 1977, *55,* 537–541.

14. Gold, D. "Women and Voluntarism," in *Women in Sexist Society,* Ed. V. Gornick and B. Moran. New York: New American Library, 1971.

10

THE POSTPONED
SEXUAL SELF

JUST AS WOMEN POSTPONE THE ACHIEVEMENT OF A PERSONAL
identity, they also frequently defer a separate sexual identity.
The achievement of a personal sexual identity in some ways
has been even more hamstrung by the historical distinction
that men "do," women "don't." It's been convenient, even
for women, to think in terms of two kinds of women—not
only, as we've learned, in terms of personal definition, but
also in terms of sexual identity. Historically, women have
been categorized as either virgins or whores, either passive
partners, waiting to be fulfilled, or predatory creatures selling
sex for the sake of sex. Still, such polarities are consistent
with the historical pattern of women's dependence on men.

Obviously, women and the social institutions are currently
in a dialectical transition—and perhaps there is no topic that
generates such an extravagance of emotion as the "new" sexuality. Before we explore the circuitous paths of a separate
sexual identity, let's consider this question of sexual "liberation," a subject that has given rise to hyperbolic interpretations.

The freedom of self-determination, self-knowledge, and
self-development is similar, it seems to me, whether we speak
of woman's right to equal opportunity in work or in bed.
Equality, however, doesn't signify that women and men, or
even all women, are identical in their sexual needs, sexual
wishes, or endowments. It does mean that we should possess
the equal opportunity to develop according to our endowments and our lights.

The woman of the seventies feels freer to engage in sexual

activity in and out of marriage, with the one and the many, and to derive pleasure from her sexuality. But, like the unleashing of any newfound aspect of the self, liberation is not enough. Genuine freedom always requires genuine choice. Our work is just beginning. The mere act of freely fornicating, like the mere act of working, is not necessarily a mark of our freedom or even of our definition. In fact, there are those in feminist circles who believe the sexual revolution is not all that it appears. In the past, nice girls weren't supposed to; now they are. We're free to engage in sexual activity, some feminists point out, but we're not free not to.

Unhappily, singlehood—whether one has chosen to remain single, or has experienced divorce or widowhood—is currently predicated on a "dating" scene of impersonal, casual sex. And paradoxically, rather than enhance the woman's independence, definition, or self-esteem, sex has become another pressure to perform. For the married woman, another "best" has been added to her list of superlative performances: Not only must she be the best wife, the best mother, the best homemaker, but she also must be the best bed partner.

According to Marabel Morgan's best seller, *The Total Woman*, the best wife is one who fulfills her husband's fantasies and puts the "romance" back in her marriage, not merely by being a submissive sex partner, but also by being a "sizzling" lover—like greeting her weary husband at the door in pink baby-doll pajamas and white boots. But there's really little that's revolutionary in that. Women have long been schooled in sexual performance.

A sexual identity, like a personal identity, however, has little to do with performance. If we can speak of a sexual liberation, it is in the freedom to know ourselves sexually as we've never known ourselves before, and as a result, to know those we love with greater understanding and intimacy. As one woman, experiencing a newfound self and a newfound sexuality, confided: "I suddenly am able to give and to share in ways that hadn't been possible before." That after thirty-three years of marriage.

We have been flooded with new feelings that will take time to sort out. Our "new" sexuality, like our "new" identity, is still in process. The view of sex as an athletic meet, a performance, or "being the best lay," it seems to me, can only result in little more than female performance anxiety. Monolithic pursuits don't do much to enhance the quality of our lives—single or married. If the desire for sexual fulfillment were to become another routine, or another demand on our stockpile of expectations, quelling rather than stoking the fires of passion, we would be diminished. Rather, with the integration of a new identity and a new sexuality, sex can become the capacity for greater intimacy.

WHERE WE'VE BEEN

Historically, it's been virtuous for women to blinker their vision and celebrate their innocence. The child-bride has been cherished and esteemed. And we've exploited those attitudes—it's less disruptive not to see and not to know. Still, women's sexual definition cannot be understood, even partially, without considering the whole context in which it is rooted: the unquenchable quest for self-knowledge, with its full measure of conflict and contradiction. Remember Eve? Characterized as Adam's rib, an afterthought, a companion for the loneliness and lust of man, she has been a sharp metaphor for woman's sexual image. She also can be an eloquent metaphor for her process of awakening.

Developmentally, woman's separate sexual voice, like her personal voice, must be achieved, and that requires the labor of sorting and separating ourselves from those incorporated parental and social sexual mores and attitudes. Let's consider the first of those central influences.

Rites of Passage: The Parental Paradox of Inhibition and Liberation. What happens when the girl, whose identity until adolescence has been ascribed, begins to pull away from the woman she has mirrored, to seek her own sexual voice? And what happens when the older woman—in poet Anne

Sexton's words, "the old tree in the background"—looks upon the burgeoning sapling?

In the woman's psychosexual development, mother's image is larger than life. Her attitude and posture during those central rites of passage—puberty, marriage, childbearing—directly affect her daughter's expectations and sexual attitudes.

Concretely, what happens when the older woman must face and attempt to meet her young counterpart's sexual coming-of-age? At best she is conflicted, greeting the event with diluted joy. Her response is multidetermined, recapitulating her own unresolved conflicts and often communicating a double message. Frequently she doesn't know where she stands. On the one hand, she may experience her aging with a resurgent nostalgia, or even jealousy of her daughter's growing attractiveness and open future; on the other hand, she is bent on seeing all her yearnings come true through her daughter. At this stage the daughter's "popularity" is the measure of all future happiness. Her offspring's passage to womanhood is to be "better" than she had it, or at least as "good." What constitutes better or good, of course, is a function of mother's vision. Like fashion, sexual styles swing from the excesses of inhibition to the excesses of "liberation."

Those stances are reflected to a greater or lesser degree in the sexual upbringing of all daughters. The social fashion, the mother's sexual development, and the daughter's sexual needs and endowment are the fine networks determining the female's unfolding sexuality.

In this age of "enlightenment," the family doctor has been replaced by the family gynecologist. And family gynecologists have some striking tales to tell. Dr. Helen Beiser comments that when a girl shows the first pubertal signs the mother generally needs as much help as the daughter. She traces several factors contributing to those familiar antagonisms between mothers and teenage daughters.[1]

On the one hand, there is the enlightened mother. Too many "liberated" mothers are signaled into action too soon. The mother who is determined to "make it better" paradoxically often denies or sublimates her own ambivalence or envy by flooding her docile daughter with an excess of information and advice. A number of mental health practitioners and sex therapists view the implicit push for an early sexuality as hostile. They report that it has interfered with the unforced evolvement of relationships that would permit a natural unfolding of caring and sexual familiarity.

In our eagerness to be different from our mothers, perhaps we've thrown out the baby with the bath water. Unfornately, too few of these "enlightened" mothers are sufficiently concerned with supporting the development of autonomy in their adolescent daughters as well. Few question: Is the girl succumbing to outside pressure? Is she free not to? Can she support her sexuality emotionally? The rise in teenage pregnancy and VD, despite our enlightenment, makes such questioning patently relevant.

The ritual trip to the gynecologist, whether the daughter requests it or not, to fit her with a diaphragm or to get a prescription for the Pill, robs our female children not only of the necessary growing pains of adolescence, but also of their freedom to choose. Well meaning or not, overprotective or envious, we're paradoxically subverting rather than buttressing an increasing personal responsibility and independence. Overcontrolled girls docilely go along, and also somehow manage to get pregnant.

On the other hand, there is the inhibited mother. There are women who deny their daughters' development, either by choosing not to notice, giving no information at all, or by infantilizing them. In extreme cases, the daughter's adolescence is a time for opening her mail, "cleaning out" her dresser drawers, interrogations, accusations, and an attempt to ferret out every detail of her social life. It is also a time when daughters, given half a chance by their fathers, turn to them for the emotional support denied by their mothers.

Those are the influences that have left their imprint, whether we are old daughters or young ones. Women grow in the dark shadows of fear and anxiety: we're either too interested in sex, or not enough; we aren't as good as Mother, or we're better.

Social Mores. Parental and social images often so thickly intertwine that it becomes almost impossible to separate them. Nevertheless, apart from the parental attitudes in which we've been raised, social attitudes and postures have been known to make their special inroads.[2] If I may be forgiven an unforgivable analogy, the social influence on actual sexual practice is quite similar to what we've learned about athletic firsts. We know, for instance, that once a record is broken, like the four-minute mile, a mental set is also broken. We discover that the impossible is possible!—and others soon follow suit.

Thus, when the social posture has been that women don't have sexual feelings and that female sexuality is primarily for procreation and the satisfaction of men's biological needs, then more women are more likely to be non-orgasmic. When the social attitudes, moreover, have been that old people shouldn't and that young ones should, then there is a mounting pressure for old people not to, and for young ones to.

Change is a slow and laborious process, and although some of us may be "liberated," the sexual patterns persist. Women, by and large, continue to cloak their sexual drive in the idealized image of a one true love. That's been equally so for Maggie, our septuagenarian, as it's been for Erica, our young feminist. It's been equally so whether we're career women, wives, and mothers, or whether we're exclusively homemakers, or unmarried and living together, or unmarried and having an affair, or married and having an affair. Melding sex and a one true love, women have made intimate relationships the fulcrum of their identity, security, and worth. The commitment or the absence of a commitment to a loved one occupies most of our waking and dreaming hours, and nearly all of our energies.

Female sexuality is a fine, multistranded network. Since traditionally it wasn't perceived as satisfying the woman's physical needs or as giving her pleasure, or even as an expression of intimacy, it became for many women a manipulation. And for many a "total woman," it still is. It's been used to get her what she wants—a baby, a bigger house, "love," security—or simply for control. It's part of our historical dowry, tucked in with the embroidered pillowcases. It is also part of the anxiety surrounding female sexuality—our own brand of performance anxiety.

Take the protagonist in Marge Piercy's novel, *Small Changes*, a "liberated" young Miriam, struggling to make her way. "Kissing him back, she was suddenly, totally delighted. Ha, he did want her, he found her attractive. It was like an enormous vindication, a proving of her. . . . All the soreness of the last six months, the insults and jostling, the bad vibrations coming out of him, abrading her, all fused seamlessly into her victory. She briefly remembered then that she had wanted him to like her, not to want her."

The extent to which our sexual heritage has held fast with most women, homemaker and professional, was strikingly brought home not long ago, when I was asked by an institute to conduct a nine-hour session as part of a training program. By an unexpected stroke of good fortune, the group—social workers, psychologists, and psychiatrists—turned out to be all women. What did we talk about? Men, of course. Supervisors. Teachers. Husbands. Fathers. Bosses. And the sexual encounters they weren't having with supervisors, husbands, bosses.

The inequality between men and women is threatening, even, or perhaps most of all, to the professional woman. Threatened, women whittle men down to a manageable size. That's part of the historical baggage of the days when women knew their place. Traditionally, women learned to use sex not from feelings of strength or desire, but rather from deeper feelings of inadequacy as a passive-aggressive wielding of power in an attempt to control or define their future—an unfortunate, but understandable spin-off of our cultural position. Listen.

"Partly it's been a resistance," Margo was saying. "A kind

of fight or flight. But it *is* also fact. There aren't many women around in a supervisory capacity. We're being trained by men." Her voice grew animated as she continued: "Once a week we meet as a group for supervision of our psychotherapy groups. On one side of the table are the supervisors—Men; on the other side us—Women. I hate what happens to me. I have visions of lying on the floor, kicking my heels, wishing I could be accepted just for me."

"I envy you," Mildred interrupted. "You make an impact. You're so . . . so seductive. It's true we're dog-tagged. Men see you a certain way and you respond that way. I'm mother earth. But I've used it. When Bill Greene, my supervisor, gets really angry, I say to myself, well, he's a little boy having a tantrum. That way I can handle him."

"Isn't that funny," Katherine volunteered. "I dreamed I was holding Christiaan Barnard in my arms. He was an infant." She added as an afterthought, "My husband is a surgeon."

Kim smiled sheepishly. "It's not so funny. The other night I dreamed of Bill Greene—he's my supervisor too. I was cradling him."

"And sex?" I asked. "Is that cut from the same cloth?"

"I know that if I can give Bill an erection," Margo volunteered, "I'm in control. It's disarming. I need to disarm because I feel so inadequate. I think about having an affair a lot; I've never slept with any other man but my husband. And after so many years with one person, what's left but fantasies about other men? But I can't risk it. I'm afraid that a younger man would reject me, or that I wouldn't perform according to standards. Besides, I'd jeopardize so much; my husband is a very traditional guy. Can you have an affair and also love the person you're married to?"

Kim rose to pour herself some coffee. "I have fantasies of being in bed with a whole roster of men," she said. "For years that's how I got orgasms. I used to feel guilty about it. I've had sex with only one man other than my husband, and that was before I married. I can't risk an affair either.

I'd like a hit-and-run thing—like at a convention. I worry I'm too old. My breasts are too small. My performance won't be the best. I've got to be the best lay. I'm competitive."

A slow smile spread across Katherine's face. "I've had affairs, but I've always kept it quiet. My mother was very competitive. She took away every boyfriend I brought home. No wonder I'm tongue-tied in a woman's group. It's dangerous to make an impact."

Those of us who are in our middle years, particularly, are more likely to have been raised with the excesses of inhibition. Sex was unacceptable, except for the conjugal bed. Premarital or extramarital sex—particularly if it was pleasurable —was a sure indication of lust and ensuing damnation. One common way to have our sex and be blameless too was to anesthetize ourselves.

Unless, of course, we were raped. In which case we were completely devoid of responsibility. Rape fantasies have thus served their function in the economy of sex. One certainly can't be held accountable, if one is given no choice. Undoubtedly, the universality of those rape fantasies has contributed to the still-popular fiction that all women want to be raped, or that no woman can be raped against her will. According to Susan Brownmiller, author of *Against Our Will*, those are the deadly male myths, the distorted proverbs that govern female sexuality and strip women of their worth and their freedom.

Female Fantasies of an Awakening. Men and women are different, and perhaps nowhere is that difference as striking as in their sexuality. Our social and parental legacy is different; our sexual fantasies are essentially different; our biological endowments and our development are different; and there is a difference even in the nature of our sexual dysfunctions.

A psychiatrist and coordinator of a sexual therapy center, Avodah Offit, lyrically writes: "The web that creates sexual suffering has many strands. Men are usually caught on only two: their parentally fostered personality disorder, or a crisis precipitated by some traumatic transaction with another person later in life. . . . Women, however, suffer not only the effects of early and later blows to self-esteem, but must also cope with societally and parentally induced sexual guilt and shame, cultural misconceptions about sex, and a high level of ignorance. They are caught in such a complex net of repression, inhibition, and fear that each element must be dealt with separately. . . . When a woman is culturally conditioned to believe that sex should be one type of experience, but becomes aroused by another, she often inhibits herself in sheer confusion, if not total despair." [3]

Of course, the one experience we've been culturally conditioned to expect is romantic coupling, although we may be aroused by anything but romantic images. Those plastic passions of the kind we're fed by the beautiful, virginal heroines of such novelists as Barbara Cartland, for example, plunge us into still more contradictions. Often it is that very attitude of a passive and submissive recipient that results in the woman's lack of satisfaction—sexual and otherwise.

Our conflicts and contradictions proliferate. The woman's passive attitude concerning "romance" is alive even in women who are otherwise active participants in the world. A thirty-one-year-old woman who'd recently been made an assistant vice-president in a brokerage house comes to mind. She'd been married four years and felt that suddenly the "romance" had gone out of her marriage. I asked to meet alone with her husband with a view to initiating couple therapy. He'd hardly hung up his coat when he began: "I know you'll find this hard to believe, because Kathy is such a dynamo, but being in bed with her is like lying next to a dead mackerel. She just lies there waiting for things to happen. She's so competent in everything else. I've been afraid to confront her with that. But I don't understand it—it doesn't make sense."

It really isn't hard to fathom. Being done to, "overpowered," not only permits us to have our sex and enjoy it too, but also allows us to hold fast to the Sleeping Beauty promise of an extravagant awakening. Unfortunately, it also serves to keep us children. The reported gender difference in sexual imagery, if nothing else, is consistent with our sexual attitudes. By and large women want to be done to—even women whose ingrained submissive images in no way reflect their active, creative lives. By and large, men want to do.

Among the most common female fantasies leading to orgasm are still those of being overpowered, or of being exposed, spread-eagled—a common enough position for any woman who has had a baby or a gynecological examination. Even those women who do report sadistic fantasies give fantasies that are more in the nature of a fight for survival than the male's fantasy of subduing and conquering.[3]

The contradictions continue to amass. Although there are a larger number of women who are non-orgasmic, whereas a non-orgasmic male is rare, women's capacity for orgasm is considerable. Women's sexuality lends itself to controversy because it clearly has not been as easy to define and label as men's performance. Some feminists say that a coital orgasm for women is an accidental happenstance. The clitoris, they say, is the only organ that provides pleasure.[4]

A more moderate view is that of Dr. Helen Kaplan, who describes female sexuality as distributed in a bell-shaped curve along a continuum. At one end there are the women who are totally non-orgasmic and at the other end there are women who are capable of multiple orgasms. In between are women who achieve orgasm through masturbation alone, and those, in the majority, who are orgasmic by partner stimulation, before or after intercourse, with a minority achieving orgasm through coitus alone.

Awakenings. It is notable that woman's adult erotic responsivity, like her adult development generally, is not age-determined, but identity-determined. We're all too inclined to think of aging in terms of decrement, and loss. But as we'll learn, women in their middle years experience greater sexual release than women in their twenties or early thirties.[2, 5] That fact is noteworthy when we consider that woman's responsiveness is strongly affected by her self-image, self-esteem, and sense of self. Conversely, it's been reported that women who experience conflicts about their own identity frequently also experience a sexual crisis manifested in orgasmic dysfunction.[5, 6] (But more of Awakenings later.)

Although it is true that woman's sexual desire and response is more sensitive to psychic inhibition and more easily suppressed than male sexuality, her potential is boundless when those inhibiting factors are diluted. It is that very potential, Dr. Kaplan suggests, that has caused men to fear and muffle women's pleasure. The nineteenth-century legacy of our gynecological fathers, she points out, has been one of suppression. It was just such a physician who warned "that an aroused woman can have destructive effects on the man with whom she is copulating." Dr. Kaplan explains: "The fear of a sexually aroused woman as corrupting, distracting, enervating, and wasteful of a man's precious sperm seemed to be a way of coping with a simple and devastating fact of life: A man's capacity for orgasm is limited, while a woman's is not."[7]

Woman in Flux. Some of us have swung from the staunchest belief in absolute commitment, to an indiscriminate non-commitment, to a complete, bewildered abstinence. Those of us who've been taught that "nice girls don't" look upon sex-for-the-sake-of-sex as the ultimate liberation. Those of us who've grown up under the pressure of Doesn't everybody? look upon this new "freedom" in quite another light. No longer able to live by the old values, the younger woman has yet to find new ones that she can live with. Just turned thirty, one woman consulted me because she'd become non-orgasmic and felt she was withdrawing from all relationships. She'd run through what she referred to as three "divorces"—relationships where she had moved into the man's apartment, lived with him for a period of two or three years and then suffered through a breakup that found her rootless, without a home or a future.

Still, the woman of thirty has been raised by the woman of fifty, who has been raised by the woman of seventy. And so we carry the excesses of each generation, melding them into a pastiche of our own. Masked in what seemed like sexual freedom, she in reality suffered a profound fear of male dominance and of losing control that kept her from forming a more lasting relationship. Just as some men experience their sexuality as conquest, some women experience it as submission. Intimacy is equated with a passive dependence, autonomy with living alone. We find it difficult to bridge the two.

Hand in glove with those attitudes is still another: the steadfast belief that the intense pleasure of orgasm is a gift, and not something in which the woman has been actively involved. Abandonment again becomes capitulation. We seem not to experience our participation in our own sexual pleasure. "The release of orgasm," Dr. Offit explains, "although not an act of will, does reflect some decision whether to be active enough to tense her muscles appropriately and passive enough to allow the tension to release." [6]

The swing toward a casual and early sexuality inevitably has given rise to its own antagonistic counter-pull—often a bewildered withdrawal from all commitments. It has been assumed, especially by those of us raised in a more repressive climate, that the earlier a girl becomes sexual, the more experience she has, the more mature she is, and the more she knows who she is and what she wants. Enough time has elapsed for health-care researchers to observe the results and to disagree.[1, 8] They report that girls who have become sexual in their early teens are not necessarily the girls who make good sexual adjustments later in their marriages. The one is not, per se, a "preparation" for the other. Early sexuality is not even an index of the teenager's emotional development, sexual satisfaction, or involvement.

One twenty-year-old woman observed that despite her sexual experience, she felt more invisible than ever. She'd been intermittently sexually active with different partners since the age of sixteen, and had climaxed only once. Gradually she came to realize that intercourse had replaced the good-night kiss, and was only another measure of her popularity. It also served, paradoxically, as a replacement for mother's warm embrace—something that she'd missed. She sought to "find" herself through her sexual encounters and found instead that she felt increasingly less identifiable.

Let's look at sex and marriage. Clearly, we don't entirely understand the role of sex in marriage or in a person's life. As young psychotherapists we were taught that the sexual relationship is a microcosm of the marital relationship and that a good sexual relationship invariably meant a good marital relationship; conversely, a poor sexual relationship meant a poor marital relationship. Well, not even that's true anymore, if it ever was. Once more we're entrapped in our attempts to determine cause and effect. But we're discovering that sexual satisfaction, love and commitment don't necessarily bear a one-to-one relationship. Although women were once stoned to death for adultery, for example, few couples today find extramarital affairs sufficient cause for divorce.

And we're also discovering that some women, like some men, compartmentalize their sex and their love. Take Belle. Married seventeen years, mother of one son, she became increasingly aware that she carried too much of the emotional and financial responsibilities of her marriage. Over the years her husband had fallen into one misadventure after another, never quite making it on his own. In bed, however, they had what Belle called "great sex." Pressured to earn more, she changed jobs and there she met a man several years her senior whom she came to respect and admire. After a few months they began an affair; after a year and a half, she asked her husband for a "friendly" divorce. Although she and her lover had a good relationship, their sexual encounters left much to be desired. Despite his age, he was inexperienced in the ways in which women take pleasure in lovemaking, and he suffered as well from premature ejaculation. Where once she'd experienced multiple orgasms, now she rarely climaxed. Frustrated and unsure, she accepted a date for dinner with her ex-husband, and accepted as well his bed once more.

In the not-too-distant past, female sexuality was synonymous with romantic love and marriage and commitment—more commonly referred to as fidelity, a term that has come to conjure up images of a loyal Fido. With the explosion of still another fiction—men are polygamous, women monogamous—we've worked ourselves out of one set of chains to slip into others. Take partner-swapping—better known as *wife*-swapping—a kind of extramarital sex where the couples swap partners, together. This is hardly as radical a change as it sounds. It seems to me that partner-swapping really isn't much more than another slightly askew form of Togetherness, another Shared Project. Will we continue to share everything, even our extramarital experiences?

Or take that other version, or what couples have taken as that other version: open marriage.[9] If that concept has made a contribution, it's been in questioning the fixed image of a couple identity—a transition, at best. As one young woman asked: How open can a marriage be and still be a marriage? The woman of the seventies, who seems to carry a legacy of contradictions, confides that although she feels freer to engage in extramarital sex, the thought of her partner exercising the same prerogative plunges her into irrational jealousy, competitiveness, and feelings of betrayal! What's new in that response?

We're in a period of transition, clearly. But it's time we get on with it. We've examined female sexuality in terms of some critical but discrete parameters—biological, social, and psychological. Like most human phenomena, the whole gestalt is more than its parts. Let's consider woman's sexuality over her life span—adult female sexuality stretched out over the years of our historical and personal development.

SEXUAL LIFE LINES

Who Am I Sexually? Remember the women's Life Lines? They graphically depicted the quest for a personal voice, with its postponements and renewals, thrusts and antagonisms, turning points and transitions. Well, women's sexual development takes much the same route. As we'll learn there is an advantage in considering women's sexual development from a life-span perspective, since in one sweeping stroke we're able to observe the multistranded network of internal and external factors that has contributed to the "new" sexuality.

For the first time in history, perhaps, we're claiming ownership of our psyches and our bodies. At the least, we're no longer buried alive or burned at the funeral pyre. But that is not to say that we're completely free of our historical scars. Too many women continue to be buried alive in marriages, if not in actuality, most certainly in attitude. The complete absorption in a couple identity commits us to the expectation that a woman, particularly a married woman, ceases to have a separate existence—sexually and in all other ways. We've been taught that two people become one in marriage—and we all know the one we're supposed to become. Our body, our desires, our fantasies are acceptable only as long as they mirror, defer to, and serve the couple identity. In part, it also has served women, and so we've clung leech-like to that idealized image of the beloved, Mr. Right, the one and only.

With such historical images burrowed into the very muscles of our being it is amazing indeed that even the *idea* of a separate sexual existence has emerged. Still, time seems to have taken care of all that. In the past women inexorably reproduced and many died at childbirth or burned themselves out—leaving widowed husbands the sexual variety of many wives—with hardly the time to ponder their short lives. The urgency of that time-left-to-live, or the fear of aging, was a philosophical abstraction. There was no worry about an After, or a mid-life crisis, when women barely made it to fifty. Currently, however, the actuarial tables have turned; women are outliving their men, and the urgency of a separate existence is anything but a passing thought. That image of a one true love, forever and ever, is slowly dimming. It is not only possible but probable that we will outlive our mate by as much as fifteen or twenty years—sometimes finding ourselves single again at the very time when we are about to put an end to our postponements. Perhaps, in a historical first, the contemporary woman has both the luxury of time and the freedom from certain biological and social restraints to turn her thoughts to the issue of human fulfillment.

The changing historical image of woman has been reflected in her changing sexual attitudes. A recent Morton Hunt survey, for example, reports that three times as many women are having extramarital affairs as a generation ago, catching up with the figure for males, which has remained stable for the past twenty years.[10] By the same token, counselors in the mental health disciplines are also reporting that most sex is taking place in marriage and that, by and large, it is more of a celebration than ever before.

Consider the woman's journey and this time let's listen to her sexual voice. But before we do: Earlier I suggested you draw your life course—a line representing your life. Now try drawing your sexual Life Line—a line indicating all the important sexual events in your life—and label those events. Put down the approximate age at which they occurred. With a plus or minus, indicate whether you considered the experience as positive or negative. Not what you *think* it was, but how it *felt* then. Now sit back. How does your sex life look in black and white? How does it compare with Ariel and Edith?

Women generally think in terms of love, sex, commitment

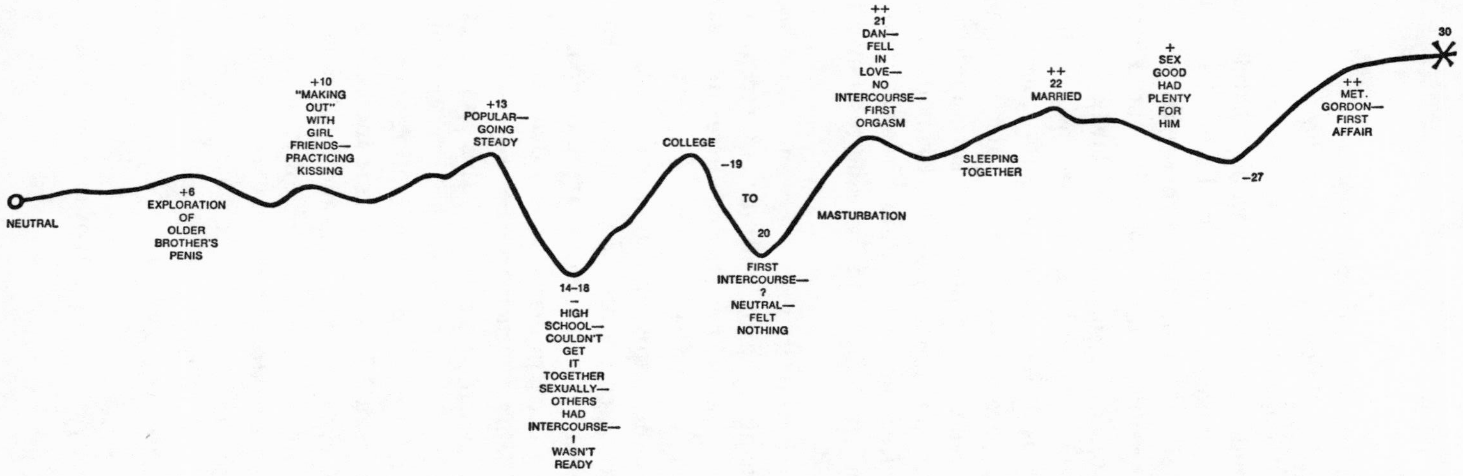

FIGURE 17 / Ariel

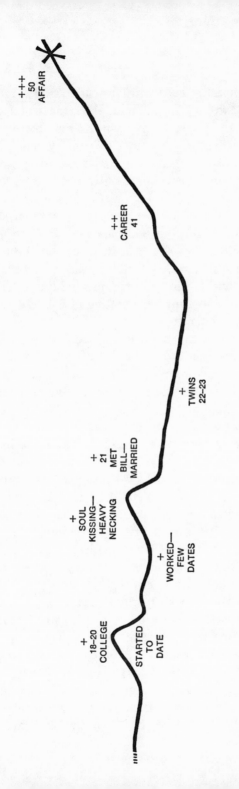

FIGURE 18 / Edith

and babies—sometimes even in that order. Ariel (Figure 17) who is of the sixties generation, typifies the usual generational kaleidoscoping. Her Life Line is noteworthy for its early "going steady," which in her case meant one boy with whom she could share things, and who would identify her as popular. Although her generation experienced a pressure for casual sex, she resisted intercourse, but not without considerable self-doubt. Finally, at age twenty, she felt she *had* to. "He showed me how, but that's about it. It was a nothing experience." Only when she "fell in love" did she feel sexually alive. She and Dan (her future husband) slept together on their first date: "No intercourse, just holding each other; and I had my first orgasm. That feeling of love! It was overwhelming; it can generate anything."

Edith, from a generation which prescribed sex only for marriage and procreation, describes a more muted sexual evolvement. She had no recall of any active sexual desire until she met her husband-to-be, and that was expressed in "soul kissing" and "heavy necking." She also didn't recall masturbating—until after her extramarital affair.

Despite the generational distances and differences in sexual mores, what is common to both women—the one thirty, the other fifty—is an abrupt sexual awakening: an awakening that unlocked their sexuality from its total submergence in the other and identified it as separate and personal. And contrary to popular myth, it wasn't a Prince Charming who precipitated their growth—even though both mention an extramarital affair—but a coalescing of "shocking" events that led to a greater awareness of a separate self.

The nature of a "shock" to the status quo, whatever the precipitating event, is to dislodge and isolate. It forces us to stand apart and sort ourselves out as that image of exclusivity—a *one* true love—is disrupted. Some women, for example, are "shocked" to discover that they are "happily married" and yet attracted to other men, or that they are "happily married" and still fantasize about a former lover. Others are shocked to learn that their husbands are sexual beings and that as such they're capable of being sexually attracted to more than one woman.

The shape of those developmental disruptions and the consequent awakening to a separate sexual voice is as different as the women. For some it has been an abrupt confronting of singlehood once more, leading them to face a sexuality that had been closeted away. Sometimes that leads them as well to a replay of former rescue fantasies, reigniting unrealistic expectations—a last-ditch attempt to find fulfillment through a man. For others, it's been an affair—their husband's—that jolted them into reassessing their lives. For still others, it's been part and parcel of a stock-taking, bringing forth a sexual self from among those postponed aspects of the self.

What is noteworthy in the woman's sexual life course is not the commonality of any specific event, but rather the commonality of sexual upheavals and abrupt awakenings. In the developmental scheme of a lifetime, concomitant with other transitional changes, the periods of the early thirties and early fifties seem to be pivots of change. I was especially interested to find that observation supported by some sexual therapists and researchers as well. Dr. Harold Lief, director of the Marriage Council in Philadelphia, and Dr. Ellen Berman report the highest incidence of sexual dissatisfaction for couples in "the late twenties and around age fifty." [11]

Tracing the woman's journey, we've discovered that the late twenties and early thirties is the time when that couple identity, which was to have resolved the woman's Who am I? conflicts, is experienced more realistically. It is a time of feelings of loss. Her innocence leaking away, she wonders: Is this all there is? I have everything a woman is supposed to have. Is this all I want from life? It is a time of beginning questioning and of urgency, a time when she begins to worry about that *bête noire* of most women: time-left-to-have-a-baby, and a time for pondering what that will mean to her life. Or, if she's already in the early throes of motherhood and the baby is just a baby, and not the sweetest joy, and if her husband is just a man, and not that shining knight, then it is a time of disillusionment and of awakening. It is a time of disruption.

Is that what she wants to commit herself to for the rest of her life? The question pursues her. What of that self she'd feared to face? The self that she'd let fall by the wayside in order to root her future?

Consider Ariel. When she married she had just gotten her bachelor's degree and was toying with the idea of going to law school, uncertain whether she had the intellectual capacity or the stamina to see it through. Then she met Dan, married, set up house, and got a part-time job as a secretary in a law firm. She was twenty-seven, married five years, when she began feeling the pinch of time. She knew she wasn't getting any younger and that she'd have to start having babies soon, if she were to have a family, but she also knew that she was afraid of settling in. At any rate, that's what she thought her dreams meant. For the past several months she had slept fitfully and would awake bewildered. She always awoke to the same dream, or a variant of it. She would dream that she was on an open road, driving a trailer. Another time it was a bus. Finally she dreamed that she was piloting a plane, soaring into the great beyond.

It was during that period that she met Gordon, a young bachelor and an impassioned consumer advocate. His enthusiasm ignited her. Each time they'd run into each other at lunch, she'd linger behind and get back to the office late. They'd talk and talk until they'd solved every injustice. Somehow Gordon had seen the rebel in her, and in some strange way he seemed to give it a voice. She'd always been so sensible, making sure to keep everything under control. But he didn't see all that. It was as if he'd given her another identity, a new name. He seemed to be her other half; the one she hadn't expected to meet. After working late one night, he took her to dinner and then they went to his hotel. She thought, why not? As she knew it would, the affair ended after a half dozen such encounters when he left for Washington.

That spring she sent in her application to law school and she also told Dan it was time they began thinking about a baby. She knew somehow that she could become a mother without losing her direction, now that she'd found her direction. Dan never learned of her affair, but he did know that Ariel was changing. Less fearful of losing herself, she became more giving and also less demanding. Dan was no longer there just to fulfill her dreams. Sexually, they had fewer fears to bring to bed, where previously their negative as well as their positive feelings for each other had been played out—a common enough occurrence. Most of us don't succeed in putting our attitudes and expectations out for the night with the cat. The humdrum in our daily lives, or fear—of losing control, of trying something new, or of change—has a way of creeping into bed.

Ariel was quick to acknowledge that she'd married Dan because he was familiar and safe. She thought he, most of all, would accept her as she was. In the "security" of the familiar, however, she also discovered that she needed more.

Is this all there is? Setting that question aside, we commit ourselves to getting on with the business of Shared Projects—babies, house, etc.—but only to experience their re-emergence in our forties and fifties, this time with an equal but different urgency.

Woman Set to Bloom. Edith was sitting opposite me on the couch, looking as sparkling as the Perrier she was sipping. It was difficult to think of her as just Bill Johnston's wife, although her husband was not a man who faded easily into the background of one's mind. Within the past month he'd been appointed to a prestigious position on an advisory council to the federal government—something he'd worked toward from the day he was married, if not the day he was born.

"As far back as I can remember," Edith was saying, "people would come up to me at parties and ask: 'Oh, you're Bill Johnston's wife, aren't you? He's such a dynamic guy.' Then I'd be left to fade into the wallpaper—or that other thing would happen: I'd be flocked to by his young protégés and 'Ma'm'd' to death as they'd look around me to catch Bill's eye. I simply was Mrs. Johnston."

For a long time that was all Edith allowed herself to be. She shared the low visibility of a number of women whose husbands set out to "make it." She provided the backdrop for his ambition and the tranquillity of a home life. Bill had begun his career as a hardworking corporate lawyer with an eye to his future, and she had been framed by his work. The skills she acquired along the way were designed to enhance his position. She learned to set the most beautiful table, dripping with lace, beeswax, and orange pom-poms— only the lace and candlelight were meant for his public image and *not* for those intimate moments with her husband.

Married thirty-three years, Edith had been with her husband longer than she'd been with her parents. How foolish, she thought, in looking back, that she'd believed her growing up would be all behind her by the time she'd leave home. Home for her had been a straitlaced Calvinist town in New England, with a population of forty thousand. Marriage held a promise of space, her own place, unfettered by mother's do's and don'ts. A stolid and undemonstrative woman, her mother made the kinds of sharp judgments one learned to avoid.

At twenty, she dropped out of college, worked briefly in a small city, met Bill and married. Under the cloud of World War II, he entered the Navy and they moved to the West Coast. Although neither had had intercourse before, Edith dreamed of those initiation rites of passage that Bill was to have led her through.

They had scarcely settled into their new apartment when they discovered that Edith was pregnant with twins. She was crestfallen, and her dreams of high romance crumbled around her. She'd longed to go dancing with all the other newlyweds at the post; instead, she felt awkward and clumsy. To add to her discomfort, they became the butt of his buddies' humor. Would she ever feel like dancing again? she wondered.

Their playground for sexual romps soon turned into a bedroom for cribs, bassinets, and diaper pails. They decided it best for her to return to her parents' home to await Bill's return East. Several years later, when they finally settled in Connecticut, the twins were two and a half, and Bill was eager to make up for lost time. He entered a large law firm and traveled the country, negotiating contracts.

Edith plumped the couch pillows and briskly placed them behind her back. "In marriage," she said, "I put my sexuality in a deep freeze and kept it there." The couple identity merged with their corporate identity and like some fungus spread into every crevice of their living—what they did, where they went, who their friends were, and even how they related to each other sexually. As he was under continuous pressure to perform on the job, Bill's sexual encounters were pressured as well. There was little that was play in their lives.

Edith grew to accept that as the way things were. He was simply overtaxed. She learned to keep busy with the house, the children, the family, shopping and entertaining, moving in ever-narrowing circles. And everything was going according to schedule. In the spring they planned to add a wing on the house. Everything was as she'd been taught it was supposed to be. She was a wife and a mother now, and Bill affectionately called her Mom. Still, why did it irk her so? Why did she feel . . .

At night she'd lie awake to wait for Bill to finish his briefs, then she'd grow weary and give in to sleep. She knew he was pitched for the top. If she showed anything but joy in his achievement, he'd scowl. "I don't understand you," he'd say. "I'm doing it all for you and the twins." Then he'd grow quiet and brood.

Bill had always been a private person. Reared by a mother

who'd been overcontrolling, he quickly learned to withdraw from an emotionality that threatened to envelop him. He didn't need as much contact as she, she told herself. Being in the public eye so much, she thought, had made him circumspect. His cloak of propriety kept people at a distance—even her.

Still, he was the hub and she clung willingly to the periphery. She'd been raised to believe that there is one man for each woman, and when she finds him she learns to adapt her life to his. She'd chosen Bill and she was governed by his opinion on everything—her clothes, her grooming, the food she bought, the candidate she voted for, the house they lived in, and the weekends they spent away.

Weekends. Those were indelibly inscribed in her memory. How overwrought she'd be then, and how grateful she was now. The girls were twelve that summer when every weekend they would pack, get into the car, and drive to Bill's protégée's summer cottage. The summer place was rented by a bright young law clerk who worked for him—a woman.

Edith crushed her cigarette; a flurry of soft gray ashes dropped on her camel's-hair jacket. She was fifty; her pants suit hugged a willowy, calorie-conscious figure. Only her nicotine-stained fingers marked an otherwise flawless portrait of "femininity."

"The biggest shock I've ever had in my life," she explained, "was when I discovered that there was no such thing as marrying and living happily ever after with the same person. It took me years. There just isn't one woman for one man."

During those weekends away she began feeling like a fifth wheel. At first she refused to believe it. She had an overactive imagination, she told herself. Then she'd catch those tender glances between them. He seemed light, and gay, and young. Those furrows that settled around his eyes had melted away.

Suddenly she felt old, sapped of her usual vitality. Small splinters of pain shot through her; it came to her that Bill might leave. With that thought, she knew she'd never be the same. The child-bride slowly died, cursing her innocence. She'd been securely rooted like an old oak. Now her doubts uprooted her. Bill had found her lacking; she hadn't measured up. She wasn't nearly as gifted or as young or as stimulating as. . . . Their lovemaking had been an empty gesture. She felt the metallic taste of terror. What would she do? How would she support herself? Her fears fanned her angers. Was a wife the same as having a two-car garage, a country home, and a twenty-one-inch color TV? she wondered.

She'd been marking time. She'd put herself aside without so much as a thought about her life. Soon the twins would be leaving. Bill, who'd always led with his brain, now suddenly seemed liquid and warm, perhaps even in love.

The summer was over, it was fall, and they approached winter. Her anger turned to bewilderment. His young protégée developed a metastasizing cancer and died. But not even in the darkest corner of her heart could she rejoice. She confronted Bill. "A girlish crush," he said, and dismissed the matter. Still, he grew troubled. A month, sometimes two would pass without his being even vaguely interested in sex—and then he'd release too quickly. His attention was focussed elsewhere.

Edith knew as she'd never known before that there wasn't any real Mrs. Johnston. After all, if it hadn't been for her terminal illness, perhaps that young law clerk would have been Mrs. Johnston. She also knew with an urgency that she had to make her own way.

She reached for another cigarette, lighting one on the other. "I tortured myself for months," she explained. "Should I go back to college and get my degree? His Washington appointment was in the air. I felt threatened. He'd outdistanced me. I felt an urgency to do something. Should I try something else? But what? Before I married I'd worked for a large commodities firm and I liked finance. I even flirted with the idea of becoming an executive, maybe trading. But that had been so long ago and I was too terrified to think about it now. I thought of the local day-care center. They could use me. But I also knew that I shouldn't spend the last twenty years of my life with kids.

"Finally, just to break through, I enrolled in a workshop on antiques. I'd collected some for the house. That was the beginning. I started buying and selling—like commodities. Eventually, I became so good that I opened up on Madison Avenue. It opened a whole life—traveling on my own, new people, and a new me. I began to identify as being somebody different."

She contemplated that small private life of her own, that essential self she'd shared with no one, neither Bill nor the twins. She now treated herself with a new regard, a little amazed. She was proud of her wholeness. Despite the wear and tear, she hadn't been diminished.

Several years passed. Edith had established a reputation with her antiques when another of life's jolts fell on them. It had been storming all day; outside the roads were coated with ice. It was growing dark and an eerie calm seemed to surround the house when the shrill ring of the phone broke the stillness. She was told that their daughter had met with an accident. Her young escort, driving the car, escaped without injury, but she'd been thrown from the vehicle and had suffered a concussion. Edith recalled the anguish of those days, not knowing whether their daughter would live, and if she did, not knowing whether she'd suffer permanent neurological damage. Happily, the girl survived with minor scars.

Although Edith was overjoyed at her recovery, the heavy sadness left its mark. It was another first. "It made me suddenly realize that the time we have on earth is so very short. So unpredictable." Her eyes shimmered with tears as she attempted to keep her voice from choking. "It did something else, too. It brought us all closer together. I became more than just Mom and we really started talking to each other.

"It changed my outlook on life. You really can't let a day go by without some experience, some feeling, or something happening. Something where you can learn more about yourself, even on a quiet day. It became an urgency to experience new and different kinds of things, to do something that I'd never done before. I came alive again. It was as if some part of me had died and I came alive again."

An excitement permeated her life that hadn't been there before, a curiosity and enthusiasm she'd never known. "I suddenly saw people and liked them. Not just men. Not just my husband. Not just a sexual kind of thing at all," she explained. "It was an emotional high of being able to look inside myself and seeing me as I never thought I could. I opened up. I was a warmer, more interesting person."

The more she took stock, the more she saw that she'd sealed herself into a way of life, growing old and dying, without ever having known any other way, or any other intimate relationship. Still, what she'd shelved in herself, she'd also remanded in Bill. They'd enclosed each other, each threatened by any change in the other, each dragging their own ghosts, each finding it difficult to be truly open. They clung to the familiar. Who, after all, wants to marry a stranger?

"I'm not absolutely sure why it happened," Edith said. "All I know is that something emerged in me, an enthusiasm that others began to feel and respond to. And some of those people were men."

Awakening to a single voice, abruptly and without planning to, Edith discovered as well her own sexual voice. "All of a sudden, it came to me that I was a person in my own right, that I was being seen apart from Bill. People were interested in *me*. You're seen as a separate person, and you *are* a separate person! It's an interacting chain. I wasn't only Bill's wife, and he wasn't the only man on this planet. And that feeling wasn't only sexual. All my friendships changed. I've got more and different friends. Some happen to be men and others women. But the women are different from those I'd known before. They're all doing something, not just talking about their kids or their husbands. It's a completely different kind of man and woman I'm attracted to and that

I attract. I think home and children are important to a woman, but they can't be all. At a certain age, your children leave, and that's all behind you."

As she became a more complexly textured person, others responded to her differently; this, in turn, further supported a personal devlopment. As she came in touch with that essential self, she also came in touch with an aspect of herself that had been put in the deep freeze—her sexuality.

Bill and Edith had been invited to the home of a couple they'd met on their travels. It was there that she met Ned. He was married, Bill's age, and very courtly. They discovered they had a mutual interest in antiques; they also discovered they could talk with each other. "We just drifted into it," she confided. "I was still an innocent, and didn't really realize what was happening, how I had affected him. Finally, he made direct overtures, and that's how it began."

As with any first, Edith was anxious, fearful that she'd spark something she wouldn't be able to control. She experienced pangs of guilt, and the first time they had intercourse, she was upset. Why? Why had she done it? What had she unleashed? She worried that she'd become too emotionally dependent. And in the first few months it had been like an addiction.

She experienced a sexuality she'd never known before. That disturbed her. She began to peel away coverings, exposing the layers of her psyche. Abruptly, she saw her affair for what it was—a transition, "Once I told myself, Don't go into the future with it, I could accept it for what it was. If I had done what I did at twenty-one, the forever-and-ever, one-and-only thing, I'd be getting into another jail."

She knew that her feelings for Ned had little to do with the love and affection she felt for Bill—even though Ned admittedly was a warmer and more outgoing person. She began to understand her husband with a compassion she'd never known before—perhaps because she no longer demanded that he be responsible for fulfilling her expectations.

Gradually the excitement of her first affair waned, and

they drifted out of the relationship much as they'd drifted into it. "It was a wonderful experience," Edith confided, "and I'm glad it happened. It was an intimate, warm friendship, a relationship with a different kind of man, and I got as much emotionally as I did sexually. And it's helped Bill and me. Now there can be two very desirable people in bed! I have more to give, really give, than ever before. I never knew what it was like to give sexually. And Bill and I have broken the humdrum routines of marriage; we're more stimulating to each other. I'm a woman now who has something to give and share.

"And do you know what? Bill's not just my husband anymore. He's a person. A man. My friend. I understand myself better—I'd been looking for the emotional support I'd had from my father—and I understand Bill better. I understand his infatuation with his protégée; she was more yielding. And I even understand my mother, who is undemonstrative like Bill. It's all come together. And do you know? I don't need all that emotional support so desperately anymore— now that I feel different about myself."

Edith had come out of the shadows. With an uncommon resiliency, she'd passed through a stretch of firsts—those ineluctable losses, those blows that shatter our illusions of a one-and-only, of a life everlasting, of a love affair with an all-embracing replacement for Father. She'd been swept along a bittersweet journey as if lighted by a thousand candles. The match had been put to the tallow. The first ignited the next, and the next ignited the one after that . . . illuminating the way.

On and on it goes, conflicts tumbling over contradictions like acrobats. She had tasted the sweet side of independence, and she was reluctant to give it up. She toyed with the thought of living alone. Total autonomy—that was what she wanted, she told herself.

"It was another phase," Edith quickly explained. "And I've passed that point too. Not that I ever intend to give up my sexuality, now that I've discovered it. I know that we can never be completely autonomous. You can't cut yourself off. Being me, I'll always be involved with someone. And Bill has been all for my growing up."

Edith fell into a frown. "You lose something," she said finally, "but I'm not sure it's all bad. I've come to the sad conclusion that no man can completely understand a woman. I can face it now. Until recently I couldn't handle it. Everyone is really separate and alone. And you learn that you can take care of yourself, whether it's a husband or a lover. Gradually you can be comfortable with that thought."

She had relinquished the fantasy of salvation through another—father, husband, lover—and she'd come alive. "It's a wonderful high to know yourself, and to feel that in every relationship you are yourself, that in every relationship you can take care of yourself—to know that you aren't identified only through your husband or your children. There's a big freedom in that. Maybe that's a woman's liberation."

She pulled out a tortoise-shell mirror, dabbed at her eyes with a tissue, and got ready to leave. "I amaze myself," she said.

A word about affairs in the scheme of a lifetime. The concept of an affair, single or married, has become one of those catchalls, covering a myriad of experiences from a one-night stand with a stranger to a protracted, intense relationship. For Ariel and Edith the extramarital affair was an outgrowth of a relationship that gave voice to unexplored aspects of themselves—personal and sexual. Unfortunately, some words are highly connotative, and too often we're caught up in reacting to an event with what we think it means. Labeling a sexual encounter an affair, however, really tells us nothing about the internal processes of growth, or about the woman and her personal and sexual development. To understand the woman's psychosexual journey, even partially, we cannot view the "affair" with its usual static connotations. For some women an affair signals changing attitudes about themselves as a separate, single identity. For others it is only a replay of shopworn fantasies of recoupling and rescue.

Released from old fantasies of a passive Awakening, the woman's "liberation" has been in the development of her identity, her autonomy, and her capacity for intimacy. Thus, women have started on brand new careers, resumed former interests or discovered new ones, gotten jobs, and confronted sexual disruptions as well. And the younger woman has kaleidoscoped that process from innocence and dependence to self-awareness and self-reliance.

The Hovering Shadow of Singlehood. What triggers our journey from innocence and dependence? It's been almost a commonplace for the middle-aged woman to point to her husband as the trigger to her own sexual development—but not necessarily in the way we might think. More often she speaks of the rude awakening as she's forced to face and meet the challenge of her partner as a separate sexual person.

Often that confrontation comes in the shape of the "other" woman. And so another myth goes awry: She discovers that they are not, and possibly they may never have been, as One. Isolated and set apart, she is shadowed by singlehood, and even the possibility of being single once again.

Remember Kate, whom we met in Chapter 5? When she learned her husband was sexually involved with another woman, she felt uprooted. Her identity, which had been centered in being Mrs. George Butler, her meanings, which had been to be the best mother and wife, and her values, which were deeply rooted in the commitment to her husband for better or for worse, were abruptly shaken. His life, his fate, had been her life, her fate.

Unlocked from his destiny, Kate was free to discover that she might have one of her own. She began to take hold of her life, and thought hard about that "other" woman in herself. What did it mean to be wholly woman, a person in one's own right?

She'd been hoarding herself, waiting. And while she'd waited she'd buried herself in extra poundage and indifferent

clothes that were intended to hide her body—to hide the
fact that she had a body, maybe even the fact that she was
sexual. She'd married and gone into hiding. But that's what
a married woman was supposed to do. Complacent, she'd
thought of herself as the perfect wife, docile and submissive.
But she hadn't liked herself very much. Now, she determined to change all that. No more cover-up. No more tent-
like dresses, high necklines, and long sleeves to hide in. No
more stuffing down her feelings with malteds and ice-cream
sundaes. No more junk food to feed a junky self. She resolved to lose another fifteen pounds, and did. She bought a
whole new wardrobe for a whole new person.

Shedding the layers that had protected and defined her,
she felt a renewed energy and interest in life. Whereas once
she had been contained in her husband's interests and wants,
she now was free to cultivate her own. Her work suddenly
took a turn and she became as committed to being a designer
as she'd been to being a mother and a wife. She even put a
daydream into action: She took her first trip to Europe, alone.
Her worlds increased and as they did she was enriched. Her
circle of friends grew as well. Burrowed into homemaking
and nurturing, she'd lost the art of friendship, including male
companionship, that would connect her with a diversity of
people, stimulating and satisfying a diversity of needs.

Although her changing threatened their marriage, she also
was aware that George looked at her with new eyes. Paradoxically, as she became more defined, so did his interest—in and
out of bed. Kate no longer waited for George's final decision
and final approval. She knew in a way she couldn't before
that she was responsible for her life and at least one half of
her marriage. She chose to remain married, but she was a
very different kind of married person. There now were *two*
persons, not one, living under the same roof.

Remember Maureen (Chapter 6)? She'd also been shaken
by that "other" woman. After considerable turmoil, she decided to separate, and in her newfound singlehood, to resume
her life where she'd left off. She plunged abruptly into the

single world of the young, the widowed, and the divorced.

"I left home and got a room in a very clean, bright house in the Bronx," Maureen explained. "I lived with a little old lady, a widow who rented out rooms, mostly to students, to make ends meet. I kept busy, got a job, and joined a consciousness-raising group. I didn't know where to turn for companionship, so I tried the singles scene. Well, if I'd felt mistreated in my marriage, I'd been mistreated as a human being. But as a single, with the current sex scene, I felt dehumanized. I was treated like a sex organ on legs. You know the kind of thing—'Let's leave this place. What's your name again? You're delicious. Let's go to bed.'

"Then I met André. I felt like a girl again. He was like a big brother to me—for a while. He was different from my husband. He was a contractor, and a hard-drinking man. For a while it was a ball. He was very sexual, and the child in me and the child in him got on very well. But then I realized I was replaying an old script; three months after I moved in with him, I realized what I'd done. He became very controlling and he began to drink a lot. Then one afternoon, when I'd disagreed with him about something, he smashed a clock-radio in a fit of temper. It was an overkill response. After another such scene I packed my bags and left, and felt flooded with anxiety.

"I realized that André had saved me from facing the separation anxiety of leaving my children, my home, and my husband. I had elephants at the pit of my stomach. I'd had such a feeling of failure when I left—failure of everything I'd devoted my whole life to—and André saved me. He made me feel attractive, worthwhile, and sexually all woman. But he also began strangling those first tender shoots of independence.

"He hassled me about getting married and leaving New York. I realized that I'd been so wrapped up with him that I was doing very little about myself. All the old longings about a home and being taken care of returned. But this time I couldn't say yes when so much of me said no. Sexually, I felt like never before, but that wasn't enough. I would be denying something that was so essential in me. Well, he left the state and got involved with another woman. I thought I'd die. I'd replayed the whole bit. But suddenly I knew André couldn't keep me from feeling alone or anxious. My feeling of worth had to come from me, from feeling that I could be responsible for myself. If I had gone away with him I knew that we'd both pay a terrible price, because I would have been false to myself once again. I knew I had to get myself in hand before I got seriously involved with another man."

No New Places. As Maureen and I parted I thought of one of Anne Sexton's lines: "It was a long trip with little days in it and no new places." Maureen strikingly illustrates the polarities of female sexuality, pointing to the attitudinal changes necessary if woman's sexuality is to find "new places" and a new voice. For her, sex, whether in an impersonal encounter or in a relationship, had no meaning when everything else she was melted away. She discovered that sex and love and commitment were a process, not a final goal. They were a way of being with another person intimately and also a way of being with another that allowed each other to be apart.

In a continuing string of contradictions, never before have women been so "free" and never before have our expectations of rescue and sexual fulfillment been so great. In the past, if a man was a good provider and a good father, nothing more was expected. "Liberation" has changed all that, and with the greater emphasis on instant fulfillment, some women seem more burrowed into their rescue fantasies than ever.

"What did you expect to happen?" I asked Nina, who'd been describing her first sexual encounter since her divorce. "Instant fulfillment," she replied. "Sex with my ex-husband felt as if I'd been rammed into. I expected this would be the way I always thought it was supposed to be. I met Jules on a blind date. We went to bed that first night. I expected him to bring me out. I expected his erection would reach me so deeply that I would be transformed; I wouldn't be a plain Jane anymore. I'd expected we'd both be transformed. As I look at it now, I don't think that either of us really wanted to go to bed. He probably felt it was expected, and I felt I had to prove I was a woman. I was looking for some-one to turn me on."

On being turned on. Russell Baker, a witty and sardonic essayist, recently wrote that women think of their sexual role as that of an appliance.[12] And so it appears. Accustomed to not having any sexual needs, women have been reluctant to express sexual preferences. Accustomed to a passive role, they reason it's for the other to "turn her on." Like an appliance she waits her dose of power—and we all know to whom we've relegated the power.

But woman's passivity isn't only that. It's often been a subtle blend of angers, feelings of betrayal, and broken promises. Nina was embittered by her divorce, and her passivity was not without its masked aggression. She'd been raised to believe that women should be taken care of, and that attitude was reflected in her sexual expectations as well. She resented sharing the responsibility for her own sexual plesaure. Still, in another of those paradoxes, her lack of responsibility and identity in the sexual act contributed to her lack of sexual fulfillment.

In her marriage Nina had been reluctant to identify her sexual needs and to make known what "turns her on." She'd also refused to make use of her own sexual experience and persisted in assuming that her husband "should know." Those attitudes, moreover, continued to plague her after her divorce in the expectation of an instant turn-on, a push-button response.

Sex used in place of a personal autonomy, to erase a life-time of self-doubt and low self-esteem or to prove that we measure up, becomes a focus for all the anxieties related to female performance—the fear of failure as well as the fear of success. Sex used in place of a personal identity to fill the gap of self-knowledge—know me; intuit me; turn me on— is as unrealistic as the romantic notion that only one person can fill our complex and varied needs, or that only we, in turn, can fulfill his.

Female Routes. The difference between male and female response early creates a disharmony of feeling. For women, it creates Herculean feelings of self-doubt. The woman generally is slower to respond, and her response is more finely calibrated. Too often, rather than feel a participant in her sexuality, she feels invaded, cheated, or worse still, frigid. And her partner, threatened by her lack of responsivity, is likely to compound her feelings of self-doubt. Their measuring stick, after all, until recently, has been the male's response.

With marriage and early pregnancy, some women suffer an added insult to their body image. Pregnancy, birth, and the postpartum period, as we've learned, can be times of heightened stress, and of hurts that spill over into the sexual relationship. Masters and Johnson, for example, report a decrease of female sexual desire during the first trimester of pregnancy. Settling into the routines of Shared Projects, we often settle also into the routines of sex.

As that tight little circle of nurturing begins to loosen, however, the sex that has gone underground begins to surface. We try to turn back the clock. Middle-aged women report an increase in sexual interest but a decrease in sexual activity.[13] The asynchronies proliferate. Consistent with their increased desire, interestingly, is their increased capacity for sexual release. Whether we consider the work of Kinsey in the fifties or that of Masters and Johnson in the seventies, women in their middle years (from thirty-five to sixty) report greater sexual response and release than their younger counterparts [2, 5]—despite all the talk of the "liberated" young. Only recently, however, has the sexual asynchrony surfaced as a problem. In the past, couples admitted sexual problems mostly when the husband's needs went unmet.[13]

Paradoxes. Those are the dynamics of growing up female. This is the shock of recognition and the loss of innocence: when we discover that there is no forever; when we learn that death is a reality, and that relationships change, whether we will them to or not. Paradoxically, as we let them change, we also may discover new affection and respect. We may suffer the pain of knowledge, but we suffer equally the pain of innocence. The extravagant expectation that any one person—spouse or offspring—can fulfill our dream is costly. As we blur our own identity in exchange for being loved, we blur as well the sharp limits of the other. Paradoxically, with an increasing consciousness of self, there is an increasing consciousness of the other. Bill was no more an extension of Edith than she was an appendage of his.

The paradox of paradise. Mom. How many women do we know who are affectionately called Mom by their husbands? I seem to count more among the older generation. Soon after the twins were born, Edith became Mom, not only to her children, but also to her husband. But it took a little while before she really heard it. "I'm not *your* mother," she lashed out at Bill, and then wondered what prompted her outburst. Yet, somehow she knew—the person she wanted to be was not Bill's Mom.

It was Freud who alerted us that, for some men, parenthood recapitulates their original tie with mother. The more a woman is perceived as the nurturing or controlling mother, the less likely is she to be the focus of his sexual ardor. Those are the Oedipal prohibitions. It's another version of that old joke: Why spoil good sex with marriage? Some couples report that is exactly what they do. Unhappily, the situation tends to feed on itself. The more her spouse withdraws in self-protection, the more panicked and demanding she's apt to become.

The paradox of marriage. Today, marriage and sex seem

less connected than ever before, but there also seems to be a greater marital openness and intimacy. In the past, marriage was a refuge, a source of security and an insured future— and sex, for some women, was a means of control. As we begin to experience a truer self-knowledge and self-reliance, a need for a more genuine intimacy is emerging: an intimacy in which marriage and commitment and sex are genuinely intertwined, perhaps for the first time.

Like Edith, I, too, am amazed at our regenerative powers. But why not? Aren't the French the ones who speak of the orgasm as *la petite mort*? I never really understood the reach of the term. We do die a little with each ruptured innocence. We do pay the price for that irresistible desire to know ourselves, and subsequently the other, more intimately. We take that sometimes painful passage from dependency to responsibility, from innocence to knowledge and, phoenix-like, we rise again from the ashes.

Chapter 10. / The Postponed Sexual Self

1. Beiser, H. R. "Sexual Factors in Antagonism Between Mothers and Adolescent Daughters." *Medical Aspects of Human Sexuality*, 1977, April, 32–42.
2. Masters, W. H. and V. Johnson. *Human Sexual Inadequacy*. Boston: Little, Brown, 1970.
3. Offit, A. *The Sexual Self*. Philadelphia: J. B. Lippincott Co., 1977.
4. Hite, S. *The Hite Report: A Nationwide Study on Female Sexuality*. New York: Macmillan, 1976.
5. Kinsey, A. C., W. B. Pomeroy, C. E. Martin, and P. H. Gebhard. *Sexual Behavior in the Human Female*. Philadelphia: W. B. Saunders, 1953.

6. Offit, A. "Common Causes of Female Orgasm Problems." *Medical Aspects of Human Sexuality,* 1977, August, 40–48.

7. Kaplan, H. S. and D. C. Anderson. "Sexual Revolution —The Time of the Woman." *The New York Times Magazine,* July, 1977.

8. Shope, D. F. and C. B. Broderick. "Level of Sexual Experience and Predicted Adjustment in Marriage." *Journal of Marriage and the Family,* 1967, *29,* 424– 427

9. O'Neill, N. and G. O'Neill. *Open Marriage: A New Lifestyle for Couples.* New York: M. Evans & Co., 1972.

10. Hunt, M. *The Affair.* New York: World Publishing Co., 1975.

11. Lief, H. "The Role of Sex in Marriage." *Medical Aspects of Human Sexuality,* 1976, October, 42–56.

12. Baker, R. "Turning On." *The New York Times Magazine,* September 11, 1977.

13. Huyck, H. M. "Sex and the Older Woman." In *Looking Ahead,* edited by L. Troll, J. Israel, K. Israel. New Jersey: Prentice-Hall, 1977.

11

YOU CAN DO IT:
SOURCES OF CONFIDENCE

" 'OF COURSE YOU CAN DO IT. OF COURSE YOU CAN,' MY MOTHER used to tell me when I was a girl. Even then I remember thinking, first you soft-pedal everything I do, you tell me to be modest, don't make trouble, be submissive like a good little girl should, and then you tell me, 'Of course you can do it!' Well, where am I going to get the confidence from?" Although Millie is now thirty-two, the child she'd been is with her still. She'd been a "good" girl: Pink ribbons in her hair, handkerchief pinned to her blouse, she was expectant, dreaming fairy-tale dreams. Then there was adolescence. Caught in the undertow—eager to please, eager to achieve—she felt torn, and clearly unprepared.

Roberta, presently in her mid-forties, recalls her college days. "Passionate interests? Dreams when I was in college? I didn't have any. Marriage, I thought, would be more rewarding than anything else I could have drifted into. I'd been unchanneled. In college I'd majored in math because I fell in love with a mathematician. Once I was no longer in love, math no longer interested me. I drifted, sampling a lot of different courses. There was very little that drew me. As a girl, I was free to opt out of practically anything, even college. There wasn't even any conflict about my drifting. A girl can get away with that. I hadn't arrived at anything. My husband was a rescue, I think."

Those are the female remembrances of growing up. Is it possible that we're groomed for success or failure? Can it be, as one sociologist asserts, that "women have been made instruments in their own exclusion?" [1] How can we learn to get what we want if, as teenagers, we're conflicted and, as young women, we're unfocussed? That is an apt description whether we are referring to the upper-middle, middle-middle, or working-class woman. Among the younger working-class women, for example, the value placed on personal development—the desire for further education, avocational pursuits, new skills or mastery of old ones—is small.[2]

Most women are quagmired in the subtle pulls of achievement. It isn't that we don't want to achieve; it's that achievement is frequently perceived as inimical to a personal life. And who wants to pay that price? Besides, there is little that draws us; there just doesn't seem to be anything we feel strongly enough about to pursue. We haven't been raised to think there should be. So we wait for things to happen, and if they happen, we wait for them to interest us. To generate dreams of personal glory, after all, one must have a clue that they're possible. And even if we do have a glimmer of a dream, where do we get the confidence to support it? Most women are likely to be felled by the first obstacle.

I'm neither indulging in vague generalizations nor mouthing stereotypes: Women's attitudes toward achievement have come under an impressive amount of study and documentation. In recent years there have been at least two major symposia that I'm aware of, and countless papers reporting and evaluating the results of dozens of studies.[3, 4, 5, 6]

Sex Differences: No Myths. Before we explore the unique wellsprings of confidence, let's examine the common patterns found among women and their motivation to achieve. Sex differences in our attitudes are striking, especially when we relate them to the differences in the socialization process of girls and boys.

It begins even before we're born, with such insinuating attitudes frequently expressed by women as: I'd like a boy first, to carry on the name. Or to please his daddy. Or for his daddy to play football with. Lois Wladis Hoffman recently conducted a survey, interviewing 1,500 married women under 40 and one quarter of their husbands. She reported that although most couples wanted children of each sex, the preference was clearly for boys. Furthermore, if the couple had only girls, they were likely to continue having children. The usual reasons for wanting a girl, moreover, are noteworthy. Those were: For the companionship. To dress up and fuss with. To help with the house. Because they're easier to raise—more obedient. They're yours forever. They don't stray too far—a boy you lose. They're cuter, sweeter, not as mean.[6]

In short, if girls are preferred, it is precisely for those attributes that leave little room for the development of confidence. Girls are valued for what they can *be*: Compliant and "loyal." Boys indeed enter the world with a different set of expecteds. They, in contrast, are valued for what they can *do*.

Those starkly differing parental and societal attitudes leave their mark. Take the early years: Differences in the handling of girls and boys have been observed from infancy. Girls are presumed to be the more vulnerable, despite all medical facts to the contrary. Boys, therefore, are handled more roughly and allowed more freedom for exploration. In an interesting study that Dr. Hoffman cites, mothers of four-year-olds were asked such things as at what age they thought parents should expect or permit their children to cross the street alone, use a sharp knife without supervision, or be permitted to play away from home for long periods without first telling their parents where they would be. Consistently, the mothers of boys gave younger ages than the mothers of girls—despite the fact that girls mature earlier and are less impulsive.[6]

Where *are* we going to get the confidence from? The cultural male stereotype is rooted in his early training for independence. His is the greater power to control his fate. He must be toughened; he must be reared to venture; he must be trained to cope with the competitive world. Girls are walled within narrower boundaries. Even in our fairy tales the youth travels far and wide while the damsel lies dormant in wait.

By and large we behave the way we're expected to behave. Those are the expectations that we've incorporated and translated into goals. Those are the groundings for our priorities, values, and meanings—the context of the sexual differences in our orientation toward achievement.

Success Phobias. Most of us are acquainted with Matina Horner's substantive breakthrough on the gender difference in success imagery. Females, she reported, were motivated by fear of success, males by success. Beginning in the sixties and continuing in the seventies, Dr. Horner studied the differences in college women and men. "It is clear in our data," she states, "that most of the young men and women in the samples we have tested over the past seven years still continue to evaluate themselves in terms of the dominant societal stereotype that says competition, independence, success, competence, and intellectual achievement reflect positively on mental health and masculinity, but are basically inconsistent with femininity. These young people have apparently learned, accepted, or taken it for granted that the right to master Erikson's 'outer world space' belongs to men. . . . It [is] especially difficult for a capable, achievement-oriented young woman whose sense of self-esteem includes feelings of competence or a desire for success in nontraditional areas to maintain any stable sense of identity or self-regard as a feminine woman." [7]

Dr. Horner asked college women and men, eighteen and nineteen years of age, to write a story based on the opening sentence: "After first-term finals, Anne (John) finds herself (himself) at the top of her (his) medical-school class." [8] The women were to write about Anne, the men about John. She found that significantly more women responded to the story with what she identified as "fear-of-success" imagery. Those women, it seemed, were not as fearful of achievement as such, as they were of the negative consequences of achieving. Success, they feared, might lessen their popularity and their likelihood of getting married and having children. I'm reminded of a homemaker who reflected that she was glad her career hadn't taken off—because if it had, she might have forgotten to marry! Fear of the loss of intimate relationships with men and the social rejection—going counter to what has been culturally determined as feminine—certainly are aspects of the success phobias.

That was borne out by other researchers when they changed "Anne's" story to read that she was top of her class not in medical school, but in nursing school—purportedly a "feminine" profession. With that the success stories told by women rose significantly.[5] The image of "femininity" keeps women from striving beyond the socially acceptable boundaries, even in fantasy!

Furthermore, when Horner's study was repeated by still another investigator, this time using adolescents (ages 10 to 16), asking them to write stories about *both* Anne and John, *both* sexes gave stories telling of the painful consequences for successful girls. In fact, even more boys than girls were negative about female achievement. And true to form, both sexes were equally positive in their stories about the successful boys.[5]

But that's not all. Consistent with those findings is another study in which the researcher asked high school and college women and men to read and evaluate a number of articles that were identified as having been written by women, and then those same articles were shown to another group and this time they were labeled as having been written by men. The results, unhappily, were predictable. Both sexes, regardless of the age-group, devalued the work when it was identified as the work of women. That study, I should point out, was done in 1974.[9] So much for our changing attitudes! Those attitudes speak volumes not only for men, but also, more disastrously, for women's self-image and low self-esteem.

The next step for investigation was to determine how far

down the age scale those attitudes extended. In a review of a symposium on achievement motivation, Thelma Alper cites an intriguing study of lower-middle-class and middle-middle-class children. Second to sixth graders were asked to write a story to follow this beginning: "When the report cards came out, Linda (David) had the best report card in class." Dr. Alper reports on the response of one second-grade girl who summed it all up with an elegant economy. "Linda," she wrote, "like a doy. The doy didn't like Linda. So she desided that the next time she would get an F⁺. She did. And now the boy likes her." Lest you are writhing in anguish, Thelma Alper adds: "We have hopes for this little girl on two counts: (a) She allows herself a plus on that F; and (b) she finally spells 'boy' correctly." ⁵

That's how girls learn to please. And then? Those attitudes only escalate. Consistently, the success phobias increase as the girl grows, peaking in adolescence, while they decrease in boys. Girls drop in their levels of aspiration, motivation, and achievement. Why not? Adolescence is a time when their desire for popularity is also peaking.

I don't mean to imply that boys don't crave popularity as well. We're all aware of boys' showing off, displaying their mastery. But that's just the point. Popularity for the adolescent boy is an extension of his status and power. Almost always his popularity requires an increasing independence and mastery. Such is the case in competitive sports or in academic pursuits, whether he is captain of the football team or editor of the yearbook.

A popular girl? To be popular a girl must be pleasing, and her appearance often becomes the measuring rod of her self-esteem. Remember the endless hours before the mirror, agonizing over a less than peaches and cream complexion or a flat chest, or the wrong tilt of a nose? Or, on the flip side, remember blurring past mirrors for fear of what you would see? If a girl can't be beautiful, then she must be ingratiating. Maggie graphically labeled it "bullshitting the boys."

"As a teenager, an image of *myself* in the world?" Kate

repeated my question, incredulous that I'd asked. "I had none. Not even in my twenties. In my teens I remember I had this image of myself as a shrimp. I'm only five feet tall, and all my friends were growing tall and beautiful. Then one day this boy asked me to the Prom, and he turned my life around. He said, 'Gosh, you're pretty.' And I said, 'But I'm so short!' And he laughed. 'You're not short. You're petite!' Finally, in college, I was voted The Most Good-natured, The Easiest To Get Along With, and The Class Sweetheart. It made my whole life. I worked hard at it."

A number of studies support the universality of those attitudes. Characterized as the easier to raise, a joy to their parents, girls define themselves largely in terms of relationships. We're expected to be human weathervanes, sensitively registering others' moods. But we're also expected to do well in school. We're caught in conflict: Do well, but not so well as to threaten pivotal relationships. And so there arises the tension between striving to satisfy ourselves and striving to satisfy others. Following our personal inclinations, suggests one researcher, may lead to isolation, while following the others' may lead to a loss of self.[10] Women gradually come to experience personal development and careers as antithetical to a personal life. Men have no such antipodes. Thus, some women abandon professional goals; others abandon intimate relationships and sometimes become diluted versions of men. In either case, their self-definition and their choices are derivative.

In an extensive review of the research literature, Lois Wladis Hoffman states: "Females seem to have more pronounced affiliative needs, and the affiliative motive more often influences their behavior in a variety of situations. They have less confidence in their ability to perform many tasks and are more likely to seek the help and reassurance of others. . . ." She is then moved to conclude, "It is probably too crude, but it would not be inaccurate, to generalize from the findings and say that females in the United States tend to be less aggressive, more affiliative-oriented or nurturing, more empathic, less independent in their coping style, and less motivationally pitched toward outside-the-home occupations." [6] That's the price of the "good girl" syndrome.

Woman's bind, however, doesn't melt away with the end of her academic years. More often it becomes a pervasive life-style in her work and even in her marriage. In the work world we're all aware of the "loyal" worker syndrome, with her steadfast commitment to one boss, or to a corporate identity. Those are women who are expected to be as gentle as kittens with the boss, and as aggressive as crusaders with the corporate interests—the Rosemary Woods of industry.

Consider the fundamental difference between men and women in their response to implied criticism. In one study, a group of high school seniors, all of approximately equal ability, were tested and deliberately scored too low. Then they were interviewed and asked to explain their "failure." Boys tended to question the results—surer of their own ability —and pressed the interviewer for an explanation. In contrast, girls accepted the low evaluation and were inclined to blame themselves.[11] Those attitudes, moreover, remain constant. In *The Managerial Woman*, authors Hennig and Jardim state: "Ask a woman and ask a man: 'When your work is criticized, how do you react?' On the average, far more women blame themselves." [12]

Even among women who achieve, the pattern of success runs pretty much along the same route. By and large, the successful woman either confines herself to the "traditional" female occupations, or her achievement is haphazard and by chance. In the words of one distinguished scientist: "I'm in the area of research that I'm in as much by luck as by anything else." By that she didn't mean the unpredictability of scientific discovery, but rather her early unfocussed, ambivalent commitment. Still, it also is true that all the luck in the world can't make a difference in our lives if we're not there to embrace it. What makes the difference, it seems to me, between achievers and nonachievers, all else being equal, is that the successful woman is open and available to her environment. She may not always make things happen like her male counterpart, but indeed she is there when it's happening.

Thus, the female success phobias have been observed as early as the first grades of school, peaking in adolescence and making their inroads in later academic and occupational achievements. Until well into their middle years, women don't feel worthy of being accepted for *who* they are, but only for *what* they are to others—an aggregate of functions. With the passing years, and a stretch of central transitional events, the woman's self-image slowly shifts from her relationship to others to her own abilities and feelings. One study suggests that the separation from children can be viewed in that light. Freed from the daily obligations and nurturance responsibilities, women may finally feel that they can be more readily accepted for who they are.[2]

Enough of the universal patterns of women and achievement. In order to better understand the woman's situation, we must also take into account the flip side. Fear-of-success imagery is at best a diagnostic tool, like taking someone's blood pressure—one of those classifications that is effective for identifying the state of our health. But it falls short in illuminating how some women *do* achieve, how those immobilizing fears and tensions concerning achievement and autonomy are circumvented or rechanneled. Let's consider, then, the women who've achieved, some sooner, some later.

YOU CAN DO IT!

Take a moment and try to remember. Can you recall the implicit or explicit messages you grew up with concerning achievement? Can you remember what fired or dampened your spirit to do? Was it You Can Do It? You *Have* To Do It? You Can Do It *But?* Or, You Can Do It Only *Through* a Man?

I asked that question to women who were exclusively homemakers, to women who were late bloomers, and to women who launched on careers first and later married. You may recall some who, in their middle years, abruptly and seemingly from nowhere, burst into newfound interests and careers, and others who launched on careers first. They too have been exposed to the prevailing social stereotypes, and some even swallowed them for a time. Yet somewhere they found the confidence to change and to achieve.

The Parental Mold. Parents spin us off, beginning our process of self-definition, identifying aspects of ourselves. They are those voices out of the past which, to paraphrase Virginia Woolf, don't leave us alone but are at us, like "some conscientious governess," abjuring us.[13]

You remember the kind of thing: Elaine is a good girl, not like Bill—he's a daredevil—but he's a boy, after all. Or Carol is the brainy one, Dee is the beauty. Or Maureen is good-natured and considerate, Jason is mean. Those are the identification tags. They carry, in part, the parental messages of expectations, which are incorporated and shape our self-image, our means of identifying ourselves. And at this point, it's of little significance which comes first, the child or the tag.

Parents give us the first authoritative picture of the world and of ourselves in that world. In so doing they also communicate what's possible. It's important, therefore, that we sort out, even incompletely, those dialectical supports that nurture woman's image of an achiever, a doer, a prime mover.

Two central strands have been observed in the family constellation of women who've achieved, and in the parental messages that grounded their motivation for success.

Consider family patterns. Consistent with what we've learned about the gender differences in the socialization process, women who've achieved have not been raised with the common social stereotypes. Those women are more likely to be without siblings, or to have one or more sisters, but no brothers. In such cases the father, in particular, tends to give his daughter(s) the place usually reserved for the boy of the family. Or, if the successful woman had a male sibling, either she was the firstborn, garnering her father's attention, or the father was indifferent and sometimes openly hostile to his son, favoring her position as the "doer."

The other pivotal influence is the mother. Despite the admonition that maternal deprivation will be the fate of the child whose mother works, working mothers are more likely to have working daughters who achieve. The woman who is actively participating and responsible in the home and in the world breaks the stereotype of what a woman is supposed to do. Despite the "after the children are grown" rationalizations, the image of a working mother has been especially beneficent during adolescence, when a girl's concerns with femininity increase. How a girl looks upon femininity and competence is affected by her mother's self-image and values.[14]

Moreover, mother's image lingers. In a study of women psychiatrists—who, by the way, also limit their achievement relative to their male colleagues—those women who had working mothers also had a more positive esteem for women. Furthermore, over half the women (57 percent, as compared to 29 percent of the men) had professional mothers.[15] There is evidence that mother's working has small effect on the male offspring, while it has a significant influence on the girl. By the same token, the father's position, per se, has little impact on his daughter.

Another survey of women in politics showed similar trends, with those women also limiting their goals, hesitant to aim for the high posts. When 800 high school seniors were surveyed, however, it was reported that among the girls whose mothers held high-status jobs five times as many girls were strongly inclined toward politics as those whose mothers either didn't work or held nonprestigious jobs.[16]

Either or both family patternings insure a training for independence that bodes well for the girl's image of woman as competent and doer. Together with the family patterning is also the implicit and/or explicit parental message about achievement. For example, if achievement for the parents has meant making a good marriage—You Can Do It Only Through a Man—then almost always that daughter will marry, either bypassing any other goals or abandoning them. Prospects mean that *you* can't. On the other hand, if the parental messages have been You Can Do It, or even You *Have* To Do It, or You Can Do It *But,* they mean that *you* are expected to achieve.

Consider some of the women we've already encountered. Elaine abruptly launched into a career after five children and two marriages. She explained: "It's ironic. There was just my younger brother and me, and my brother was programmed to misbehave. He did. So my father, who was only involved with his business anyway, blotted him out. I was programmed to behave and to do well in school. I did. But that inhibited me for a long, long time. When I was fourteen, my father suddenly took an interest in me. He came home one night and announced that he wanted me to go abroad to study. The sudden thrust into independence terrified me. I backed away, but it planted a seed. The following year I did go away to school in the States and there I blossomed, at least socially and as far as schoolwork was concerned. And my brother seemed to drift." That tender image of herself as an achiever, however, remained dormant until after she had established a permanent relationship in marriage.

Take Edith. After years of homemaking and rearing children, she "mysteriously" burst into a newfound self and a career. I'd asked her where her get-up-and-go had sprung from. She explained, stringing out her thoughts: "My husband was very definite when it came to women. He wasn't about to be controlled by me, as his mother had tried to do. We were married fifteen years before I realized that he held the upper hand. I'd been just his wife, taking care of things. And really Bill wasn't to blame. That's the way he'd been raised. He was to bring home the paycheck, be a success, and I was to manage behind-the-scenes.

"But as time passed we had less and less to say to each other. I was living a fishbowl existence and it got to me. You see

I was brought up in a family of girls where my father and my mother both worked. We had a small-town family business and my mother was as responsible for the family finances as my father. The truth is that she did all my father's bookkeeping and accounting. She had a very sharp mind. My father was a good businessman but I don't think he was as keen as my mother."

Reaching for a cigarette, she tilted her head. "I didn't like my mother," Edith said, letting the words jam into each other. "But only now can I see it. She was much more of an influence than I've ever given her credit for. Now I realize I owe her more of a tribute than I ever gave her. Growing up, I was closer to my father and wanted to be more like him. He was warm and people liked him. My mother was too forceful; I resented her strong voice about what I should and shouldn't do. But throughout her life she showed strength, intelligence, and determination. And I saw something in her that I felt I had to have, but it never occurred to me that I was developing it along the way. Only later I found that I had some of her strength, and of her forcefulness too, I'm afraid. It could have been my downfall, but it meant my survival. I couldn't let myself be swallowed up by my husband or be consumed by his life. I knew inside that if I did, I'd never get out from under. If I hadn't some of my mother in me, I couldn't have survived with the man I'm married to, and also go on to develop myself.

"My mother was very disappointed that I didn't finish my degree. I never really understood her; she had deep yearnings, but I'm not sure what they were. She taught Sunday school, and was a religious woman. But when I asked for dancing lessons, which were frowned on, she not only took me to dancing school, but she made me a beautiful costume of pink satin and sequins. I can still see it. She showed me how to stand on my own."

And then there is Carol, who was the middle child in a family of three girls. She has a Ph.D. in physics, has been actively engaged in a career since the age of twenty, and married in her thirties. Carol described her father as a self-made man, a man who put himself through school to become a country teacher. Carol reflected: "We weren't the kind of family that would automatically go to college, but my father made a tremendous commitment to his girls, despite the fact that he didn't have a son. Both he and my mother sacrificed and committed themselves to giving us an education. They always stood behind me, no matter what I did or wanted to do. I could commit murder, I think, and they'd be there for me. My mother spent her whole life working for her girls, and if it was a question of whether she ate or we ate—we ate. Although I'm more like my mother in temperament, she's a distant person; my father had a tremendous influence on me. All my life from the time I was four my father would go over my lessons. He'd say: 'You can be a success. You can do it. I'm going to help you.' And he did."

For Carol, both parents set an example by their own lives of sacrifice and achievement. Although her mother wasn't an educated person, the parents shared a unity of purpose. Both communicated determination, perseverance, and support. Moreover, the girls received particular attention from their father. All were active in sports, for example, and one sister became a champion athlete. Carol, who was tagged "the brainy one," of course, set her sights to achieve academically. (More on that later.)

The father's role in women's lives is noteworthy. Presenting us with the *fait accompli* of success, one study of twenty-five top women executives—all company presidents or vice presidents—describes them as generally only children, or first-born, raised by their fathers without the usual sexual stereotyping.[12] The father's occupation, per se, may be unimportant to his daughter's achievement motivation, but his presence is not—especially in the realm of mastery. That is strongly suggested by an innovative group of researchers who weren't satisfied with the common parental reports of "we treat all our children equally." They set up an experimental situation where parents, placed in a classroom situation with their preschoolers, were observed. Although both girls and boys are expected to do well in school, some significant differences in the fathers' behavior toward the pressure to achieve were recorded. "The fathers of boys were more concerned with the child's achievement and emphasized the cognitive aspects of the teaching situation, while the fathers of girls appeared to be more attuned to the interpersonal aspects of the situation and were less concerned with performance." [6] The researchers suggest that we've underestimated the role of the father, particularly in the cognitive achievement of his daughter. Related to that is the fact that the father of one or more daughters, but no sons, in developing expectations for the girl as if she were a boy, has given her the impetus to achieve. Similar differences have been reported in terms of parents' goals for their children. A significantly greater number of fathers will give career and occupational goals for their sons as compared to their daughters.[6]

Can it be, I wondered, that the mother's role as the primary socializer of her children is more strongly felt in training them for independence, and the father's role in training them for cognitive achievement, for mastery, and for self-esteem? And aren't mastery and autonomy the seminal ingredients of achievement? And aren't focus, channeling, and confidence the humble beginnings of that journey?

With those questions swimming in my head, I turned to Millie and listened. A contemporary woman, she is fresh from a muddle of conflict, still laboring with the traditional prohibitions. And she is also of the generation that seems to experience and to cope with those binds of achievement sooner.

A Voice of Her Own. Remember Millie's Life Line? Round and round it went, in ever-expanding spaces. In college Millie was unfocussed; she knew she was going to marry Don. After she married, as her husband gradually became immersed in his career and her little daughter started nursery school, she found herself thrown more and more on her own resources. It was then that she realized that living in a dollhouse existence was not enough. It also was then that her early interest in the theater reemerged—and, with it, the traditional conflicts.

Still, in her early thirties, Millie decided to pursue her former passion, theater. Where did she get the confidence from? What was it that contributed to her ambivalence about achievement and also eventually sparked her achieving?

At lunch, Millie sat condensed into herself. Compact, she took up as little room as possible. She dropped her eyes to her salad and gave it a weak stab. "You've picked the right week for us to talk," she said finally. "It's been hectic with Tabby, who fell and broke her tooth, and Don, who was away, and my trying to do things that I want to do too. There are times when. . . ." She let her voice trail, and made another attempt to down her lunch. "There are times when, well, when this gets to me, and I think that maybe I shouldn't have started the whole thing. Maybe I should quit and stay home like my mother. It would be a lot easier."

The eldest of two daughters, Millie had been tagged the docile, considerate one; her sister had been labeled the rebel. She spoke again, arguing those internal voices. "The trouble is that I feel guilty in leaving Tabby so much to do what I want to do. I have all the responsibility for her. Don knows how I feel, but he has his career to think of. He's been told that he's slated for the top. Besides, he thinks it's great that I do as much as I do, and he tells me I shouldn't worry so much about Tabby."

This Is the Way It's Done. In an attempt to exorcise those nagging voices, Millie began to rethink her life. She could still hear her mother, disapproving, looking down on women who'd leave their children in order to work—even if they had to. "We don't leave you with baby-sitters," her mother used to say. "We want you with us." And so Millie grew, kept close to the hearth, given very little opportunity to venture and explore.

"It's hard to get her out of my mind—even though I know I shouldn't be feeling guilty. That's what my guilt is from," Millie explained, reassuring herself. That, I thought, and striving to be a "better" mother than her mother.

As if answering my unspoken, inevitable next question, she continued: "I really want to be a better mother than my mother. I'm glad I have a closer relationship with Tabby. I hope she doesn't feel about me as I feel about my mother. I've always envied girls who've had a close relationship with their mothers because it's so very special. I hope I can do it. I think I can.

"My mother? She's harder to figure out than my father. She was . . . I should be completely honest with you . . . she was terribly overprotective. And still is. She encouraged me to be dependent on her and didn't allow me to assume responsibility that I was perfectly capable of assuming. She was *always* there. If I'd forget my homework, instead of letting me face the consequences, she was right on the phone, smoothing things over with the teacher. She kept that up until I went away to college. Until she couldn't get at me anymore. So I learned to grow up. I only realized what abilities I had the past few years when I saw other people's reaction to me," she explained. "They would tell me I was capable of more. Somehow I don't entirely believe it.

"And I still don't know how my mother really feels about me. She still makes me feel incompetent. She'll say she's proud of me but . . . I wonder if she isn't a little jealous. She hasn't done anything with *her* life. And she'll say things like: 'Well, you wouldn't have all the problems you have if you'd stay home like *I* did. You wouldn't get yourself in those messes.'"

Caught in a common double bind, Millie grew with a maternal message that told her: "Of course you can do it, but let me do it for you." In infantilizing her daughter, Millie's mother not only deprived her of the necessary independence for achievement, but she also implied: "Do, but not so well as to overreach me. Of course you can do it, but I can do it better." That's hardly the sort of message that fires self-confidence.

Going away to college proved a boon. It offered Millie other ways of seeing herself. "If I hadn't read all I did in school," she confided, "gone away and had friends who saw me differently, my mother's attitude of seeing the worst might have gotten to me."

At college she'd majored in English literature. Soon after graduation, she married and worked as a secretary until Tabby was born. Still, as long as she could remember she'd been interested in the theater. She'd gone the route of grade-school, church, high-school, and college drama clubs. But she only toyed with the idea of acting; she never seriously entertained the possibility. It had been one of those fragile dreams she hadn't dared acknowledge. She lacked the confidence, she explained. It just hadn't been the image she had of herself.

Nobody Ever Told Me, You Can Do It! "I felt I had the wrong temperament to be a performer. I get terrible stage fright. I thought I shouldn't consider it. I was just too young—not in age, but in outlook. *Nobody ever told me that I should be an actress, so I thought I just better not.* I'll keep it as a hobby. A serious hobby.

"My parents, my mother especially, really thought . . . I guess they thought I wasn't strong enough. Or something like that. I don't know. It's not exactly what was said. Maybe it was the impression I got. So I thought I didn't have it. My mother used to say I was a very pliable child, no trouble at all. What I was supposed to be, what I was told, and what I had stirrings of, the real me hidden someplace, I just never found it . . . until now."

In the past few weeks Millie had auditioned for a supporting role in a leading theater production and gotten it, after competing with several seasoned professionals.

Where did she muster the drive to pursue her dream?

My Father Expected a Lot of Me! "My mother ran things," Millie was saying. "On the outside my father can seem harsher; he was impatient with us as children. But it masks a very sensitive man underneath. For good or bad, I admired and was influenced by him a lot. He's a self-made man. He put himself through high school and college. He's bright. He had to overcome a lot of problems. *He made something of his life.* My father expected a lot of me. And if he knew I could deliver, he expected even more.

"I think he's proud of me—my accomplishments. He's happy with what I'm doing even though he feels compelled to soft-pedal it. He likes the fact that *I'm making something of myself.*

"And, you know, as guilty as I feel, I know I'm a happier person than my mother. And Tabby might suffer the results if I didn't have my work, as I did with my mother. I hope when she's a little older she'll respect me for having gone out and done as much as I could with my life."

Exorcising Mother's Voice. "So what should I do?" Millie asked. "Do I stay home and provide a cozy nest for Don and Tabby? Or do I get the guts to go out and do what I feel is this nagging urge to see what I can do with my life? I'm torn between wanting to strike out on my own, and doubting that I can really do it. I get so mad. I tell myself: Don't be silly, *you can do it. Of course you can.* Quit hiding." Our eyes met. A slow smile spread across her face—the first all day.

Her mother's values and priorities were wearing thin, yet they threatened to swamp her every time they talked. Clearly Millie was in transition. She was rethinking those attitudes she'd been raised with, trying them for size. And she was exploring the new, knowing full well that it all was still too new and untried to feel solidly grounded.

The child in her had been incubating hurts and resentments all these years and suddenly they were released, unedited and unlicensed. "I didn't know that that was going to be part of my twenties," she reflected, "having all that anger toward my parents. I suppose I had to get it out, recognize that it was there, before I could start to do something with my life."

Millie puzzled, then sorted and sifted herself out. And as she deepened, so did the image of her mother. She explained: "I would never call my mother a weak woman. She's a strong personality and she's put up with a lot. She's a determined person. She must have shown me how to be strong, although I don't exactly know how she did it."

Although Millie possesses the usual female ambivalence about achievement, she also possesses the urgency to achieve. Despite her parents' You Can Do It But . . . their silent models communicated strength and determination. Her father had shown her that it was possible to be "self-made," and that he expected a lot of her as well, which, after all, is a vote of confidence.

And her mother? As we listen to Millie, she suggests an intriguing possibility. Millie certainly hadn't identified wholesale with her mother, but she had identified with certain aspects of her mother's behavior. As a child she'd reacted essentially to mother-as-overprotective; mother-as-controlling; mother-as-rival; mother-as-hausfrau. As she grew in her own sense of herself, she was able to see that mother was also mother-as-determined—the source of her own indomitable will. Thus, it isn't enough to say that we do, or don't, identify with our mothers; rather we need to look to what aspects of our mother's behavior we identify with. That, it seems to me, makes the difference between a dried-out or a renewed source of confidence—those roots of strength and independence that are there when we need them most.

Mother's Image. Clearly mothers have exposed us not only to multiple messages about achievement, but also to multiple images of what a woman is supposed to be. If in one light they've deprived us of confidence and independence, in another they've also been the source of our salvation. We've focussed too much, to our own diminishment, on mother-as-hausfrau and not enough on mother-as-person.

Even our most traditional mothers have aspects of nonconformity and independence to bolster their daughters. If we look back at Edith's mother, we see that despite the fact that she was bred in a small, straitlaced community where dancing was frowned upon, she not only saw to it that her daughter took dancing lessons, but she made her a costume as well. In symbol and in reality, Edith's mother had shown her how to stand on her own two feet. Edith observed: "We all have facets in our person. I understand that now. And when life was rough for me, I wasn't lost. I had something within me to cling to. My mother showed me how to be strong. I know that if this is the time in my life for me to be strong and a hard-nosed businesswoman, *I can do that too!*" Edith discovered that mother-as-too-forceful and mother-as-homemaker was also mother-as-independent-thinker.

I was interested to find the women's personal reflections supported in another context by psychologists Katz and Shapiro, who wrote: "In cases which we have seen, professional women with mothers who were exclusively housewives did not identify wholesale with the woman-as-housewife, but rather with part aspects of the mother such as woman-as-perfectionist, woman-as-competent worker, woman-as-follower. In some cases, these women unconsciously identified with the mother's unrealized, sometimes vague longings for a professional life. There is evidence that the mother's own yearnings, in contradiction to her actual achievements, play an influential part in the formation of the ego ideal. Some of the women were consciously motivated by a wish *not* to be like mother-the-housewife, although they were unconflicted about identifying with her in certain other respects." [17]

Anaïs Nin writes in her diary: "We receive a fatal imprint in childhood, at the time of our greatest plasticity, of our passive impressionism, of our helplessness before suggestion. In no period has the role of the parent loomed so immense, because we have recognized the determinism, but at the same time an exaggeration in the size of the Enormous Parent does not need to be permanent and irretrievable.

"If they gave us handicaps, they also gave us their courage, their obstinacy, their sacrifices, their moments of strength. . . . We cannot forever await from them their sanction to mature, to impose on them our own truths, to resist or perhaps to defeat them in our necessity to gain strength." [18] And if, in our eyes, mother becomes less of a cardboard figure and more fully a person, can daughter be far behind?

Training for Independence. Separating from mother is a first step toward independence. It is mother who first, consciously or unconsciously, supports or inhibits our strivings as infants. It is she, after all, who responds to those very first steps—actual and metaphorical—that we take, moving away from her: the beginning steps of the process of individuation.

The significance of the quality of our separating, of the loosening of those early symbiotic bonds, has long been recognized in psychoanalytic circles.[19] Some believe that the nature and outcome of the early separation even determines our subsequent experiences with all kinds of separations.[20] Recently, however, we've begun to reexamine that process and to relate it significantly to the development of independence, as well as to those ambivalences about "standing on our own two feet."

The motivating force toward independence is the natural maturational demand. As our muscles strengthen, we begin to hold ourselves up, to crawl, to stand, and soon to take our first steps. If, as we do, we encounter mother's anxiously clenched hand or furrowed brow, we begin to perceive separation as threatening to our relationship. And if, each time we venture, we receive repeated communications of ambivalence, those perceptions become ingrained. Overtly, the child may experience the pressure to do, to perform, and to achieve—You Can Do It; covertly, she may also experience the BUT—like, But Let Me Be Number One, or But Don't Leave Me. . . .

Moreover, in adolescence, when strivings for independence increase, so do our ambivalences—if independence has carried with it the threat of incurring mother's displeasure, anxiety, or envy. For the boy, mother's role is not quite so crucial. If she does not support his strivings for independence, after all, society does.

Training for Mastery There is, as we've learned, an accumulation of evidence that the father's role carries greater weight in the daughter's motivation for performance and mastery. At any rate, that appears to be the current state of affairs, with the usual divisions of labor being that the mother is the homemaker and the father is the breadwinner. That too will change, I suspect, as more and more mothers also achieve an occupational identity.

Double messages in child rearing, however, are not the exclusive domain of mothers. Fathers, too, give off their share. Although the father may communicate a feeling of worth to his girl, he also may entrap her in a lifelong bondage. Seeking the unconditional love of the child, which his wife cannot possibly give, he subtly begins to use the daughter as his unconscious ally.

The symptoms of that relationship are replayed again and again by the kind of "loyal" female employee who remains twenty years with one firm, patiently taking those pygmy steps up the executive ladder—or the woman who enters one of those protracted affairs with her married boss because he is misunderstood by a "stupid" wife. What has been identified euphemistically as loyalty and devotion can just as easily be interpreted as the daughter's willing bondage to a seductive father.

Mothers and fathers both contribute to the later symptoms of success phobias as they subvert their daughter's motivation for independence and mastery—the central ingredients of achievement. Interestingly, women who've perceived their parents as controlling, restrictive, and overprotective are more likely to become homemakers. Moreover, parental rivalry or hostility has been reported as a central factor in instilling a fear of competition, independence, and success. And, unfortunately, homemaking as such is perceived by many women as a situation in which independence, competition, and achievement can be avoided.[21]

That's the assumption, at any rate. Our lives, however, are not quite so simple. Female performance anxieties—especially when the woman feels pulled between satisfying herself and satisfying the other, between personal achievement and homemaking—seem to be a pervasive characteristic. Even though some research studies suggest that women can permit themselves the fantasy of success in "feminine" occupations, in actual performance we're likely to see the same patterns of fear, whatever the occupation. Fear of achievement, independence, and mastery colors the many aspects of our lives. Again and again I've seen homemakers, for example, with similarly strong doubts about their performance as homemakers!

Fear of autonomy is a central concept not only in understanding woman's fear of success in achievement, but also in understanding her fears in marriage. One woman, a homemaker, is a striking illustration. She described in considerable detail the fits of anxiety and self-doubts she experiences every time she's forced to entertain—certainly a central performance for any homemaker. "I avoid having people over if I can. Maybe we have people for dinner twice a year, and then the house is full of panic. Last week I had to invite some of my husband's business associates. Well, my mother was on the phone every minute, telling me everything that could go wrong. Time the turkey so it won't be too dry. Take the ice cream out of the freezer a half hour before dinner so it won't be too frozen. The laugh is that as a kid I think I remember people coming to dinner just once! It was awful."

How was she to build the confidence to master the homemaking skills? Reared in a home that communicated panic, where guests seldom set foot, she feared being a carbon copy of her mother. And sensing her mother's rivalry, she also feared being "better" than her mother. Indeed, woman's scripting has turned words like competence, independence, assertion into masculine words and values. Assertion as a female value, for example, was perceived by a group of lower-middle-class women as unacceptable to the central function of motherhood. On the other hand, the complete endorsement of the traditional feminine role, with the passing years, was associated with feelings of unacceptability about oneself.[2]

Wending Our Way. If we haven't been groomed for achievement, how can we assume responsibility for achieving? True, women have been anchored by the other, and anchors keep us stationed—like those that label us a "joy" to our parents and that reward us for our passivity, or those that leave us unrewarded—Let Me Do It For You; I Can Do It Better. Rewarded or unrewarded, women are pretty much in the same stew.

Still, as we've seen, achievement is a mix of many ingredients, and it must be dealt with on its many fronts—in attitudes and in action. There is need, to begin, for fundamental change in women's attitudes. That doesn't negate the need for political and social action. But I am concerned that in our enthusiasm for changing the external images, we blur over the need for changing the internal images as well. Over the years, I've been with too many women of strong talents who've been too fear-ridden to move toward even the smallest opportunities. No doubt our negative internal images have been exacerbated by the external stereotypes, but as some women change so will our social and political ecology. And as the social and political climate changes, so will some women.

It isn't easy; it's necessary. Women have been reared in concerns that offer small room to stretch. We're not stimulated to stir, and most of us haven't had even the slightest conflict about not stirring. If we haven't been among the fortunate few who've been groomed for achievement, then we must learn to groom ourselves.

Where to begin? We begin by deepening our self-knowledge; by tapping the sources of confidence; by looking around us at other women; by setting up small goals. Those common female patterns of self-doubt, as we'll learn, are not predictions, nor are they irreversible. Nor, in order to achieve, do we have to lose our femaleness. I'm not suggesting that we think like men, but rather that we use our special feminine proclivities to work for us, to include rather than exclude us.

Let's begin by rehearsing what's possible—a dream of ourselves in the world. If we had been born with an attitude of I Can Do It, that's precisely what we would have—an attitude of possibility, an outlook that positions us squarely in the process of becoming. This came through clearly in an exchange I had with a colleague—a male, of course. "Ferruccio, who would you be without your career?" I asked. "The possibility of another career," he said, quick as a finger snap, adding, "My grandmother used to say, 'One door closes and a window opens.' "

If, like our male counterparts, we haven't been groomed in the attitude of "possibility," how can we achieve it? Let's open still another door, another untapped storehouse: daydreaming. Are you one of those women who feels guilty about daydreaming? Who feels it's a waste of time? Well, don't. Where but in daydreams do we encounter the ultimate in possibility? Where but in the power of dreams?

Chapter 11. / You Can Do It:
Sources of Confidence

1. Epstein, C. F. "Tracking and Careers: The Case of
   Women in American Society." In *The Radcliffe
   Symposium: The Seven Ages of Woman: Multiple
   Roles of the Educated Woman in a Changing Soci-
   ety.* Nov. 11, 1972.
2. Lowenthal, M., M. Thurnher, D. Chiriboga, *et al. Four
   Stages of Life: A Comparative Study of Women and
   Men Facing Transitions.* San Francisco: Jossey-Bass
   Behavioral Science Series, 1975.
3. *The Radcliffe Symposium: The Seven Ages of Woman:
   Multiple Roles of the Educated Woman in a Changing Society.* Nov. 11, 1972. New York: Radcliffe
   Club of New York.
4. Symposium: *American Educational Research Association.* Sex differences in achievement motivation and
   achievement behavior. Washington, D.C., April,
   1975.
5. Alper, T. "Where Are We Now?" Discussion of papers
   presented in the 1975 AERA Symposium on sex differences in achievement motivation and achievement behavior. *Psychology of Women Quarterly, 1,*
   1977, 294–303.
6. Hoffman, L. Wladis. "Changes in Family Roles, Socialization and Sex Differences." *American Psychologist,
   32,* 1977, 644–657.
7. Horner, M. S. "Why Women Fear Success: Careers—
   Other Aspects." *The Radcliffe Symposium: The
   Seven Ages of Women.* Nov. 11, 1972.
8. Horner, M. S. Sex differences in achievement motivation
   and performance in competitive and noncompetitive
   situations. (Doctoral dissertation, University of
   Michigan, 1968.) *Dissertation Abstracts International,* 1969, *30,* 407B.

9. Mischel, H. N. "Sex Bias in the Evaluation of Professional Achievements." *Journal of Educational Psychology*, 1974, *66*, 157–166.

10. Schnitzer, P. K. "The Motive to Avoid Success: Exploring the Nature of the Fear." *Psychology of Women Quarterly*, *1*, 1977, 273–282.

11. Maccoby, E. E., and C. N. Jacklin. *The Psychology of Sex Differences*. California: Stanford University Press, 1974

12. Hennig, M., and A. Jardim. *The Managerial Woman*. New York: Anchor Press/Doubleday, 1977.

13. Woolf, V. *A Room of One's Own*. New York: Harcourt, Brace & World, 1957.

14. Baruch, G. K. "Girls Who Perceive Themselves as Competent: Some Antecedents and Correlates." *Psychology of Women Quarterly*, *1*, 1976, 38–49.

15. Rosenbaum, M., and I. Ascher. A survey reported in *Psychiatric News*, October 1, 1976.

16. A survey report—special to *The New York Times*, October 1, 1975.

17. Katz, C., and R. Shapiro. "Sex-role Identification and Success." *Contemporary Psychoanalysis*, 1976, *2*, 251–257.

18. Nin, A. *The Diary of Anaïs Nin: Volume V*. New York: Harcourt Brace Jovanovich, 1974.

19. Mahler, M. *On Human Symbiosis and the Vicissitudes of Individuation*. Vol. 1, New York: International Universities Press, 1968.

20. Kauff, P. F. "The Termination Process: Its Relationship to the Separation-Individuation Phase of Development." *International Journal of Group Psychotherapy*, *27*, 1977, 3–18.

21. Kriger, C. F. Need achievement and perceived parental child-rearing attitudes of career women and homemakers. *Dissertation Abstracts International*, 1972, *32*, (11-B), 6621.

12

DAYDREAMING:
A POWER SOURCE

"WHAT TO DO? NOTHING DRAWS ME. WHAT TO DO? NOBODY cares anyway," she moans. "My husband and children certainly don't care what I do. My parents never did. When I was little they wanted me to be 'good'; when I grew up, they wanted me to be 'settled.' I'm interested in so many things —gardening, politics, interior decorating, writing. . . . I *start* a lot of thing and then. . . . Maybe I'm lazy."

"Stop nagging yourself," I say. "Put your energies to better use and daydream instead."

"Daydream?"

Mastery and success are skills. With self-confidence, we're part of the way to getting what we want. But self-confidence is only part of it. To get what we want, we must *know* what we want. We need to establish our priorities and to take a hard look at what's important to us. I don't mean what we think should be important. I mean what those things are that you *do* that make you feel whole, integrating and embodying the many different aspects of you. What ways are you living your life to enhance rather than diminish all of who you are?

To cite some true-to-life female predicaments: If you have a very important job interview to prepare for and a friend phones to invite you to dinner, what do you do? Are you tempted? Do you work off any anxiety by spreading yourself thin? Or do you zero in on the task and focus your energies? If you're finally back at school and a swarm of term papers are due and a windfall comes your way—a three-week holiday with your lover or husband—what do you do? If you like to kick off your shoes, watch the six o'clock news, and daydream about whether that attractive fellow you met will phone, when you get home from work at night, are you irked when your male colleague comes in the following morning with the solution to the problem that had you stumped? Do you stop to wonder?

Perhaps it's time for all of us to wonder what we've been doing, and also about what *he*'s been doing. In most instances, not knowing what we want to do means that we also don't know what we want. Often it's easier not to know. Knowing brings with it the responsibility of choice and of actualizing our choice—and for women that almost always brings the threat of loss. One woman explained it simply. "Making a choice," she said, "always makes me anxious, because it means ruling out a whole lot of other choices."

Knowledge again comes with a price. In acknowledging our wants, we're vulnerable. We're exposed to not getting what we want—the rejections; and we're exposed to getting what we want—the commitments and the risk-taking.

One fateful evening when I fell into daydreaming that the *Atlantic Monthly* had accepted one of my short stories, I knew with a sure gut-knowledge, even then, that I'd let loose a thousand hornets. My identity, after all, had been rooted in being a psychotherapist, not a writer. I was risking laying bare my dream, trying to achieve it, and possibly failing to. I exposed myself to the questioning of family, colleagues, and friends. I was exposed to the arduous labor of learning a new craft, to tons of rejection slips, and to an avalanche of self-doubt.

Better not to know, not to get the whole thing started, we tell ourselves, for who knows where it will end? Happily, the human psyche is reckless and seems to have a natural tendency to seek knowledge—even if the first inklings of that knowledge often have to sneak in the back door. Just as our parents, implicitly or explicitly, told us *how* to do or not to do, our daydreaming is there for us, cueing us in to *what* to do.

We've all heard stories about the girl who grew up to find

herself in a Broadway role like the ones she had daydreamed about. Or the girl who dreamed of becoming a scientist someday, and did. Admittedly, those are the more flamboyant dreams. But dreams of achievement, even those as misty as the one that goes When I grow up I'm going to be Somebody, have produced wonders.

Getting to Know You: Daydreaming? The usual response to my suggestion to start daydreaming is an incredulous silence, followed by an outpouring of protestations. "Daydream? That's been my problem. A dream world is where I've lived! I never got it together. I spent too much of my life daydreaming." Or else I'm told: "I'm much too busy for that sort of thing. Daydreaming was okay for my teens. I haven't daydreamed since." Then there is the usual pause, enough time for an oblique insight, and I'm asked: "What do you mean by daydreaming anyhow? A story of some kind in your head where you feature yourself? Or planning for some future event? I've a lot of head trips planning. But I call that planning, not daydreaming."

What Is a Daydream? We all know what a night dream is, and most of us think we know what a daydream is until we try to define it. Somehow, the more we try to delimit its boundaries, the more it slithers away. In part, that's likely to be the reason the number of vigorous research studies is small.[1, 2, 3] I suspect another reason is that before the advent of contemporary psychotherapy the potential utilization of dream imagery in the psychic economy hadn't been fully understood. In the past, psychoanalytic effort had been directed toward unearthing and interpreting the dream image, rather than toward actually *using* it for the preparatory task, the transitional step, that it can be.

Moreover, most of us who do daydream aren't aware of it —that is, we're not likely to characterize our "thoughts" as such. Yet, contrary to popular assumption, we spend proportionately little time in "logical thinking." If we make an effort to listen to ourselves, we'll find that, a good deal of the time, we're engaged in an internal monologue—babbling to ourselves—or that we're deep in a wordless reverie. In the words of one researcher: "Human beings spend nearly all their time in some kind of mental activity, and much of the time their activity consists not of ordered thought but of bits and snatches of inner experience: daydreams, reveries, wandering interior monologues, vivid imagery, and dreams." [1]

According to another study, if we live to be seventy we'll have spent twenty of those years sleeping and 20 percent of that time, or four full years, dreaming. Add to that the time we spend in wakeful dreams and we've the most eloquent case for believing, as many researchers do, that so extensive "a set of activities cannot be functionless." [1] Indeed, one way of looking at our "ideational" experiences is that, from time to time, external reality demands our attention, plunging us into syllogistic reasoning, interrupting our wandering reveries.

Still, if we've been inclined to treat dreams as so many parentheses in our lives, daydreams—characterized as woolgathering, castle-building, and cloud-lands—have been in even less esteem, particularly since we're held totally accountable for our daydreaming. Too often daydreaming has been associated with the flaky substance of children's, adolescents' or harried housewives' imaginations. We're all familiar with the youngster holding medieval jousts with his peas and mashed potatoes, or the girl looking into space dreaming fairy-tale dreams of her one true love, or the young man, 'schoolbooks pushed to one side, dreamily scaling the Matterhorn. Those are daydreams, but as we'll discover, they're also a significant aspect of our development—and so are the planning kind. In fact, memories, images, feelings, and even the anticipation of future events are all properly considered daydreaming. As such, they surely encompass a large share of our waking awareness.

For some, daydreaming is the last lamppost of our consciousness, appearing just before we're ready for sleep, or when we're alone, engaged in some activity that doesn't require our attention, like doing the dishes, taking a walk, or riding a bus to work.

With due credit to Freud's genius for pointing the way to the "royal road to the unconscious," the fact remains that we haven't begun to plumb the depths of dream images for the personal and socially salient events that they are. Dreams and daydreams are not shadowy apparitions that require special divining powers when we learn to look upon them as "real" events, unfocussed happenings. For our purposes we needn't make arbitrary distinctions between the dream states of night and daydreaming.[4] There are a number of indications that dreams and fantasies are in good measure functionally interchangeable, forming a continuous ideational current.[1]

Dream Realities: Another Way of Experiencing. Let's consider two widely different samplings: one, the dreams of a primitive tribe, the Senoi, an isolated jungle folk of the equatorial rain forest of the Malay Peninsula; the other, the reveries of the elite geniuses of our Western culture, the Kekules and Einsteins.

Is it likely for dream images to carry the same clout as our waking realities? Can they hold their own pitted against orderly, logical thinking? Is it possible for them to change our attitudes, focus our energies, and even anticipate the change in the direction of our lives?

I'm grateful for the work of the late Kilton Stewart, a psychotherapist and fellow of the Royal Anthropological Society, who has brought the Senoi way of dreaming to our attention.[5, 6] It is a way of dreaming that has found its use in both the classroom and in psychotherapeutic groups.[7]

What is extraordinary about this tribe is their claim to have had no violent crimes or intercommunal conflicts for several hundred years. What is also remarkable is that they've imbued their dreams with the same reality as waking reality, so that there is a continuous interplay between dream occurrences and waking events, profoundly affecting their waking life. The absence of violent outbursts, armed conflict, and physical and mental disease, Dr. Stewart believes, is a direct result of institutions that produce a high level of psychological integration and emotional maturity, along with the development of attitudes that have promoted creative rather than destructive interpersonal relations.[5]

And the cornerstone of those institutions is the dream! Dream events are used as an impetus to personal as well as communal actions. Stewart explains: If a young man dreams of a new trap, "the elders help him construct it, to see if it will work. If he dreams of a song or poem, the elders encourage him to express it for criticism or approval. If he dreams of a girl he is encouraged to consummate love with her in his dreams and to court her while he is awake." [5]

Each morning breakfast in the Senoi household is like a "dream clinic." Before beginning their day, the father and older brothers listen to the children's dreams. Each member of the group then responds to the dream as they would to a "real" happening, following through with possible actions.

In view of what we've learned about training for independence, the Senoi methods of dealing with children's fears, angers, and anxieties are of particular interest. Have you ever had a dream in which you've awakened with a start because it was too frightening to complete? Rather than comforting ourselves, as we frequently do, that it was *only* a dream, a bad dream, what if we tried to turn it around instead? Rather than running from a fearful dream image, what if we faced it?

One of the common anxiety or terror dreams among children, including Senoi children, is the falling dream. When the Senoi child reports a falling dream, the adult answers with enthusiasm, "That is a wonderful dream, one of the best dreams a man can have. Where did you fall to, and what did you discover?"

". . . The child at first answers, as he would in our society, that it did not seem so wonderful, and that he was so frightened that he awoke before he had fallen anywhere.

" 'That was a mistake,' answers the adult-authority. 'Everything you do in a dream has a purpose beyond your understanding while you're asleep. You must relax and enjoy yourself when you fall in a dream. Falling is the quickest way to get in contact with the powers of the spirit world, *the power laid open to you through dreams.'"* [5] (Italics mine.)

Stewart observes: "The astonishing thing is that over a period of time . . . the dream which starts out with a fear of falling changes into the joy of flying. . . . That which was an indwelling fear or anxiety becomes an indwelling joy or act of will. Dream characters are bad only as long as one is afraid and retreating from them, and will continue to seem bad and fearful as long as one refuses to come to grips with them." [5]

Thus, should you encounter a fearsome figure in your dream, the Senoi suggest that in another dream, or in a waking daydream, you turn and face him. Since no distinction is made between sleeping experience and waking experience, the dream and the dreamer begin to change. Such has been the power of dream images that they have been known to dissolve fears and initiate projects.

In the world of dreaming the Senoi are light years ahead of us. With minimal risk the Senoi child is supported in gaining independence, self-confidence, and mastery. With an attitude of exploration, they are reared to esteem the infinite dream possibilities. Falling, climbing, traveling, flying are vehicles, not of danger, but of discovery. In the secure playground of dreams, free play and risk-taking make possible the resolution of conflicts that have failed solution in the light of day, becoming a power source in defining a definable self. Where else could one accumulate such breadth and depth of experience?

An interesting aside: If all those references to dreaming and *men* are having an adverse effect, let me hasten to report one dream that Stewart describes that succeeded in breaking down a major social barrier—the position of women! The dream, that of an esteemed elder—suffering qualms of guilt no doubt—involved the ceremonial status of women and was directly responsible for making women more nearly the equals of men in the ritual ceremonies!

Understandably, we still may be skeptical. That seems to work for the primitive Senoi tribe; but can we, dealing with the complex textures of a modern culture, dare pay attention to dream imagery, sleeping or awake?

Dream Imagery and Breakthrough. Paradoxically, in our culture it's been the most cultivated and rigorously disciplined "logical" thinkers who have discovered the value of dream imagery. The scientific annals are full of fascinating tales of creative breakthroughs that were the direct result of the reveries of a restless, unsatisfied mind, a mind that was reaching after "I-don't-know-what." [8, 9, 10]

A story that bears retelling, even though you may have heard it before, is that of the Dutch physicist Friedrich A. Kekule, who describes the birth of the structural theory of the atom. "One beautiful summer evening," he writes, "I was riding on the last omnibus through the deserted streets usually so filled with life. I rode as usual on the outside of the omnibus. I fell into a reverie. Atoms flitted before my eyes. I had never before succeeded in perceiving their manner of moving. That evening, however, I saw that frequently two smaller atoms were coupled together, that larger ones held fast three and even four of the smaller ones and that all were whirled around in a bewildering dance. I saw how the larger atoms formed a row and one dragged along still smaller ones at the end of the chain. . . . The cry of the guard, 'Clapham Road,' waked me from my reverie; but I spent a part of the night writing down sketches of these dream pictures. Thus arose the structural theory." [8]

Kekule reports a similar happening in his discovery of the benzene ring. He'd been troubled, turned his chair to the fireplace, and sank into a reverie. This time his mind's eye was besieged with long rows of serpents, when suddenly one of the serpents seized its own tail and the form whirled mockingly before his eyes. He ends his account: "As though from a flash of lightning I awoke; I occupied the rest of the night in working out the consequences of the hypothesis. . . . Let us learn to dream, gentlemen." [10]

The troubled mind is the mind that is prepared for the creative breakthrough. What had escaped Kekule in his waking consciousness provoked the exploratory perceptions of his reveries. And so we discover still another function of dream images: problem-solving.

But is it only for primitive tribes, geniuses, and men to actualize their dreams? Sleep and daydreams have been, for a number of women, the first glimmer of a single self, a single voice. Dreams, after all, are the only things that are exclusively ours. They make up that "inner climate" that distinguishes each of us as a particular person, identifying and defining who we are. Indeed, the dream, in the words of novelist Joan Didion, can teach the dreamer how to live.[11] And it has. Those unfocussed, random "thoughts" have had the power to show women what to do. As women have become freer and more spontaneous in their daydreaming, they have paradoxically become more channeled and deliberate in their lives. The daydream became an invaluable tool for unearthing massive amounts of information about themselves, past, present, and future, that they had squirreled away—a kind of free-floating retrieval system, quite as sophisticated as any IBM programming device.

Practicing Problem-solving. Remember Maureen and her dream of the starving monkey (Chapter 6)? It was that dream, she confided, that "pushed her out the door," and started her thinking about her life. For Maureen the dream served to crystallize something that was becoming increasingly clear, yet difficult to face. She'd been trapped in marriage and in her life by an image of herself as Superwoman, while, in reality, she was starving, intellectually and emotionally. The dream image—that starving monkey in a crumbling house—reflected the death of one aspect of her, but it also made room for the birth of other parts of the Self that needed nourishing. In her consummate honesty and courage, she couldn't dismiss the dream as *just* another nightmare. She knew that she was her dream, and that she had to make a choice between dying and living.

Changing those self-defeating images is perhaps the most difficult task we face, as well as one of the most critical. Another woman, an architect, observed: "Every important step in my life has been foreshadowed by some dream. A few nights ago I had a dream that makes me feel I'm finally ready to be independent."

Her dream is all the more striking because Antoinette Rogers is a woman who had achieved. Yet, she was still dragging an image of herself as only "second-in-command"—an image that prevented her from feeling in charge of her life. Initially in the shadow of her architect father, and later in her spouse's, she continued to think of herself as fragile and in need of being taken care of. That illusion, however, came at a high price. Antoinette could risk nothing that might alienate her from her benefactors.

The dream she related followed her trip to London, where she decided to go alone to attend a series of professional conferences. She explained: "The night I was to return home I dreamed that I was walking along a narrow, winding street when my eyes were arrested by a striking-looking building. I entered and there I saw a remarkable apartment, structured in the shape of a triangle. I admired every detail, especially the skill and taste with which the architect had executed the job. When I awoke, I had a tremendous feeling of joy, as if a weight had been lifted. 'Of course,' I told myself, 'how wonderful, it's *your* dream, you're the architect!' All this time I've been imputing my own strengths onto someone else, hoping that he'd be strong enough to take care of me!"

The dream was a concretization of a major transition, a turning point. It both indicated her readiness to assume responsibility for her own person and pointed the way. She realized she no longer needed a mentor—a guiding hand—and so her attitude toward her talents changed. After years of keeping a low profile, she actively began thinking "commissions" and actually enjoyed promoting her work, which quickly gathered momentum.

Dream states, precisely because they aren't bound by the same laws of ordinary reality, can play a dual function. They can show us how we *are* in the world; and they also can show us how we *can be*. They can lay bare different ways of seeing ourselves, gradually eroding those old ideas about how we *should* be. If we pay them heed, they can and do prepare us for transitions in our growth. For some women, daydreams, in particular, have become the dry runs, the trial perceptions, foreshadowing critical events.

Daydreaming As Dress Rehearsal. As a matter of record, there is strong evidence that daydreaming is equally as significant, and sometimes more so, in giving direction to our lives than night dreaming.[3] Unlike dreams, which transcend time, reveries enact times past and times to come. Inhabiting the outer fringes of reality, they put us in touch with what is probable and possible. They familiarize us with a new environment without our even leaving our own backyard. Hilma Wolitzer's protagonist in *In the Flesh* puts it so well: "I tried to play it out in my head, a little dress rehearsal in preparation for the real thing."

Along similar lines one researcher writes: "In the course of fairly extensive fantasizing we may also encourage ourselves to further action in the pursuit of a particular goal. In this sense our daydreams can actually have motivational characteristics; they can encourage us to try new kinds of experiences, or at least to look for ways of reaching some compromise approach to these wishes."[3] They can acclimatize us to the "real" event as well. If you daydream yourself center stage in a Shakespearean play, for example, you're participating in an inner rehearsal. And when they day comes for you to be center stage, the unfamiliar has been made familiar.

Unhappily, however, we seem to lose the knack of it as

we grow older. If you're one of those who claim that you've never daydreamed, think back. Think back to when you were a girl, an adolescent, or in your early twenties. Remember, when you were growing up, how you prepared yourself for adulthood by playing grown-ups?

Childhood Play and Fantasy: Developmental Rehearsals. In earliest childhood, play and fantasy are virtually insep- arable. Childhood play is the stuff that later fantasies grow from, tracing a developmental path. By the time we reach puberty, play goes quietly underground, only to reemerge as fantasy—reflecting the focal concerns of late adolescence and early adulthood.

One team of researchers collected the fantasies of twenty- eight high school students and then ten years later studied them again as adults. They report: "Fantasy attitudes ex- pressed in adolescence play a major role in determining decisions to be made in later life. Fantasy is the 'unfinished business of personality'. . . ." [2]—an intriguing observation. Our early daydreams, it seems, are pivotal in our adult atti- tudes and in some measure are reflected in our later life- style, achievement, and even occupational choice. In short, they anticipate and prepare us for our future roles.

Farfetched? Think back, and then think ahead. That's what all this talk of daydreaming propelled me to do. Odd, I thought, that I had never given my daydreams even a pass- ing nod, despite the fact that they were a prominent aspect of my childhood. Not even in all those years of my own per- sonal analysis. They just never came up. Pity.

Cornering my sister one afternoon, I started to reminisce. "Remember that large vanity table you had in your bedroom? The one with the long center mirror and two side mirrored panels that folded at different angles? I spent half my child- hood sneaking into your room and playing with those mir- rors. I'd seat myself before the table and move the panels until I got multiple images of me. Then I'd study each image. There were dozens of them. The thought of so many Me's intrigued me, and frightened me, too. One Me I remember was an archeologist, just back from discovering the tomb of Nefertiti. Another Me was an author who'd written a book on the evils of the Industrial Revolution! And another Me was about to leave for the mission fields to take care of . . . lepers? One way or another I centered myself in some adventure; not terribly heroic ones—I was too passive for that—but I was center stage."

My sister laughed: "I'd pose in front of the mirror too, turn on the record player, and when no one was around—especially you—I'd pretend I was an orchestra conductor. In full command, I'd call in the violins, soften the cellos, and heighten the woodwinds. It was great until I hit adolescence and became self-conscious. Then I had less flamboyant kinds of fantasies. I went underground and used to pretend I was a scenic set designer." That I remembered because I was the one to inherit the discarded sets—old shoe boxes transformed into a veritable fairyland. They didn't mean much to me. After all, it was her fantasy!

Most of us internalize our let's-pretend play just about the time we reach twelve or thirteen. Those fantasies become the developmental rehearsals for adulthood. Was there really a connection between our idle play and our later lives? My sister didn't become an orchestra conductor, but she is a designer, continuously designing and orchestrating a great many home sets. I didn't pursue archeology or missionary work, but I did become intrigued with unearthing the archaic in the human mind. Although I've never traveled to a leper colony, I certainly had my share of rescue fantasies as a young psychotherapist. As for the other dream—being an author decrying injustice—that one has had a long winter of hibernation that haunts me still.

Between the ages of thirteen and fourteen most adventure and achievement daydreaming is joined by those of sex and romance. I was a late bloomer. At thirteen, the romantic fantasies I had were pure fluff, without much erotica.

I can't help wonder, however, what my aspirations would have been if my brother, tagged the "genius" of the family, had lived. I've become acutely aware of a persistent "typographical" error; I seem to spell daydream, dadydream. Indeed, the dreams my father couldn't hand down to his son spilled over to his daughters.

And on and on it goes. Kate used to play at being the prima ballerina Mia Slavenska, to thunderous applause. Later, much later, in her mid-forties, she was to become a "star" fabric designer with seasonal displays of her work—and applause. Maggie, fatherless, raised by a mother who was overworked and embittered, somehow found her art. Art? From where did that spring?

Let's explore her turn-of-the-century childhood. The year was 1913. The place was Morgantown, Virginia.

Margaret Hoffman: Patches of Color. The snow was falling on the narrow alley, blanketing the shabbiness like a coat of paint. Morgantown suffered the sharp edge of winter. Outside the street was empty and growing dark. A horse-drawn carriage made its way over the cobblestones and came to a stop. Her father was helped down by the coachman. His coat hung limply. He was not at all as she'd remembered him. Her mother and baby sister ran to the door, yet there was no joy.

He smiled and fingered her hair: She was Daddy's girl. But he couldn't talk. The consumption had attacked his larynx and he'd been sent home to die. Weeks later, at the age of twenty-seven, he was gone. Just six, Maggie had lost her one friend and ally, and her mother, now alone with two children, was plunged into a lifelong struggle. And widows then had no Social Security checks or pensions to fall back on.

Her mother was eighteen when Maggie was born. Then there was another daughter, and a son who also died of TB. Her mother had grown up in a poverty-stricken family whose men drank themselves into oblivion. At home Maggie had been taught one credo: "Be humble. Be meek. Work hard. Scrubbing floors earns you the right to drink at the bar. Everything else is a sin."

Despite the dour climate of her childhood, she saw in her mother a model of hard work. "I had the example of my mother doing all the time," Maggie said. "She went to work in a sewing factory when she was eleven. After she married my father, she did home sewing. I remember the horse and wagon coming to deliver huge piles of collars—just collars, or sleeves. She would sew them in a continuous line on the machine, and it was my job to cut them apart and turn them right side out. When my father died she had to return to the factory.

"Home," Maggie reflected, "was a bleak place to be. It was a roof overhead, food and clothing. That was it! I used to do a lot of reading. I was eight when I read *Pollyanna*. I remember looking around the house at that time, and thinking: 'Man, there must be more to life than this.'"

Those words were to echo and rebound throughout her life, urging her on. And books became a lifelong source of wonder, revealing what was *possible*—drowning out her mother's voice. "My message at home was, 'What's good enough for me is good enough for you.' There was no discussion of anything. Intellectually, I know my mother had a rough time, and that she wasn't equipped mentally or emotionally to handle us. She was bitter. I remember when her infant boy died, she said at the funeral, 'Why couldn't it have been one of the girls?'

"My mother was the reason I quit school in the tenth grade. I'd told her I was tired of middy blouses—I was bigger than I am now. And I hated the long plait hanging down my back. She said, 'If you want clothes, go get a job.'

"It hurt. A lot." Maggie grew hoarse, fighting back tears. "I'm sure the fight in me came from her. She was strong, and supported us the best she could. But holidays . . . I'll never forget those holidays. I'm scarred. You really haven't experienced life until you've gotten a Christmas poor basket.

We'd rush to the table to spread out the things, and I remember thinking, is there anything in there just for me? Or is it all beans and rice and coffee? Oh, my . . ."

Tears glistened against her parchment-like skin. She quickly added: "But I remember one special Christmas. I'll never forget it. My mother must have gotten a little money together; she bought me a set of watercolors, six tiny patches of color, and a coloring book." A faraway look came into her eyes as she explained: "I trace my interest in painting and photography to that day."

Books had enriched her imagination, fed her information, and opened the door to what was possible. They'd given her a fantasy life, so that at the tender age of eight, she already knew that her home didn't encompass all of reality. The storybooks triggered dreams, and a set of paints colored an otherwise gray existence. They brought the blue of the sky and the yellow of the sun into a room that had been blacked out by newspapers to keep out the cold. True, the daydreams were a withdrawal from a harsh reality, but they also were a necessary vehicle of escape. Years later, they proved a rescue. The child's make-believe taught Maggie how to deal with her world by exploring new possibilities, giving her a feeling of confidence and power as she conquered her severe circumstances. That confidence served her all her life.

Maggie daydreamed herself beyond the shabby walls of Morgantown, to not one, but two homes, and eventually to a room of her own. As a photographer, she alighted on something that was singularly hers. Her dreams gave her incentives and motivated her: She always knew she'd be Somebody.

Clearly childhood play and fantasy serve a pivotal developmental need. Dr. Jerome Singer observes: "If he [she] can effect some combination of actual achievement and a continuation of a varied and increasingly elaborate but partially reality-oriented daydream life, he [she] can move into adulthood armed with a significant skill and with an important adaptive potential." [3] (Inserts mine.) If we take a new look at our past, we too may find that even the poorest childhood has been rich in dreams.

And the adult? Those fantasies continue to inhabit and to serve our adult life as well. In a study of college-educated and some working-class whites and blacks, it was reported that regardless of race or education, most people engage in some form of daydreaming daily. This frequently deals with planning for future action and dealing with significant relationships, enabling them to explore a variety of alternative actions.[3]

Regarding change in the occurrence of daydreaming over the lifespan, there's been a tendency to believe that fantasies gradually decline through the fifties. A study, however, based on one hundred and seventy males, aged 24 to 91, suggests a far more intriguing possibility. It isn't daydreaming as such that declines, but rather some kinds of daydreams decrease with age while others are not at all age-related.[12]

And for the adult woman? Although the early female fantasies follow the common stereotype of women's concerns, I heartily agree that daydreams, as such, don't decline appreciably with age, but that they do radically shift in content. I suspect that had I asked the women to plot their daydreams as I did their personal and sexual development, we'd observe a similar series of valleys and peaks, postponements and actualizations. The achievement fantasies characteristic of the teenage boy, for example, are not likely to surface in the traditional woman until her forties. Only when those imperatives of merger are behind her does a vision of herself in the world emerge.

Let's trace, then, still another postponement: Women's fantasies of achievement.

ACHIEVEMENT FANTASIES

The Four R's of Female Fantasies. Small wonder that we lose the art of daydreaming as we grow older. Not only has daydreaming in general been regarded as a frivolous pastime; women's daydreams in particular have been looked upon as not only frivolous, but also as neurotic—even by women themselves.

There are, unfortunately, a number of reasons. For one, the early psychoanalytic thinkers did nothing to assuage our shame. Freud, in his paper on "The Relationship of the Poet to Day-Dreaming," writes: "Happy people never make phantasies, only unsatisfied ones. Unsatisfied wishes are the driving power." [13] He goes on to explain that the driving power, the impelling wishes, vary strongly according to the sex of the person, that is, either they are motivated by ambition or by erotic desires.

Of course, since women reputedly lack ambition, it fell to us to be driven by erotic wishes. So, behind every female fantasy, it was said, there lurked some hidden erotic desire. Freud writes: "In young women erotic wishes dominate the phantasies almost exclusively, for their ambition is generally comprised in their erotic longings; in young men egoistic and ambitious wishes assert themselves plainly enough alongside their erotic desires." [13] For the traditional analytic thinker, the primary function of fantasy, then, was the release of forbidden drives. Obviously, to fantasize meant that we were frustrated, or unsatisfied, and to be frustrated, or unsatisfied, meant that we were neurotic.

So, better not to fantasize. Intellectually, if not emotionally, we've come a long way in our understanding. We now know that, except for those antagonistic pulls, those antithetical dissatisfactions of the heart and the mind, it's unlikely that we'd venture and develop. Speaking of poets, it's unlikely that Anne Sexton's poetry would have erupted as it did at the age of twenty-eight had she been totally satisfied with her life as a suburban housewife.[14] It is also unlikely that she would have withstood the ravages of her psychosis as long as she did, except for her poetry.

We have to admit, however, that on the face of it some of our fantasies aren't the kind that we find particularly enhancing to our self-esteem—certainly, not those of a romantic or sexual turn. For the most part, if we aren't fantasizing of Rape, then it's Rescue, and if not Rescue, then it's Revenge —a woman scorned. Or if not rape, rescue, and revenge, then it's likely to be the Ravishing Beauty kind—the *femme fatale* who drives men out of their skulls. I suppose there is a certain power in being victim, even if only the impotent power of being the victim of men's "desire."

Admittedly, that kind of daydreaming doesn't seem to have much that can serve us. Fantasies of being overpowered, or rescued—swooped up and going off arm-in-arm into the sunset—are, as one woman observed, a nice place to visit but no place to live. Nor are those Medea-like vengeance vignettes a place to be too long—shackling us, as they do, to the object of our wrath.

In their twenties and in the early years of their marriages, women spend a good deal of their time daydreaming. Usually those dreams are vague and misty, a restless reaching after I-don't-know-what. "Who knew? Who knew what I wanted to do with my life," one woman explained, echoing a common plaint. "I spent the first eight years of my marriage day-dreaming I was a movie star, walking down the aisle in a flowing chiffon gown, claiming my Academy Award. I wanted desperately to be successful, but I didn't know how. Being an actress was totally unrealistic. I'm not beautiful. And I can't act!" Nor did the passing years crystallize that diffuse image of herself. "So I forced myself to stop dreaming. Now I just go blank as if I've drawn the shades."

The Four M's of Men's Make-Believe. Contrast that with the young man's reveries. As boys begin to grow, their dreams —and consequently their self-images—grow sharper. So does their identity. Typically, the young man's dream is concerned with doing. He is centered by the actions he'd like to take. His reveries are of: Medals; Money; Mastery—of skills and of women; and, somewhat later, of the Memorable "good old days."

Nothing in the woman's movie-star dream, unfortunately,

is concerned with mastery or autonomy. Fame and success are hers just for being beautiful and pleasing—pleasing enough, perhaps, to attract a Robert Redford, or whoever is the current idol. Nothing accrues to her in the development of confidence in mastering her life situation—even in fantasy. In at least one study, Singer points out, "there are indications that women who showed a great many achievement-oriented daydreams were also characterized by having more frequent guilt-oriented fantasies." [3]

Our dreams have been used to bolt us down. If men can be said to have narrowed their sights for power, what of women? What have we forfeited for adoration? Still, while the daydream identifies the nettles and brambles of the female psyche, it also foreshadows who and what we can become, pointing to untapped resources. Even that movie-star fantasy?

Remember Carol Anderson Salant (Chapters 4 and 11)? Carol is now a professional woman and the wife of Brian Salant, a luminary in cancer research. But once she was a girl, with all the "slushy" dreams of girls. When we met, she was thirty-five and had recently married.

And How We Grow. "Who am I?" Carol broke into self-conscious laughter. "Married or unmarried, I'm the same person I've always been—somebody who copes and who does things somehow or other. I see myself as a *doer*. I feel strongly that I'm a person, and that I have an identity and that Carol Anderson is somebody who is . . . who has her feet planted in the world. And I'm not going to be shoved to one side."

What could be construed as a declaration of war was actually a statement of fact. Carol is disarmingly forthright. But she hadn't always felt that way about herself. Like most women, she was once filled with the restless longings of the growing girl, and the self-doubts. What caused her to turn herself around? If you were to ask her, she'd reply, quite simply, that she learned to daydream!

She'd been raised in the austere days of war-torn Europe. From the age of eleven to eighteen, she'd been cloistered in a convent school. There, in a community of women, she flourished. It was a time of gestation as she developed an intellectual curiosity and discipline. But then, her parents had tagged her the "brainy one" and taught her to value hard work and intelligence.

Once in the larger world of the university, however, all the conflicts of a postponed adolescence besieged her. "I'd been in a girls' boarding school for seven years," she explained, "and all of a sudden I was back home, going to a university and exposed to men! I had never felt pretty. So I withdrew emotionally as well as in my work. The ability to learn just seemed to vanish with my confidence.

"I never felt pretty growing up, but now it became worse. As a girl I had terrible eyes so I had to wear thick glasses that make your eyes look like specks. And I never made friends easily. I lived in a dreamworld. My parents went crazy. My mother just couldn't understand. She thought I was being snooty. And to make matters worse, she was critical of the way I looked. I was always very thin, but my legs were heavier than the rest of me. Well, my mother would continually comment until I ended up wearing skirts down to my ankles.

"In one way her attitudes were horrid, but I'm grateful to her for making us aware of wanting to look well—even though I fought her most of my girlhood. We had no money, so she taught us to sew, knit, and crochet. And if it was a question of eating or looking well-dressed, my mother decided you looked well-dressed.

"My dream world? My daydreams were the slushy kind. My dream was to be very elegant and beautiful and to dress well. I could see myself walking down the main street of our town, dressed like the most elegant woman you ever saw. Sometimes I even dreamed I was going to be a star. But then I gave that up. I decided that if I was going to wear glasses I couldn't possibly be an actress. That was a terrible trauma, wearing glasses."

Vague longings stirred. But because Carol didn't look a certain way, or behave a certain way, she felt she was lacking. Then she entered the university, ill-prepared for the social and intellectual competition. She explained: "I was in a tremendous emotional upheaval, so I started failing. I failed math and physics. I lost all confidence in myself. I decided to switch my major to biology. Finally I had to take an extra year to complete my course work. But that turned out to be a boon. I somehow got myself together, and I ended up winning a prize! I graduated and gradually I felt my confidence return."

Her hazel eyes, now fashionably set off behind contact lens, seemed deep in thought. "But you know, at the same time I had all those problems and was going through all those doubts about myself, I also had a total commitment to work. Even though in my daydreams I never projected myself in a work future. . ... That's been one of my great failings, I think.

"I've never looked at the track ahead. *I didn't feel I had to, as a woman.* Unlike Brian, my success has been as much by luck as by design." For a time Carol's life ran along two parallel tracks. Despite her intellectual interests and perseverance, she experienced an emotional lag that is typically female. She endured all the inexpressible longings of wanting to be ravishing and admired, of wanting to be swooped up and adored—by that special someone.

Dissonance. Carol explained what she saw as the contradiction of her teens and twenties. "That didn't jibe," she reflected. "Those romantic daydreams, and the fact that I always knew I was a doer, didn't go together somehow." But they do, if you're growing up female. It is just those dissonances and contradictions that give us an opening wedge, a handle to latch on to later.

"Soon after I graduated I came to the States," she continued. "And those first years saw a lot of changes in me. My sister Dee had married and gone to live in Washington. She had a small baby and felt lonely. I came over to be with her. But I had no money. I arrived with just seventy dollars. I told myself I'd stay for two years, but I never went back.

"My brother-in-law was a bit callous, and I knew I *had* to find a job, and pretty fast. Although I had little confidence in myself and was very timid, I started going around to the employment agencies two days after I arrived. I'll never forget it. My brother-in-law took me down to the center of Washington and then left me. He said he had to get to work. I guess he knew I had a fighting spirit.

"My confidence quickly returned because I found that I got several offers. As a matter of fact, I came home one afternoon, and Dee said, 'Some crazy man has been trying to reach you. He's so desperate to get you to work for him, you're to call him at home.' That was Brian! He was head of a research team and wanted someone who could work along with him. So he hired me."

Autocatalytic. Her work, as well as the respect that Brian showed for her ability and dedication, acted as a catalyst. Seeing herself reflected through the eyes of another, she began to define herself. Carol has a word for that process: Autocatalytic.

She explained: "After two or three years of working, everything changed. I joined a ski club, and since I've always been athletic, I skied well. Then I began to realize that people liked me. It's an autocatalytic thing. All you need, really, is somebody to start you off—somebody to see something in you that's been there all the time but that you haven't felt as you. Soon you start telling yourself, well, maybe you're not so bad. And then you begin to make an effort. I started to do things. I got my teeth fixed. I got my hair styled. Those things may seem frivolous but they make a difference in how you feel about yourself. Also, they're a *reflection* of how you do feel about yourself. That's the autocatalytic thing again.

"And then I got a boyfriend. That made a big difference. Actually, I used to get really mad at him. Alex used to say things like, 'I'm not going to have anything to do with you unless you get contact lenses.' I thought to myself: 'What a heel!' But really, he helped; he recognized that I looked better without those big glasses, and so he decided, come hell or high water, he was going to get me to wear contacts."

Slushy Daydreams vs. Ring-Around-a-Molecule. With her parents' support, Carol grew to be hardworking and ambitious. Still, that gnawing desire to be Somebody could just as easily have gone into deep-freeze, as it has with so many women.

She'd been scarred by the common female dissonance—wanting to be beautiful and admired for her beauty, and still wanting to be an achiever and admired for her intelligence. Not one to be overcome by the first obstacle, she persevered and completed her studies, but she felt buffeted. Playing devil's advocate, I asked Carol: "Do you think that, hamstrung as women are, they're incapable of greatness? After all, how many really great women scientists are there?"

She laughed. "I don't think there are *many* great women scientists and I'm not sure why that is. I suspect that we get sidetracked in so many different things. I can tell you about myself in my twenties. I would start out my daydreaming about some mythical man, or it may have been the man I'd met the night before, and it took a tremendous effort on my part to make myself into a thinker! I distinctly remember when I set my mind to doing it, and even then I kept wandering in and out of the old daydreams. The thing is, women have too many escape hatches, I think.

"I was about twenty-three when I realized that all I was doing was spending my time on silly daydreams. So I decided I had to make myself think. But it never would have happened, I never would have learned how, except for

Brian. I never would have been aware of all the time I spent on slushy dreams if it hadn't been for him.

"It was watching Brian. I watched him work, and he kept saying something like: 'Oh, you know, I daydream all the time.' And I thought, well, *I* daydream all the time too. Then I discovered that *we were talking about two different kinds of daydreams*. My daydreams were of some improbable romantic adventure. His were constructive; he was *doing* something.

"I would talk to Brian one day, and the next he'd come in with another idea! I'd wonder, *where did he get that?* And how does he have the time? We both worked late. Then I realized something. It came to me that, while I went home and wasted my energies daydreaming about my next date, or whether So-and-So would phone, he had done something."

Carol paused, reliving a vivid moment. "Then I thought, maybe *I* could be as good, if I did that too. I could daydream, but daydream with a footing—the kind of dream that gets you going in some direction. Brian's been fantastic for me. Much more than being a husband, he's a superlative person. It took me exactly three months of knowing him to realize the importance of having somebody that you can talk to who really has made something of his life. I've watched and he's been a model for me. I'm tremendously lucky for many reasons—not the least of which is the fact that I'm in a field of work where really at the end, you feel you've done something. You've really created something."

Not the least of Carol's creations has been herself. In her early twenties, her energies had drained into the common longings, shored by the common illusion that a man would be her savior, and that love, like magic putty, would fill all the lonely spaces. As it happened, a man did prove a cardinal force in her life. And, as often happens, dreams may come true, but not quite in the shape we dreamed them. Brian was her rescue not because he eventually became her lover, but because he was a creative thinker whom she grew to respect and admire and emulate as a thinker. Watching him at work, she beheld the creative daydream in process. Being Carol, she learned to imitate—ultimately imitating unformed aspects of herself. She saw how she was and rehearsed how she wanted to be.

That something or someone that ignites us can be a book, an idea, a dream, a teacher. It can be someone we admire and would like to emulate. Or it can simply be someone's recognition and affirmation of who we can become.

Mentors and Models. Most of us are weighed down by fixed ideas about ourselves and our future that limit and entrap. Women, particularly, are wont to perceive themselves in ways that are self-defeating. The function of models and mentors lies precisely in their capacities as editors. They significantly edit the parental message, enhancing what was positive, diluting what was negative, and honing that beginning dream. There is little doubt, for example, that Carol's childhood groomed her for the mentor of her adulthood. Simply by being who he was, Brian returned her to the home ground of her past, reinforcing her father's esteem for hard work and intelligence, directing her to what was possible and probable, and showing her the way.

The young Anne Sexton writes to an early mentor, the poet W. D. Snodgrass: "And I know we will be uncomfortable until we are on a like level of growth. So I'll just get me up and grow taller. I am a bean sprout stretching toward you." [14] Later, the apprentice became the accomplished poet and in turn a mentor and model to other aspirants, giving back what had been given to her and what she'd learned the hard way. "Her attitude metamorphosed," her biographers write. "And now it was her turn to teach students what to leave out." [14]

The life cycle in a capsule. Being Child and becoming Parent. "Force discipline upon madness," she writes a troubled young poet. "You can do it. I did it. Why not you?" [14]

Why not? I asked one woman. "Why not look around you

and see what's possible. Look at Tina. She'd left school, devoted her life to homemaking, and now, at forty-four, her life's been renewed. She always loved gardening, but it was just a hobby. Today she runs one of the most successful gardening services in Georgetown. Or take . . ."

"That's how you look at it," she interrupted. "When you say look at Tina, I feel worse. It's like looking at those Jack LaLanne or Main Chance posters with pictures of svelte beauties in bikinis. All that does is make me think I'd better get in shape quick before I dare walk through their door!" Those common hindrances. For many women a model stands for perfection, and rather than being someone to stretch toward, the model becomes someone to shrink from and fall short of in comparison.

From the other side of the fence, for women—especially older women—to become mentors has not been an easy transition. Perhaps because women of the older generation who've achieved really don't believe they have. Achievement for the older woman has been arduous and most likely feels like it's built on quicksand. Morover, too many women in their late forties, fifties, and sixties still slosh in the backwaters of old rivalries in which every woman, be it mother, sister, daughter, or a stranger, is competition for her spotlight, and thus a threat.

And the fact that women still continue to undervalue the personal achievement of other women adds to an already tenuous relationship. In the 1974 Roper Women's Opinion poll, women were reported to respect political and social status achieved by other women, but the respected status was not necessarily a result of the women's own achievements. Of the top five most respected women, only one, Golda Meir, gained her place through her own accomplishments.[15]

If the women I spoke with could think of any *woman* to admire, they too were likely to be women of political status, but not primarily of political accomplishments. The names of Eleanor Roosevelt and Rose Kennedy, for example, came up with an uncommon regularity. What was it about those political wives that seemed so enviable? It seems that what was admired was not a personal "success" but the fact that each, despite potentially repressive marriages, maintained her own identity. Each projected the ideal—the combined image of devoted wife and her own person.

What *men* do women respect? Men who have considerable personal accomplishments, of course, such as public figures in the media and in world affairs. Male mentors? They too have their thorny aspects. Currently a professor of mathematics, Evelyn Keller writes of her graduate days in the physics department at Harvard. "I had so successfully internalized the cultural identification between male and intellect that I was totally dependent on my (male) teachers for affirmation—a dependency made treacherous by the chronic confusion of sexuality and intellect in relationships between male teachers and female students." [16]

Even the ancient Romans knew that script. Wasn't it Ovid who wrote of Pygmalion and Galatea, the sculptor and his creation with whom he falls in love? For the woman, it is indeed heady to be affirmed and recognized for gifts that not even she has recognized in herself. It is exhilarating to suddenly discover something so deeply lodged in you; the unborn you that had been stoppered and plugged. It is that larger-than-life Hollywood cliché of the wise teacher to whom one imputes all sorts of sexual qualities—for a while.

A male mentor, however, can function only as a limited model. He is a man, after all. Although Brian taught Carol how to daydream, he couldn't possibly have taught her about being a woman. Moreover, male mentors are even less likely as informational models for the middle-aged woman who is developing her first occupational goals.

To be sure, women haven't had the wide diversity or the same availability of models as men. When present residents and recent (within the past ten years) graduates of a psychiatric training program—sixty men and twenty-three women—were asked to describe their most significant professional role models and to specify age, sex, and professional capacity, there was a preponderance of male role models for both women and men. In part, that reflected actual availability. Another finding, however, is striking. The researchers state, "whereas 13 percent of the men out of training mention female role models, 50 percent of the men in training . . . specified women as role models." [17] The attitude toward the professional woman is changing, but perhaps the professional woman is also changing.

I was startled to hear similar attitudes reflected by a friend in his mid-thirties and in the vastly different profession of TV journalism. He explained that although as a young man his mentors had all been men, he now finds that his present mentors are women. He has not only learned from a number of books about the executive woman, but also he looks to the corporate woman who is juggling her many roles, and is equally, if not more committed to her work than any of her male counterparts. (His reflections were totally unsolicited.)

Enough of obstacles. Let's turn to the flip side and explore those mentors and models women have found, sometimes under their very noses.

A Friend. Married and with two daughters, Liz was in her early thirties when she decided to go back to college for a year and finish her degree. Soon after, she got a job at the now-defunct *Life* magazine. I hadn't see her for nearly ten years when she called to say she'd be in New York and let's have lunch. I'd remembered her as an intelligent, attractive, impeccable social creature who could quite easily have become the chairperson for this or that social affair or this or that charitable occasion. She'd come to New York not on a shopping spree as I'd imagined, but on business as a high-level executive for a multinational conglomerate.

"What made the difference? What really set me off? It was a friend. I had one real friend at *Life*," she began in a voice bursting with vitality. "She was a secretary. We used to walk home together every day after work. I'd stroll along as usual, window-shopping, making mental notes about one gown or another. One day she stopped me short. It was like a wallop. She took me by the arm and said, 'Liz, if you stopped constantly looking at party dresses and put just half that energy into thinking by-lines instead, you'd be a lot better off.' " Her words seemed prophetic. A few years later, Liz was divorced, left with small children to raise and a job that was uncertain at best. Today, Liz tells me, thanks to her friend, she thinks by-lines.

Colleague-watching. Sharon, a fashion coordinator, explained: "I used to spend all my time dressing like a million on a $15,000-a-year salary, using all my time putting outfits together. Then I went to work for this large corporation and the head of publicity was a woman, a young woman, who was making closer to $55,000. She was a dynamo and she didn't look like she'd just stepped out of *Women's Wear Daily*. In fact, she was a wee bit scruffy. She was an eye-opener for me. But that's not how I'd been taught to think. My mother would look at women and says things like: '*She's* married to a doctor and she's got such a big behind?' "

The Man You're Living With. Odd as it may sound, I heard myself ask a woman who was in a quandary about what to do with a sticky political situation in her firm: "Well, what would Jim (her lover, who is also vice-president of a large corporation) do in a similar situation? How would you handle it, if you were Jim?" "I'd be on the offensive, not the defensive," she countered before I finished my question. And it worked.

A Teacher. Dan Rather, in *The Camera Never Blinks,* traces the evolution of the youth turned esteemed newsman. One statement riveted my attention. He wrote: "The dream begins, most of the time, with a teacher who believes in you, who tugs and pushes and leads you on to the next plateau, sometimes poking you with a stick called truth."

Teachers can be a never-ending source of inspiration, particularly for the woman who comes to her dream later in life.

Edith burst into a radiant smile, explaining: "I took that first course in antiques with fear and trembling knees. I was so green; I had been out of school for twenty years. Then I met Mrs. Ellis, the instructor. She'd worked in the field for many years, although she was still a youngish woman. During the months that we worked together, she prodded and supported me. She was strict about our learning, but always cushioning. I got to know her well. I thought to myself: Hell, here she is, she teaches, she works, she markets, she runs a home. If she can do it, maybe I can too."

The Media. Kate's first teacher was a mellifluous voice pouring from a small wooden box—a radio. "I know that sounds funny, but my first mentor all those years I was washing diapers, gardening, cooking, and canning vegetables was an extraordinary woman, Martha Deane. She had one of the first talk shows. And day in and day out she brought into my home people that I never would have even known existed—authors, playwrights, politicians, artists—people from all walks of life. She stretched my narrow little world, and in some way prepared me for stepping out into that world."

Watching and listening to the be-ers and do-ers of the world was for Kate like an actor trying out for a role. Ultimately she rehearsed those closeted facets of herself and when it came time for her to be center stage, she stepped into the spotlight with the ease of a professional.

A Special Interest. A special interest, be it political, industrial, or in the arts, carries the promise of potential mentors and models. It can be the local political club, or Bella; it can be the industrial networks mushrooming in support of working women; or it can be a book such as this, where you may encounter a woman who'll move you to think, She did it—maybe I can too!

Since ours has been an exploration of the woman's lifespan and since this is really a chapter on living creatively, it is fitting, I think, to say a few words about creative living and "successful" aging. To nobody's surprise, I'm sure, research studies have found that greater satisfaction is reported by old women and men who've combined their aggression and dependency, who've accepted both the family and work roles, and who have insight into themselves. There is strong evidence, moreover, that those qualities are broadly subsumed into a larger characteristic: flexibility, specifically, role flexibility. It is suggested that role flexibility—a blurring of what is considered strictly masculine or feminine—is what makes for creative living and successful aging. One study is of particular significance. In investigating the personality traits of long-lived persons, it was observed that those were people who had the ability to combine "independence, interest in work, activity, and strength with adaptability, nurturance, family concerns, and acceptance of emotions." [18]

Achievement Skills: Refurbishing a Wilted Image. Where to begin? Let's begin where we left off as children, in our playground of fantasies and dreams. A good time to start is at the end of the day, when you're ensconced in bed, about to drift into sleep. Close your eyes. Relax. What image, feeling, or thought comes to you? Like some women, at first you may not like what you see, or feel, or think. I'm reminded of a passage in essayist Nora Ephron's *Crazy Salad*. With wit, wisdom, and a bit of pathos, she ponders this business of women's fantasies. "I wonder if our fantasies can ever catch up to what we all want for our lives. . . . Is it possible, through sheer willpower, to stop having unhealthy sex fantasies? I have several friends who did just that. 'What do you do instead?' I asked. 'Nothing,' they replied." What a pity that, in so doing, we're throwing out the Power along with the "bad" daydream.

Dissolving fears and initiating projects. "What do you daydream about?" I asked Joan, who'd just reached her twenty-second birthday. "Up until last year I had two recurrent fantasies. In one I was being raped, and I froze. I tried to scream and my voice wouldn't come out. I tried to fight, but

I couldn't move. It was awful. The other one was more like a recurrent scene. I'd see myself jumping out of a car going at a good speed.

"How did those fantasies stop? A strange thing happened. I was going to a small-town college where all the kids used to hitch rides from one place to another. One afternoon I was alone when I hitched a ride. I was in the car just a few minutes when I realized that something was very wrong. The driver, a young guy in his twenties, took a wrong turn and was heading toward a large wooded area. I asked him what he was doing. I asked him to stop. He only kept driving faster and faster. I knew I was about to be raped, or even worse. Without even thinking, I opened the door and jumped out of the speeding car. It happened so quickly that he didn't even have time to turn around. I was bruised but I ran, screaming for help.

"Since that time I haven't had those fantasies anymore. And I'm not scared anymore; I know I can take care of myself, no matter what. Now I daydream about having my own apartment. Or running a TV panel. I'm so different in my fantasies. I'm so assertive. I also dream about being in love. But in that dream, the guy and I are each doing our own thing and then we get together at night."

Certainly we have "unhealthy" daydreams of impotent withdrawal, or of escape into the improbable; but even fantasies that seem self-defeating can lay the groundwork for changing. Joan's fantasy of rape and impotence became a reality of rescue: self-rescue.

Have you ever stopped to observe how you position yourself in your daydreams? Could you go back into your rape fantasies, for example, and rescue yourself? Or maybe you need to try giving orders! One woman put me on to that. Divorced after twenty-five years of homemaking, she'd re-entered the job marketplace. A capable, energetic person with considerable organizational skill, she found a position in a travel agency. After some time, she confided: "You know, lately I find myself daydreaming all the time about owning *my own* travel agency . . . except that, each time, I seem to block at the same point—Giving orders!"

Reenacting her daydream out loud, she heard herself say to the teenaged stock clerk: Would you mind going downstairs and getting some travel brochures on London? Battle scarred—living with a rebellious teenaged daughter—she was understandably timid in couching her requests. In subsequent daydreams, she learned not to *ask*, but to *tell* the stock clerk what had to be done.

Or are you like Ruth, who has her own built-in obstacle path? Ruth ends every fantasy with Yes, *but*. . . . A professional woman, she felt at an impasse, worried about her future. "Imagine yourself in a beautiful mountain resort," I suggested. "Can you picture it?" [19] She nodded. "Describe the scene to its smallest detail." She began: "I see some mountains close by, and some far off in the distance covered over by mist. I stroll to the foothill of one mountain; it's still green. I walk around. I'm aching to climb to the top. But I can't find any path."

"No matter," I said. "Try to imagine another scene. This time imagine launching on a new work-project." With her eyes closed, Ruth detailed an idea for a professional panel. She had the theme; she described the various subtopics; and she listed the speakers. Then, she abruptly opened her eyes and said: "Yes, *but* they wouldn't come."

Try that one—without any Yes, *buts*. Place yourself at the foothill of a mountain and watch what happens. Are you willing to look around until you find a path? Are you willing to journey, even though the path may be rocky? Will you hang in there when it gets slippery? That's what it's all about: the journey. The top is only one frozen moment of time. The journey is all the rest of our lives.

Women, it seems to me, need not only to raise their consciousness, but in the sensitive phrase of poet Anne Sexton, their unconscious as well. In our daydreaming, play, and fantasy, we're given a whole supermarket of choices and incentives—an opportunity to try out new roles and broaden our

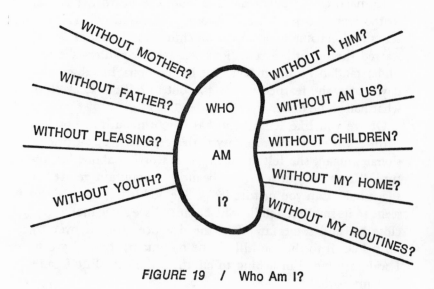

FIGURE 19   /   Who Am I?

repertoire. If the women we've met in these pages have shown us nothing else, it is that our future need not be like our past. Those worn, ill-fitting Rape, Rescue, Revenge, and Ravishing Beauty fantasies can be turned into another set of realities.

It's time, I think, for you to go into your own private lab and look into yourself. Have you asked yourself lately: Who am I? Who am I *without* . . .

And who am I with him, us, all of them? . . .

Now you're free to be your most creative. Invent yourself. Dream yourself up. The possibilities are infinite. Nurture the dream that draws you on, the dream that taunts and won't let you be.

Chapter 12. / Daydreaming: A Power Source

1. Klinger, E. *The Structure and Function of Fantasy.* New York: John Wiley & Sons, 1971.
2. Symonds, P. (with Arthur Jensen). *From Adolescent to Adult.* New York: Columbia University Press, 1961.
3. Singer, J. L. *The Inner World of Daydreaming.* New York: Harper & Row, 1975.
4. Chalfen, L. "The Use of Dreams in Psychoanalytic Group Therapy." *The Psychoanalytic Review*, 1964, *51*, 125–132.
5. Stewart, K. "Dream Theory in Malaya." *Complex*, 1951, *6*, 21–34.
6. Stewart, K. "Culture and Personality in Two Primitive Groups." *Complex*, 1953, *9*, 3–23.
7. Greenleaf, E. " 'Senoi ' Dream Groups." *Psychotheraphy: Theory, Research and Practice*, 1973, *10*, 218–222.
8. Ghiselin, B. (ed.) *The Creative Process: A Symposium.* New York: The New American Library/A Mentor Book, 1952.
9. Gordon, W. *Synectics: The Development of Creative Capacity.* New York: Collier Books, 1961.
10. Selye, H. *From Dream to Discovery: On Being a Scientist.* New York: McGraw-Hill, 1964.
11. Didion, J. *Slouching Towards Bethlehem.* New York: Dell Publishing Co./A Delta Book, 1961.
12. Giambra, L. "A Factor-analytic Study of Daydreaming, Imaginal Process, and Temperament: A Replication of an Adult Life-span Sample." *Journal of Gerontology*, 1977, *32*, 675–680.
13. Freud, S. "The Relationship of the Poet to Day-dreaming" (1908). *Collected Papers*: Vol. IV. London: Hogarth Press, 1950.

14. Sexton, A. *A Self-portrait in Letters*. Edited by Linda Gray Sexton and Lois Ames. Boston: Houghton Mifflin, 1977.
15. Roper Poll: *The Virginia Slims American Women's Opinion Poll*. Vol. III. A survey of the attitudes of women on marriage, divorce, the family, and America's changing sexual morality. Spring, 1974.
16. Keller-Fox, E. The anomaly of a woman in physics. In *Working It Out*, edited by Sara Ruddick and Pamela Daniels. New York: Pantheon Books, 1977.
17. Rosenbaum, Maj-Britt, and I. Ascher. Results of a survey reported at American Psychiatric Association, Miami Beach, 1976. In *Psychiatric News*, Oct. 1, 1976.
18. Sinnott, J. D. "Sex-role Inconstancy, Biology and Successful Aging: A Dialectical Model." *The Gerontologist, 17*, 1977, 459–463.
19. Hammer, M. "The Directed-Daydream Technique." *Psychotherapy: Theory, Research and Practice*, 1967, *4*, 173–181.

EPILOGUE

ENDINGS AND BEGINNINGS

WHATEVER HAPPENED TO EDITH? THAT IS THE SORT OF QUES-
tion we so often find ourselves asking about women we have
known in the past. The answers, years or even decades later,
are infinitely varied, unpredictable, and sometimes startling.

Woman, any woman, almost always leads a serial life—
with times of hibernation and times of renewal, with times
of postponement and times of actualization—whether we
look at her personal development or her sexual development, or even at her inclination to dream. At any rate,
those women who grow and change do. Their lives are never
a straight line.

Despite the broad differences in personality, temperament,
rearing, talents, and achievement, women's lives are bound
by certain common threads. By and large, women are late
bloomers; by and large, we postpone ourselves. We live a
life derived from the male experience, whether we perceive
the world through the kitchen window or the rungs of the
corporate ladder.

We've been squeezed under the umbrella of man, despite
the fact that women have radically different developmental
patterns. What's been expected of us has been different. We
haven't been expected to think about what to do with our
lives. As boys spend their adolescence establishing an identity, dreaming dreams of achievement, girls use their youth

laying the groundwork for an "Us," dreaming dreams of rescue.

And there we encounter the first of our female Selves: The "I" of which the largest part is Us—a common circumstance. Woman—career-oriented or home-centered, single or married, with cultivated talents or yet untried—invents herself around a man because it's expected and because it suits her fantasy of rescue. In men's development identity precedes intimacy; in women, intimacy precedes and postpones a separate identity.

How, then, do women develop? "Most of us have to be transplanted," sculptor Louise Nevelson observes, "like a tree, before we blossom." To be wrenched from their early rooting in relationships, women need to be disrupted. Simply, we grow and develop through contradiction and conflict and paradox.

Starting with Eve and her expulsion from paradise, women develop through the loss of innocence—their many innocences. Transitions, those predictable life events, are not development per se. More often, we grow *not* through the common, predictable transitions of graduations, marriage, motherhood, and aging, but through the "unpredictable" events, those central critical events that dislodge and "shock."

We begin to journey into adulthood in a haze of vague contradictions. There is the one side of the female Me that reaches for Adventure; the other, for Stability of hearth and home. There is the Me that longs for the excitement of Romance and Adoration and the Me that desires the security of a Permanent Relationship. There is the Me striving for achievement, independence, and self-reliance, and the one that yearns to be loved and taken care of.

We elect to merge, or hope to, for its promise of stability. To be a good wife and mother, we've been taught, is the center of a woman's life and the source of all her meaning. Only later do we discover that there are many meanings.

In the wake of instability, we grow. We're "shocked" to discover that every merger bears the seeds of its own distancing; every enchantment, of disenchantment. Those are the female "shocks" of change. Those are the jolts that disrupt the dream of rescue—the shocks that trigger self-knowledge, laying bare the many cloistered aspects of the womanly Self.

How we perceive those shocks and what we do with them determines our development. The woman's life course traces a series of valleys and peaks—postponements and renewals—of which two stand out from the rest.

At first the shaping of a personal identity is so labyrinthine as to defy detection. It begins with a subtle turn of events, a broken promise, a feeling of betrayal. We merge to "settle"; life, we find, is not for settling. Sometime in their thirties, women suffer the loss of the first of their innocences—a central transition that jars the promise of Togetherness. Still, the female "I" remains riveted in the Other. Quicksanded in the fear of loss, we often grip those we love in the stranglehold of the drowning. To cement bonds, we have houses, gardens, septic tanks, station wagons, and children. The Us unravels and reshapes itself around another center, the family, and once more the separate "I" is postponed.

Then, sometime in our late forties or early fifties, erupting like a groundswell, we begin to listen to our own voices. Perhaps, freed from the imperatives of union and motherhood, the "I" turns inward and takes stock of itself. Abruptly, seemingly out of nowhere, we become concerned with our personal and sexual identity, and often even unearth a buried dream—one we quite forgot we had. In the future that she foresees—in opening up choices—it is, in fact, very "normal" for the Life Line of the woman in her forties more closely to resemble that of the young man of twenty than that of her fory-year-old male counterpart. Women indeed are twice born.

We've explored the woman's lifespan, with its fantasy of rescue, its loss of innocence, and its labor of combining the many threads of Self. We've considered the woman's strivings to combine a separate identity with intimacy, and to achieve independence and mastery. With that behind us, can we characterize the "successful" woman?

It seems to me that at this time in history, the successful woman is one who's been sufficiently flexible to integrate and synthesize those contradictions of the youthful self. She's been sufficiently flexible to harmonize conflicting roles and internal tasks. In short, those dissonances among biological, psychological, cultural, and environmental demands triggered both her conflicts and her development. She is also one, according to documented study, who lives creatively and reaps the rewards by aging "successfully" and even living longer!

As a matter of fact, one unexpected finding revealed by this study is a cause for celebration. It is the discovery of a "new" woman—one who, despite what we may have thought, is *not* necessarily in her twenties, but in her forties, fifties, and even sixties—a mutation and a new female experience. She is the woman who learned that her existence on this earth is not only as a companion to man, but also as a person in her own right.

Just think what "unexpecteds" may be lurking in your life to prod you on, to stretch your stride. So that old dream has been reignited? You've caught it on the fly? Now step into the lead. Go ahead—you can do it. We can only write our story as we go along.

INDEX